LIFE AT SCHOOL

THE UNIVERSITY OF
WINCHESTER

To be returned on or before the day marked above, subject to recall.

Excerpts from Reviews

'This is a serious, theoretically informed, conscientious, intensive stuffy of an ideology-oriented school.'

—Journal of Education and Social Change

'This book is a micro-study in which the author reconstructs the subjective interpretation of school life as perceived by teachers and pupils.'

—Contributions to Indian Sociology

'... a well-considered, well-executed analysis of an Indian public school with a difference.'

—Times of India

'...a fine piece of work in a field in which good research and good writing are equally rare.'

—Indian Express

LIFE AT SCHOOL
An Ethnographic Study

MEENAKSHI THAPAN

OXFORD
UNIVERSITY PRESS

OXFORD

UNIVERSITY PRESS

YMCA Library Building, Jai Singh Road, New Delhi 110 001

Oxford University Press is a department of the University of Oxford. It furthers the
University's objective of excellence in research, scholarship, and education
by publishing worldwide in

Oxford   New York

Auckland   Cape Town   Dar es Salaam   Hong Kong   Karachi   Kuala Lumpur
Madrid   Melbourne   Mexico City   Nairobi   New Delhi   Shanghai   Taipei   Toronto

With offices in

Argentina   Austria   Brazil   Chile   Czech Republic   France   Greece   Guatemala
Hungary   Italy   Japan   Poland   Portugal   Singapore   South Korea   Switzerland
Thailand   Turkey   Ukraine   Vietnam

Oxford is a registered trademark of Oxford University Press
in the UK and in certain other countries

Published in India
by Oxford University Press, New Delhi

First published 1991
Oxford India Paperbacks 2006
Third impression 2010

ISBN-13: 978-0-19-567964-9
ISBN-10: 0-19-567964-4

Printed in India at De Unique, New Delhi 110 018
Published by Oxford University Press
YMCA Library Building, Jai Singh Road, New Delhi 110 001

For
Jyotsna, Ayushya, and George

Contents

Introduction to the Second Edition*

In the fourteen odd years since this book first appeared, the sociology of schooling has focused on dissimilar paradigms and approaches that focus on issues such as race and ethnicity, gender and class, social networks and policy issues, theoretical advances and practical posers, and the engagement of all these factors with schooling practices in various and complex ethnographic sites. Conflict, violence, and terror have necessitated new perspectives on understanding their impact on schools and on children. World events and the shaping of particular ideological debates and practices, for example, in the former Soviet Union or in contemporary France, have evolved an understanding of schools in particular social and political contexts.

The complexity characteristic of childhood in vastly changing, 'modern' societies, beset with rapid technological advances of every kind, has demanded an understanding of some of the issues involved. The impact of the media in the creation of not just modern technological skills but also an early preoccupation with embodiment, and its many aspects, has resulted in the 'loss of childhood'. Children are sexually aware and active at a much earlier age now and 'counselling', not only for career choices, is an important component of school life. Childhood is in a sense no longer an 'innocent' moment in an individual's life cycle. It may be traumatic, turbulent or 'divine' depending on location and acquired capital. The 'poverty of childhood' has also been addressed in this context as indeed has the childhood of those living in extremely impoverished and marginalized conditions. A sociology of schooling has also considered the space of schools as sites of struggle, contradiction, and change. Resistance in the space and location of schools has moved from an early understanding based on Paul Willis's study (1979) of working class boys in a school near Manchester to other acts and types of resistance. These changes are

*I thank Ray McCoy and the Krishnamurti Foundation Trust (UK) for permission to quote from Krishnamurti (1995). I am also very grateful to all at Rishi Valley for cheerfully putting up with my frequent visits, endless questions and requests for information, and for allowing me to remain an ethnographer in their midst.

related to methodological shifts in the sociological study of schools and inevitably of participants in schooling.

Life at School (1991) was written at a particular time when everyday life was central to an explanation of schooling practices through the experience of the participants in this process (cf. Woods 1979). Other approaches have elaborated on understanding schooling from different conceptual perspectives although the methodological tools may often remain the same (for example, Willis 1979; McLaren 1985; Walkerdine 1990). Appendix A in the first edition delineates the theoretical approach undertaken in the study of Rishi Valley School (RVS). In the penultimate paragraph, I expressed my views on theories advocating 'resistance' and indicated that I was somewhat sceptical of the transformative value of resistance especially in the context of the 'educational code'. However, I now consider such resistance crucial to educational practice and to an individual's relationship with the social world. My interest in such resistance stems from my understanding that the individual is not a mere cog in the wheel of human life but plays a significant role in constructing the social world through an active engagement with the processes and practices that constitute her environment.

The individual self is constituted always in relation to the social but this does not happen only as an arbitrary imposition or inculcation; it is always a simultaneous creation and engagement, albeit, informed always by the limiting, constraining, and restraining aspects of such engagement. It is in this sense that sociology ultimately views schools as sites for the evolution of power through the various nerve centres that constitute the school whether these are spatial or intellectual, moral or material, academic or social, personal or public. In this process, how does the human subject find space for articulation, voice and resistance? And how indeed is the self constructed in the school vis-à-vis the 'pedagogic encounter'[1] that remains essentially a political act charged with intent and meaning? There are undoubtedly elements of negotiation, challenge, and acceptance as well as ambiguities, conflicts, and tensions that reflect the multiplicity and complexity within which selves are constructed and reconstructed. This multiplicity of perspectives, of voice and subjectivities, is critical to the pedagogic encounter and suggests that there is no single ideal community; rather, there are webs that create and recreate the possibilities of engagement among different subjectivities.

Life at School (1991) does not explicitly provide an explanation of the nuanced nature of this engagement. It does however draw out the perspective that the individual is significant to the schooling process in terms of the worlds that are created, managed, negotiated, contested, and developed. Moreover, the school's 'ideology', in the case of Rishi Valley, is especially explicit in underlining the catalytic role of the individual in transforming the social world. The reiteration of this 'ideology', even as an implicit presence, and as a world-view and guiding force in the lives of participants enhances its effect on human engagement with school processes. This is what drew me to the school twenty-five years ago as a sociologist seeking explanations for the question, what life at school is all about, not merely in terms of processes of interaction but as an engagement with the human and social world.[2]

Rishi Valley in 2005: Everyday Life in the School

In many ways, Rishi Valley remains unchanged. In terms of school organization, academic goals, student culture and teacher culture, interaction in different spheres and between various groups of people—all located at the twin levels of the transcendental and local orders of the school that both define, as well as constrain its existence. One criticism of the book, for example, in a review by the late Suresh C. Shukla (1991), has been that it has neglected to study conflict or resistance in school processes. While the book does examine the dilemmas and contradictions in the functioning of the transcendental and local orders in the everyday life of the school, it also points to the fact that the students and teachers learn to negotiate their way through these contradictions and the conflict they may generate. In a way, the goals of teachers and students are realized, in the different arenas of school life—whether this is in terms of teaching, learning, passing examinations, achieving good examination results, giving voice to independent and often divergent views, expressing doubt and criticism. This was present in the school in 1981 and this is present in the school in 2005.

Conflict is present in school life and is evident, for example, in the lives of those participants in the school process, who may not conform to school expectations and do not accept the regulations and guiding practices of school life. Conflict is also endemic to everyday student culture in terms of student evaluations of school culture and the norms and regulations that circumscribe their existence. Such conflict and the many forms it takes is not a deterrent however to the strategies of contestation, negotiation and circumvention that both teachers and students evolve to resist rules, norms, guiding principles, and behaviour in their quest for being a 'good' teacher or student. This view of conflict suggests the possibilities for an engagement with the causes of conflict through an understanding of the issues involved and the explicit desire and will among participants to push for their own perspective to prevail. Often students are unable to change a particular rule but they nonetheless offer a challenge to those who frame rules and in this process set the ball rolling for the re-thinking and re-framing of rules. Similarly, teachers may not be able to completely change school processes in a perceived direction but they frame the possibilities for change in their very articulation of their perspective and its difference from the dominant/prevailing view.

Such an approach to the study of schools allows for a multiplicity of voices and perspectives in the everyday life of such institutions. This multiplicity is complex as participants have competing perspectives on the purpose of schooling, on their roles and on prevailing school practices. Participants are also endowed with different kinds of social and cultural capital that provide different mental frames within which dialogue take place.[3] The complexity is heightened by very divergent *experience* of schooling among the participants and this tends to be the most contentious among the participants in any one school. Hierarchy and power are critical components of this process of negotiation that allows for the multiplicity of voice and experience. It is in this aspect that a school like Rishi Valley scores in terms of an absence of hierarchy in everyday school processes although a clear hierarchical structure exists in the organization of school life.

The recently established Senior School and the Junior School staff committees are an example of the greater involvement of teachers in the decision making process. The Coordinator of these committees is usually a teacher and all groups of teachers are generally represented in them. For example, different subject areas—music and the fine arts, house parents, and sports—find a voice in the committees. The participation of teachers in such committees, apart from their physical presence, is enhanced by the role of the Coordinator to whom any teacher can present an item for discussion. In this manner, the school seeks to involve all teachers, to the extent that it is possible, in those aspects of school life that traditionally seemed the preserve of the Management and administrators alone. However, it is also possible that power is not explicit and therefore the undercurrents of the exercise of power remain hidden even to the participants themselves. Their involvement in the committees nonetheless ensures that their perspectives are shared and heard.

The overwhelmingly significant division among teachers that was present in the school, as 'ideologues' and 'pedagogues', has vastly changed and become somewhat more complex. There are now sixty teachers (including ad-hoc and part-time) in the school (of whom twenty six are women),[4] a much larger figure than in 1981 and includes teachers with differing forms of social and economic capital, with varying ideological persuasions and religious commitments. The sharp distinction between 'ideologues' and 'pedagogues' was a somewhat over-simplified analytical tool that was unable to capture the complexity and variation that must have been present at the time. There can, at present, be no analytical distinction between teachers on grounds of either modes of recruitment, or types of commitment. The avenues of recruitment remain more or less the same as in 1981 but what stands out sharply is that, commitment on the part of teachers, of different subjects, with varying forms of capital, is to similar goals.

The academic life of the institution is an important aspect of everyday life. This does not mean that teachers are not engaged in activities that are concerned with their professional development, including publication of their work in curriculum development, for example, and participation in workshops outside RVS, and students with life in the 'house', workshops, theatre, clubs, excursions, sports, discussion groups, exposure to village life, and interaction with a resident poet, among other things. Moreover, teachers who are committed to more than their teaching goals are encouraged to do other work. In this, they are also supported with grants, administrative help, study leave, and the opportunity to participate in exchange programmes, workshops, gatherings, and retreats. As teachers are more or less free to pursue their own interests, and Krishnamurti or his perspective is not 'being shoved down their throats', teachers are not resistant or aggressively against it and this allows them to do their own job diligently and with commitment.[5]

In a sense, there has been a merger between the 'ideologues' and the 'pedagogues' which is the outcome of a movement in two directions.

One, the so-called ideologues, those with an explicit commitment to Krishnamurti and his views, are not, as of now, 'propagators' of the ideology. They do not pontificate or promote Krishnamurti's world-view as one that needs to be accepted by one and all. The kind of doctrinaire ideologues who were present in the school in 1981 do not really exist any more. In a sense, and to a large extent, the ideologues have made a 'common cause' with the pedagogues.[6] There is clearly a sharing of values and practical work on the part of both the ideologues and pedagogues. They are both there to teach, define and shape the curriculum, discuss texts, provide an intellectual ambience and contribute to academic excellence. As they share similar goals and concerns, they are now therefore at greater ease with one another. In addition, those who are there because of their commitment to Krishnamurti and work in the manner they think best without any explicit conflict among the teaching body.

Secondly, there is a greater awareness among many teachers, whether or not committed explicitly to Krishnamurti's view, of the degeneration of the world in general, in the degradation of nature, in the excessive violence, heightened nationalism and therefore there is a greater acceptance of his view now than in earlier times. Krishnamurti appears to make sense to many socially aware teachers in RVS at present and this helps to bring teachers together in a common cause not just as teachers but as a body committed to making the world a somewhat better place. This new coherence among teachers of different religious and ideological persuasions, whether Buddhist, Roman Catholic, Hindu, or agnostic, results in a different kind of ideologue: academic teacher and the socially aware and committed practical worker.

Krishnamurti is not therefore a continuous and explicitly stated presence; the emphasis is on 'work' in RVS and in all the concurrent programmes and ventures the school is engaged in. The new ideologue is a conscientious and diligent worker, practical and seeking to be the best in the field she chooses whether as teacher in RVS, in Rishi Valley Institute for Educational Resources (RIVER), ornithologist, conservationist, builder, sportsman, or just as one who takes time off from regular assignments to spend time at Rishi Valley before deciding what to do with his/her life. It is a different kind of ideologue today in RVS: one who is committed to the students and the teaching programme in RVS, the environment, to rural education, health and nutrition programmes for the villagers, to alternative and indigenous health programmes and practices, to yoga, to music, and climbing mountains, and other creative pursuits. However, it would be naïve to assume that ideological praxis exists in a congenial atmosphere of harmony and well-being. There surely must be dissonances in and among the different agents of ideological practice but the critical point is that these do not overwhelm their tasks or inhibit the fulfilment of their goals. The underlying premise is the freedom to pursue their individual and collective goals to fruition. This carries over to all aspects of their performance and remains integral to teacher culture in RVS.

The daily routine of the school remains more or less the same: a routine punctuated by rituals of consensus and collective existence. A significant departure from the routine is the absence of *asthachal* which has been curtailed due to certain practical considerations. There is a sense in which the activities of everyday life, including the pressures of a crowded syllabus, tend to interfere with that aspect of school life that was integral to Krishnamurti's perspective on Rishi Valley—leisure. He has stated that if he were Head of RVS, 'I would see, apart from games, apart from the school timetable, curriculum and all that, that they have leisure...Then I would help them to find out what it means to be silent, because when you are silent, you'll hear the trees...the birds' wings in the air. When you are silent, your senses are awakened' (1995). The pressures of a creatively organized academic programme, that is arguably among the best in the country, coupled with a wide range of group activities, compete with the presence of free time for 'leisure', quietude, and silence among the children. Some teachers and many students do not even notice this absence, and those that do have not so far managed to find ways of strengthening this dimension of school life. There are 'dramatic' elements to the routine and these remain critical to life at school such as the annual examinations, sports-days, visiting poet and painter who guides poetry workshops, art lectures, and student recitations, and the immensely popular annual visit of a story-teller who goes around to the houses and organizes after-dark campfires. Krishnamurti's death in 1986 has eliminated that other 'dramatisation' of the routine, his annual visit, a significant component of school life in 1981, as well as other activities associated with it.

The underlying character of the school with its emphasis on freedom and vitality remains central to teachers' definitions of school life and their own roles in it. Teachers are committed quite clearly

to enhancing this quality of freedom by giving the children space—
intellectual and psychological—to discover both the academic life and
their own participation in this process as well as their psychological
development and maturity. This does not however mean that students
do not experience constraint in the form of rules and norms for
appropriate behaviour and dress, of what is acceptable and possible,
within the space opened up by the freedom in school life. All students,
whether in the junior or in the senior school, experience this constraint
in one way or another. Their submission to it is simultaneously marked
by submission, rebellion, contestation, negotiation, and strategization.
Children openly argue with teachers, protest against the imposition
of some rules, hotly discuss the impositions among themselves,
negotiate with teachers and house-parents, strategize and evade
impositions and also submit to them. The forms of resistance as
individual and collective acts of engagement represent the agency of
the human subject which therefore constitutes a critical component
of everyday life at school.

The most explicit example of this agency remains the Democracy
Board in the senior school, a vibrant forum, which continues to carry
articles, points of view, poems, and prose by students about different
dimensions of school life. The dress code and the 'grub' (food other
than that available in the Dining Hall) policy in school remain the
most debated topics between teachers and students on the Democracy
Board as indeed are the more contemporary concerns of internet
use and personal music walkmans among students, relations across
the sexes, and importantly, the role of the Students' Council. The
latter is a students' body elected by senior school students who work
with teachers around issues of common concern. Periodically, this
Council becomes a dormant body and is re-activated through demands
made on the Democracy Board by students themselves. The Council
also plays a role in arranging and organizing students' assemblies,
planning and organizing relief work, whether this is in relation to
national disasters like the Orissa cyclone, Gujarat earthquake, or the
recent Tsunami disaster, and scheduling students' roles in the Dining
Hall (as dishwashers, servers, etc.). While this may suggest that the
Council's role is merely an organizational one with no input being
made in important areas of school life that are often contentious
and require student involvement and consideration for their resolution,
this indeed does happen. For example, students themselves raise
questions on the Democracy Board about Rishi Valley 'culture' being

on 'the decline' and in 2000 were asking for more involvement in the Rural Education Centre (REC) activities, suggesting that they might do so through greater involvement in the REC's annual Sports Day. Their sensitivity to their environment is expressed by their observation that 'school has been around for about seventy years and yet we don't really know the surroundings very well. We are not very comfortable around the villagers and nor are they, around us' (9/12/2000).[7]

Students understand only too well what the 'real concerns' are and articulate these when they intersect with their own perceptions and questions. It is no longer possible to be patronizing about students opinions and concerns as there is a greater exposure through the media and the internet to a variety of social processes and activities. The school at some point needs to also recognize its strength as an active and enabling forum, as it were, which helps in redefining and reshaping students' experiences and perspectives in very many different ways. These views may not always appear as mutually acceptable positions in the immediacy of the moment, as students especially would like to project themselves always in opposition to the dominant voice, but when considered in their depth, they often arise from and celebrate all that Rishi Valley stands for. Teachers, therefore, appear sometimes to be engaged in an uphill task of seeking student acceptance of and commitment to its goals which exists in any case but is suppressed or differently voiced by students. This is the nature of the human subject, to be passionate and fearless in articulating difference, and through this, voicing resistance and rebellion in the everyday practices of school life while simultaneously remaining committed, perhaps unconsciously even unacknowledged by themselves, to the goals and values of RVS.

At the same time, students' recognize the ability to have relationships with teachers in Rishi Valley that does not exist elsewhere, that they have 'freedom of speech' and the space to say whatever they want to. This 'space' also creates 'confidence' in students, especially girls, in terms of being able to express themselves, and not be put down so easily and in that sense, as one girl put it, 'has helped me grow'. More significantly, students recognize and accept the presence of that special quality that sets RVS apart from other schools: the quality of 'innate goodness' that is 'out there', 'intangible', 'inexpressible' but an undeniable part of their experience of everyday life.[8] Students say, 'You feel it. Its in the air and it enters you'. Others agreed, 'It is there'. This experience in a sense reaffirms all that Rishi Valley stands for in terms of the values that define and embody its place in the network of alternative schools in India. The point however is not only the experience of students in RVS as compared to other schools in contemporary India, but to understand whether or not the school, in the experience of its students, has attained its goal of creating a different quality of mind in a new generation. Such a mind is not concerned only with material success or well-being but cares for all forms of life, a sharing of resources, is awake to 'humanity' in all its diversity and complexity. It is such a mind that may create a different human spirit that may in turn give rise to the 'good' society that Krishnamurti envisioned for this world. Students at RVS, in their engagement with teachers and themselves, are those who question different aspects of school life, who seek an even more liberal attitude on the part of their teachers, better food in the dining hall, more freedom in relations with the opposite sex, greater liberty in wearing a variety of clothes, a relaxation of various rules which appear to have 'no rationale', and so on. They question, criticize, and doubt almost all aspects of school life; simultaneously, however, they experience and are able to voice that crucial quality that is the bedrock of a Krishnamurti Foundation, India, (KFI) school and that was not articulated in 1981: the experience of 'goodness' that somehow pervades the school and, in turn, them.

Students however are unwilling to accept the position that this goodness is not a metaphysical, mystical quality that mysteriously exists in the atmosphere but is created by the participants in the educational process that is RVS. For them, it is just there, not created by any one, especially not by teachers, past or present.[9] This dualism in their experience is a manifestation of an obvious desire to rebel against authority of any kind, even in their experience of a quality they deeply value, and yet submit to that quality in their very experience of it. The school, in a sense, succeeds in creating the 'right' attitude among students, in Krishnamurti's terms: never to accept authority of any kind whatsoever, and somehow also generate the quality of 'goodness' that remains an immeasurable, intangible experience of student culture. This is the sense of responsibility that pervades Krishnamurti's world-view, that is, 'the impulse of goodness' (Herzberger 2004).

Student culture is an aspect of school life that often endures within the academic, intellectual, and psychological spaces that the school inhabits. There are now a larger number of students from all over

India, than there were earlier, although the total number remains more or less the same, around 350 in all. There are students from regions as diverse as Ladakh, Goa, Uttarkashi, Chittorgarh, and the large and smaller towns of Karnataka, Tamil Nadu, Kerala, and Andhra Pradesh. In 1981, the students by and large exhibited an involvement with school work and conformity to school life. There appeared to be a break with, or a rejection of, components of school life that were related to the 'ideological' underpinnings of the school, namely, Krishnamurti's philosophy and activities connected with it. Student career preferences at that time emphasized careers in engineering, medicine, architecture, and computers based on their choice of academic subjects clearly being in favour of the Science stream as opposed to the Arts or Humanities. Twenty-five years later, students at Rishi Valley are far more open to career paths that diverge from the well worn options of the pure Sciences and opt for clearly innovative mixes of a variety of academic subjects that allow them to explore their interests and eventually may help in choosing very different career trajectories. Students may often take up a career in environment related projects and the social development sector in addition to the established paths of architecture, design, visual communication, economics, and so on. There is also an enthusiasm for returning to Rishi Valley after a short gap to work as teachers, almost unanimous among all students of the current school-leaving class. Among the alumni, there are many who contribute to the school scholarship fund, the environmental projects, and the rural health programme. There is an enduring relationship with Rishi Valley that lasts long after they have left and are differently located in geographical space, inhabit deeply variant ideological and occupational worlds, cultural milieus, and public spaces.

The Regeneration of Rishi Valley: Krishnamurti in Praxis

The reorientation and renewal at Rishi Valley is taking place as an outcome of an integrated approach. The focus is not on education alone whether this is at RVS, the rural centre or in the satellite schools. It is also on ecological development, health and nutrition, alternative health care such as ayurveda and herbal therapy, yoga and homeopathy. The seriousness with which Rishi Valley has undertaken conservation of the natural environment that is its location, and the linkages that are made with its educational activities, is abundantly clear in its publication, *Birds of Rishi Valley and Renewal of their Habitats* (Rangaswami and Sridhar 1993). The book includes an exposition on Krishnamurti's thought on nature and the environment (by Radhika Herzberger) and a detailed compilation of the different species of birds in the valley. Its educational component includes a history of bird studies in India (by Theodore Bhaskaran), their habitats and ecology, the basic principles of taxonomy with reference to birds, and the principles underlying their classification and nomenclature as well as colour plates with detailed notes. Some basic concepts in biodiversity and variety of plant life that provides protection to birds in Rishi Valley are also discussed. Although bird watching is an optional activity undertaken by students on Sunday mornings in RVS, the teachers who take them through its intricacies are ornithologists and apart from teaching children about the different birds and their habitats, develop in them, over time, a concern and affection for nature and the environment. The question that RVS sought to answer, in the writing of this book, was quite simple, in keeping with Krishnamurti's ideas, 'At the end of the twentieth century, living in an ancient culture to which many different religions and races have contributed, in an over-populated country with shrinking resources and exploding communal discords, how should we Indians educate our children?' (Rangaswami and Sridhar 1993: 8).

In the posing of this question itself unfolds the sensitivity of the questioners, not only to the environment but to the minds of young children, and a concern with providing a radically different education that would sensitize children to a sense of beauty, concern for and a practical awareness of the problems that beset Rishi Valley's natural habitat. Rishi Valley is a natural habitat of exceptional beauty and wealth and in it are located several institutions as part of the Rishi Valley Education Centre (RVEC) that constitute Rishi Valley today. Rishi Valley is no longer defined by RVS alone but by all the other programmes and institutions to which it is linked in a number of ways.[10] In 1981, RVS was critical to defining Rishi Valley. In the last twenty-five years, RVS has grown in many ways, become academically diverse (offering students a larger number of subject options), intellectually vibrant, with a larger teaching body, more facilities for students but it is a small component of the greater magnitude that encompasses it. This larger process is Krishnamurti in praxis: a new interpretation of Krishnamurti's teachings that has slowly shaped Rishi Valley into a substantially different kind of a place from what it was in 1981.

To begin with, let us consider Krishnamurti's perspective. In 1984, at an International meeting of the Trustees of the Krishnamurti Foundations held at Brockwood Park in England, Krishnamurti propounded his vision of what he would do if he 'were Head of Rishi Valley School' (1995). It was a time of transition. A new Principal was already in place along with some highly qualified new teachers, and a Director was planned for taking over the functioning of the RVEC. The first step Krishnamurti proposed at this meeting was to have village schools that would be built along with the villagers. This focus on the rural poor is not something new in Krishnamurti's perspective. He had reiterated 'you are the world' to his audiences across the globe, emphasizing an intimate and continuous relationship between individuals and the collective at all times. He said, 'In oneself lies the whole world, and if you know how to look and learn, then the door is there and the key is in your hand' (Krishnamurti 1972c: 158). In this manner, he sought to draw out individuals from their self absorbed lives into a sense of global responsibility towards the earth and its people: 'you are the rest of mankind' was an oft spoken phrase by Krishnamurti. This was the refrain in his talks and discussions with young people in his schools and at public meetings everywhere.

As part of his endeavour to awaken a sense of responsibility towards the world and its many problems, Krishnamurti emphasized selfless, completely non-ideological commitment towards change. At a talk in Benares, he argued, '...No one in the world is interested vitally, strongly, in completely eradicating poverty. They all say they are interested but their interest is ideational, not actual...Of the several causes that are preventing [*i.e. acting together to stop the starvation throughout the world*], the first is nationality—to belong to a nation, as an Indian, as a Buddhist, as a Christian, as a communist, as a capitalist...' (Krishnamurti 1963–4: 75). Krishnamurti clearly perceived that the fragmented identity of the human subject prevents one from translating one's concern for the poor into a movement for change. The piece-meal manner in which one perceives oneself, due to one's diverse interests and narrow commitments, is in fact the cause of a limited approach to change. At a talk in Delhi, he said, 'We have not solved the problem of starvation, and probably we will never solve it the way we are going because the problem of starvation is not of a particular country or of a particular party. It is the problem of the world. We are human beings interrelated with each other, and we all have to solve this problem together, but the politicians and their helpers prevent this. So...is there an answer?' (Ibid.: 41). Krishnamurti was concerned deeply about poverty, as he witnessed it, with an acute and deeply sensitive awareness of its everyday presence in his detailed descriptions about suffering and life in the *Commentaries on Living* (1972a, 1972b) and in *Krishnamurti's Notebook* (2003). He sought a global resolution of poverty; it was not something that could be addressed by one nation alone but had to be the genuine and common concern of the human world.[11]

Krishnamurti's vision was not utopian. He was simple and clear-headed in his obvious concern for the earth and its people: 'The Earth is ours, yours and mine, and we have to live on it together; we have to cherish it and grow things on its soil, so that all the people will have sufficient food, clothing and shelter' (Krishnamurti 1993: 41). It was a simple quest—to preserve the earth and its resources. This aspect of Krishnamurti's thought finds resonances in modern times with the contemporary global concern for environmental well-being in response to the vast degradation of natural resources and the environment. More than fifty years ago, Krishnamurti was already urging his audience to protect the environment, its pristine beauty, and its natural wealth. This is something that all teachers in RVS can comprehend and empathize with even if they do not fully understand other aspects of his world-view. In particular, Krishnamurti's world-view was being absorbed by those who felt they could live their lives in the manner most appropriate and closest to his perspective as they understood it.

The current Principal of RVS, Dr A. Kumaraswamy, came to the school as a teacher in 1982. He feels that there are two ways of understanding Krishnamurti's philosophy—one is the 'inward' approach which is the most popular as everyone wants to go inward and 'understand' themselves. The other is that aspect of Krishnamurti's thought that emphasizes 'going outward into society' and engaging with processes in society. It is therefore central to Krishnamurti's approach, to go out into society. Kumaraswamy feels more oriented to this approach and wants the students at RVS to be related to the larger world. He feels that most schools are rather 'isolated places' where participants remain preoccupied with themselves and with the daily routine. In this process, they remain disconnected with the external world. He therefore is personally committed to doing something for the people around Rishi Valley.

Figure 1

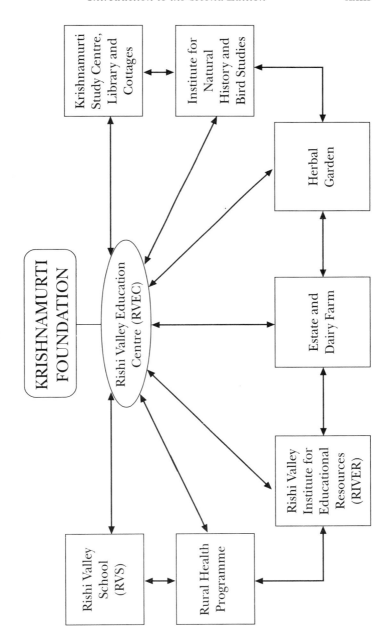

The Director of RVEC, Dr Radhika Herzberger, also came to RVS in 1982. She had a great interest in the environment and as a young person was apprehensive of, what she calls, the 'loss of landscape' and experiences a sense of urgency to preserve it at all costs. Like Kumaraswamy, Herzberger turned away from excessive self-absorption that has often been the path preferred by some of those who follow Krishnamurti's thought. That Krishnamurti's teachings remain central to Kumaraswamy's and Herzberger's lives and work is beyond doubt; what is different is their manner of interpretation and practice in the school over the last twenty odd years. For herself, Herzberger perhaps had to break the divide between the spiritual and the material in consonance with her understanding of the individual's responsibility to the social environment. In the KFI, of which both Kumaraswamy and Herzberger are Trustees, there are divergent understandings of Krishnamurti and his work which has resulted in schools that are run according to differing perspectives by members of the KFI. For Herzberger, an indispensable aspect of Krishnamurti's thought in praxis is 'work' in these directions. In her articulation of the goals for RVS that she and others, like Kumaraswamy, have envisioned, ideas engage critically with practice. Secondly, emerging from such an approach is also a concern for 'values' and the place of values in the everyday lives of teachers and students. Love and concern for the environment are two of the values extensively nurtured at RVS, both in the classroom and in the field.

Concern for the natural environment in which RVS is located became the first priority in this new re-working of Krishnamurti in praxis. In July 1991, Rishi Valley was declared a private Bird Preserve and a Declaration was signed under the sprawling branches of the old banyan tree in Rishi Valley. The role of RVS in this process is unmistakable as the declaration stated that this private bird preserve would be under the 'direct control and supervision of the Management of Rishi Valley School for the purpose of preserving, protecting and enriching the avifaunal wealth, habitat diversity and flora of the Valley as a whole, appreciating their interdependence' (RVEC, n.d.: 9).

The next step, to continue with Krishnamurti's vision for Rishi Valley, is 'the whole question of education' and the direction it must take which is the responsibility of 'all the school, not me alone' (1995). A rural centre had been maintained by the school since the 1950's as a free school for workers' children. In the 1980s, a process was set in motion to strengthen the rural education programme and reach out to nearby villages. A group of teachers and administrators explored the idea of locating schools in the heart of these villages and reviving a village commons around them. The school and its grounds could be the nucleus of this revival in which both students and their whole families would feel a sense of responsibility toward the school and the school would feel the same about the local community. They began by working with the existing rural centre school which was functioning in a shed with no clearly formulated curriculum. In 1987, with the arrival of Dr Y. Padmanabha Rao and Rama Rao, a transformation began to take place in the rural education programme of RVEC. In the last twenty years, RVEC has created a multi-grade, multi-level programme for elementary education called 'School in a Box'. This kit contains work material in the form of a series of cards in the disciplines of language, mathematics, and environmental studies. These cards break down the learning process into smaller units as groups of cards which are organized as 'milestones' leading the students from level I to level V. As textbooks have been done away with and there are several kinds of activities, deriving from the local culture and context, including songs, stories, puppetry, miming, 'metric melas' (rural science and math fairs organized by the children themselves) and greater interaction in the classroom, 'classroom management' is much better for the teachers (Singh 2003). For the children, the Raos tell us, the School in a Box is just a 'springboard for the creativity of the children' (ibid.).

'Quality' in education has been a central component of the educational process in the 16 satellite schools established by the RVEC: the child's learning experience is critical including the 'ideal location of schools', the school's relationship with the ecological environment; and the children's 'interactions within the multi-grade classroom and with the larger community' (Rao, Herzberger and Chandy 2004: 55). RVEC conceives all its schools, enriched with fruit trees and medicinal herbs, as ecological spaces for the renewal of the village community. Quality in education may begin with ensuring an excellent curricular framework and learning material, with well trained teachers, and sufficient resources, but quality in education is also, as RVEC puts it, about 'nourishing the Indian earth and the communities it sustains' (ibid.: 56). The satellite schools are the 'nodal points' of the village for the children, their parents, other villagers and visitors to the village. They serve to educate as well as to awaken an aesthetic sense, a concern for the environment, and also serve as small clinics for the visiting doctor from Rishi Valley. This ensures that children at these schools are not the recipients of mere tokenism, or expansive largesse at the cost of quality, but have access to the very best education that RVEC can offer them.[12] As Robert Kaplan tells us, 'The Raos thus reinvented what a school is' (1996: 362) and the school in a formal, organizational space with a rigid curriculum does not exist for RVEC.

Links between RVS and the satellite schools are well established. Children from RVS have been active in planting trees and building infrastructure especially in the early days when the rural schools were first coming up. Telugu-speaking teachers participate in rural school administration and activities. One of the RVS teachers has taken over as headmistress of the rural education centre and RVS music and dance teachers are regularly involved in various events and activities in the rural school. Senior students have been helping in the preparation of the educational kit, especially the Science tool-box, for the satellite schools. Students of class 11 in RVS are also engaged in projects on health and related issues at the rural health centre. The doctor at this health centre is a former student of RVS and currently he and his wife are teachers and house-parents in RVS. A former student of the rural education centre is a qualified optometerist and anchors eye care programmes for the villagers. The engagement of student alumni with rural centre activities is evident from their involvement in providing infrastructure and other financial support for the rural health care programme. RVS is no longer an isolated space for the education of the privileged few. It has engaged with its environment and the social space in which it is located and emerged as a catalyst force for the regeneration of the entire valley in very many different ways.

The dynamism that has transformed Rishi Valley, from providing a vast and generous natural expanse for RVS, to being a vibrant centre for excellence in education, is part of a genuine 'movement for sustainable development. It is a movement that no doubt has been initiated and nurtured by a leadership that recognizes the necessity of being grounded in the social, as much as in the natural, environment. It is also a movement that seeks to go beyond a focus on RVS and the immediate environment, and seeks to reach out to society and the world at large, making global linkages, gaining international recognition, and yet remaining focused on the small and the local. The village community, the multi-grade school-room, the locally recruited and trained teacher, the children and young adults in RVS, the learning and inquisitive mind, the creativity in both teaching and learning, the herbal garden, the institute of bird studies and natural history, and the vast natural landscape are all critical to both the local and global in both aspirations and in practice.

Significantly, all this, as well as the perceived relationship between the inward and the outward in an individual's personal development, as articulated by those at the helm of affairs in RVS, derive from Krishnamurti's world-view. Krishnamurti is not merely an intellectual philosopher talking and writing about the inner life of individuals in a vacuum called 'society'. In fact, Krishnamurti was making a clear statement about the individual's responsibility to society and her commitment to it in whatever sphere of life she chooses to inhabit. This complete commitment and dedication is the reorientation and renewal that has enriched Rishi Valley in the last twenty-five years and continues to shape the lives of the children and adults in the school. Rishi Valley is not however a sanctimonious haven of goodwill and generosity. Undoubtedly, there are often sharp differences, rivalries, personal conflicts, and competition at all levels and participants at RVS seek to negotiate, strategize, and manipulate, in much the same ways as teachers and children do in the classrooms, all sides seeking fulfilment of their goals and desires in different ways, using tools and devices that both fascinate and repel, liberate and constrain, succeed and fail in their quest for that perfect and final solution to humankind's eternal question, 'what does it mean to educate?'

Notes

1. By 'pedagogic encounter' I mean that engagement that takes place with persons, textbooks, the media, in diverse domains and situations in which learning takes place whether this happens in relation to the teacher, the peer group, the family, or society in general.
2. The specifically class or caste based and gendered nature of this engagement and its implications for interaction in school is no doubt a significant component of schooling processes. This aspect of school life has not been discussed in Thapan (1991) but has been the focus of my more recent work (Thapan 2001 and Thapan 2005).
3. For an excellent formulation of the different forms of capital, its uses and transformations, see Bourdieu (2002).
4. This figure holds for February 2005.

5. Interview with the Principal, February 2005.
6. Interview with the Director, Rishi Valley Education Centre in February 2005.
7. Not many students in the school are conversant with Telugu which restricts the extent of interaction between RVS and the villagers.
8. These experiences were shared with me by the students of Class 12 on 3 February, 2005, in response to my question about what special quality or experience will they take with them when they leave the school.
9. Herzberger writes that during one of Krishnamurti's visits to RVS, she asked him whether his 'long association' with the school had built 'a deep spirit of silence and goodness' in the school. Krishnamurti replied, 'I have not built it. It is there and many before me are responsible for its presence' (Herzberger 1997). In a sense, Krishnamurti's perspective supports the student's viewpoint but as any student of society will confirm, the environment is continuously constructed, reaffirmed, conserved and reconstructed by participants in the process.
10. Figure 1 depicts the many institutional and programmatic dimensions of the school's existence.
11. The manner in which globalization, for example, has overtaken contemporary society, with its problematic anti-poor policies and practices, is a clear illustration of the effect of global irresponsibility especially towards developing societies.
12. In 2004, RIVER was awarded the first prize for the Most Innovative Development Project for their work in education from the Global Development Network (funded by the Japanese government) at Dakar, Senegal.

References

Bourdieu, Pierre. 2002. 'The Forms of Capital', in A.H. Halsey et. al. (eds) *Education, Culture, Economy, Society*, Oxford: Basil Blackwell.

Herzberger, Radhika. 1997. 'Krishnaji at Rishi Valley', in *The Presence that Stays: Personal Recollections of Jiddu Krishnamurti*, Hyderabad: Jiddu Krishnamurti Centre.

_____. 2004. 'An Overview of J. Krishnamurti's Writing on Education', in *Encyclopaedia of Indian Education*, New Delhi: NCERT.

Kaplan, Robert D. 1996. 'Rishi Valley and Human Ingenuity', in *The Ends of the Earth: A Journey at the Dawn of the 21st Century*, New York: Random House.

Krishnamurti, J. 1972a [1956]. *Commentaries on Living: From the Notebooks of J. Krishnamurti* by D. Rajagopal (ed.), Delhi: B.I. Publications.

_____. 1972b [1956]. *Commentaries on Living: Second Series. From the Notebooks of J. Krishnamurti* by D. Rajagopal (ed.), Delhi: B.I. Publications.

_____. 1972c. *You are the World*, Madras: Krishnamurti Foundation India.

_____. 1992. 'Talk in Benares, 1963–64', *The Collected Works of J. Krishnamurti. Perennial Questions. Vol. XIV: The New Mind*, Iowa: Kendall/Hunt Publishing Co.

_____. 1992. 'Talk in New Delhi, 1963–64', *The Collected Works of J. Krishnamurti. Perennial Questions. Vol. XIV: The New Mind*, Iowa: Kendall/Hunt Publishing Co.

_____. 1993. *Krishnamurti at Rajghat*, Madras: Krishnamurti Foundation India.

_____. 1995. International Trustees Meeting, Brockwood, Park, September 11, 1984. 'If I were Head of Rishi Valley School', in *Bulletin Krishnamurti Foundation (India)* Bulletin, 1995/3. Madras: Krishnamurti Foundation (India): 20–1.

_____. 2003. *Krishnamurti's Notebook*, Chennai: Krishnamurti Foundation India.

McLaren, Peter. 1986. *Schooling as a Ritual Performance: Towards a Political Economy of Educational Symbols and Gestures*, London: RKP.

Rangaswami, S and S. Sridhar. 1993. *Birds of Rishi Valley and Renewal of their Habitats*, Rishi Valley: Rishi Valley Education Series.

Rao, Padmanabha, Radhika Herzberger, and Rajan Chandy. 2004. 'Reaching for Quality in the Countryside', *Seminar*. 536: 52–6.

Rishi Valley Education Centre. n.d. *Profile of a Naturalist. S. Rangaswami: In Words and Pictures*, Rishi Valley: RVEC.

Shukla, Suresh Chandra. 1991 'Schools—Ideologues and Professionals', *The Patriot*, 11 August 1991.

Singh, Sehjo. 2003. Film on Interview with the Raos. Sir Ratan Tata Trust.

Thapan, Meenakshi. 1991. *Life at School: An Ethnographic Study*. New Delhi: Oxford University Press.

_____. 2001. 'Adolescence, Embodiment and Gender Identity in Contemporary India: Elite Women in a Changing Society', *Women's Studies International Forum*. 24, 3/4: 359–71.

_____. 2005. 'Cultures of Adolescence: Educationally Disadvantaged Young Women in an Urban Slum', in Radhika Chopra and Patricia Jeffrey (eds), *Educational Regimes in Contemporary India*, New Delhi : Sage Publications.

Walkerdine, Valerie. 1990. *Schoolgirl Fictions*, London and New York: Verso.

Willis, Paul E. 1979. *Learning to Labour. How Working Class Kids get Working Class Jobs*, Surrey, England: Saxon House.

Woods, Peter. 1979. *The Divided School*, London: Routledge and Kegan Paul.

Preface

There is no doubt that Jiddu Krishnamurti has made a significant contribution to progressive education in India although his worldview is often perceived, especially in academic circles, as 'religious' or 'spiritual' in nature rather than oriented towards society and social change. Nonetheless, Krishnamurti's educational thought, with its emphasis on holistic education implying both academic excellence as well as a concern for the inwardness of life, is geared towards individual transformation and thereby eventual social change. This has important ramifications for progressive educators who are concerned with modifying or changing the existing educational process and its attendant pedagogy. It is of some interest then to explore the significant relations between Krishnamurti's ideas and the institutions that seek to implement them. The Rishi Valley School is one such institution in India and this book examines life at Rishi Valley in terms of the interplay between ideas and institutions, pupils and teachers, as well as the school's relationship with the wider society.

This work is based on my doctoral dissertation accepted by the University of Delhi in 1985. Krishnamurti's death in 1986 has undoubtedly had an impact on school processes and some of these are briefly considered in the postscript to the concluding chapter. Clearly, the Rishi Valley School has a dynamic character which is reflected in its ability to engage in a continuous process of transformation. My view of the school is based on my fieldwork, conducted in 1981, and on subsequent visits to the school. This does not however imply an outdated view of the school. On the contrary, I examine the school, within an explicit sociological framework, precisely in terms of its essentially fluid and changing character.

Earlier versions of Chapters 4 and 5 have been published in *Contributions to Indian Sociology*, 20(2) and the *British Journal of Sociology of Education*, 7(4) respectively, in 1986. I am obliged to these journals for their permission to use these materials in this book.

I am grateful to several persons in the preparation and writing of this book. My greatest debt is to Professor T. N. Madan, who supervised my doctoral dissertation, for his kindness, generosity and unfailing support. I thank Professor André Béteille for inadvertently suggesting the title of this book many years ago. I am grateful to Professor Suresh Shukla for his continuous encouragement and his faith in my abilities as a sociologist of education. I also thank Professor Krishna Kumar for his very useful suggestions.

I am obliged to members of the Krishnamurti Foundation (India) for their support and particularly to Rajesh Dalal for his friendship and hospitality at Rishi Valley. Mrs Pupul Jayakar facilitated my entry into the school as a research scholar and I thank her for her support and many acts of kindness over several years. Radhika and Hans Herzberger have provided many enriching insights into Krishnamurti's thought and educational processes in general. The staff and pupils at Rishi Valley are always most generous with their time and hospitality and I express my gratitude to each one of them. Among the staff, in particular, Mrs Thomas, Mrs Parchure, Mr and Mrs Natrajan, Mr and Mrs Hamid, Mr Prasanna Kumar, the Yoga teacher, and Fiona G. McMaster surpassed the role of informants and were very valuable friends in the field.

My parents have always supported me in my somewhat deviant ventures and I am grateful for their patience and understanding.

It was Krishnamurti who awakened my interest in education and I remain indebted to him for this and for much, much more.

CHAPTER ONE

Introduction

Introducing the Problem

This work seeks to answer questions concerning the character and functioning of a public school—the Rishi Valley School—in southern India run by the Krishnamurti Foundation (India). The questions that I pose—for example, regarding the internal organization and authority structure of the school, the nature of the school ethos, or the form and content of interpersonal relations between different categories of 'actors' in the school—are surely encountered, in one form or another, by the Foundation Members, the teachers *and* the pupils.[1] Their questions, however, primarily seek information or guidance for action, rather than an understanding of the school as a socio-cultural phenomenon through an interpretive effort. Such an effort to clarify what at first may seem obscure calls for a holistic view of the actors' externally observable behaviour as well as of their perception of their own social situation and of the school as a social reality. More precisely, the effort is to render the educational institution intelligible sociologically, that is, in terms of certain selected sociological paradigms of social reality at both the societal and the institutional levels.[2] I have attempted to do this through an ethnographic study of the Rishi Valley School (RVS). The ethnographic method imposes certain obligations: the necessity to do intensive fieldwork through involved observation followed by thick description. The ethnographic narrative also does not allow for a meaningful comparative perspective as it is essentially an in-depth approach focusing on a particular case.[3] It is possible that several structural changes, as well as transformations in the 'ambience' of RVS, have taken place since 1981 (when I conducted fieldwork) but following sociological convention, I have used the ethnographic present throughout.

RVS is a coeducational, residential, public school located in Chittoor District of Andhra Pradesh. It is not a large school by contemporary standards with only a total of 327 pupils (in October

1981) of whom about two-thirds are boys. The pupils are drawn primarily from middle to upper-class backgrounds and belong mainly to the southern region in which the school is located.

Schools in India may be broadly categorized as those managed by the government or a local body and those that are private (which are either aided or unaided by the government). Public schools fall in the category of private schools as they are managed by private bodies and trusts. The largest category of secondary schools are the private aided (57.30 per cent), followed by government managed schools (30.44 per cent), schools run by local bodies (8.71 per cent) and private unaided schools (3.55 per cent) (NCERT, 1980). Clearly, RVS falls into the last category as it is not supported by any government or local body (at least in 1981) and is managed by a private trust.

While RVS appears to belong to the smallest category, i.e. that of the private unaided schools, its significance as a model for study cannot be denied. Its importance lies precisely in its attempt to do something different while at the same time conforming to certain standard academic norms and performing similar academic functions as other public schools in the country. What is this 'something different' that RVS strives for in its very purpose? This level of its existence is primarily informed by the world-view and educational thought of the renowned philosopher and founder of the school, Jiddu Krishnamurti, whose work I examine in Chapter Two.

I must state at the outset that, in this work, I have not undertaken a comprehensive or comparative examination of Krishnamurti's thought.[4] I have only chosen the elements in his world-view which appear most relevant to his educational thought. My primary interest here is his educational thought and its impact on pedagogic processes inasmuch as it is claimed to provide the rationale for the school's existence as well as the guiding principles for action in RVS.

Krishnamurti's educational thought, with its emphasis on harmony between what he calls the 'technological world' and the 'psychological world', appears to be crucial to contemporary pedagogic practices that tend to emphasize the former to the virtual neglect of the latter. The human being is not only an individual, for Krishnamurti, but more importantly, an individual in relationship to society. If, therefore, the school seeks to provide an environment for the nurture or development of certain qualities in its pupils (such as, social awareness, a sensitivity to other people, to nature, or to ideas), these will only contribute to eventual social transformation rather than mere individual absorption that is so often feared by critics of the school. To the extent that these ideas comprise the foundation on which the school exists, it is of obvious interest to examine the relationship between these ideas and the actual pedagogic process in RVS. This work is therefore an attempt, at one level, to examine the interaction between ideas and institutions, i.e. the relationship between 'ideology' and education, as such.[5]

It is possible, however, that while ideas may seek to transform society through a holistic pedagogic process, the school does not exist in a vacuum: society acts on the individual and the institution through various agencies and avenues. The relationship between the individual and the institution with society is therefore dialectical in nature. One of the implications of such a view is that there is an element of constraint from the external order which may give rise to contradictions, cleavages, and dilemmas within the school. This work, at another level, seeks to examine the school's relationship with the external order and its influences on school processes.

Finally, and perhaps most importantly, there are the teachers and pupils—the major 'participants'—in school processes. The school is not merely a physical or an ideological construction. Its reality is also constructed by teachers and pupils through their everyday lives in the school. The school, thus, does not only exist as an institution 'out there', as it were, but acquires a social reality from the meanings brought to it by the participants through their interaction and everyday lives in RVS. Such a view of the school attempts to go beyond previous constructions of the school and the educational process in India that have tended to exclude the voices of the major participants in that process.

Sociologists of education in India have tended to look at educational processes largely in terms of their 'internal' and 'external' dynamics discussed somewhat loosely as the social background of teachers, student politics in higher education, problems of university administration, educational goals in relation to social development, and so on. All these problems, and others of the kind, indicate a concern with issues that are perhaps necessary to identify the social linkages with educational processes in general. While an understanding of these links is indeed important, it is quite obvious that there is a lack of interest in theoretical principles as informing the problematic of educational processes in India. These have been neglected to the extent that we have studies of secondary and higher education, for example, that provide us with adequate descriptions of fact and detail but do not really provide us with an account of what life at school is all about. Of course to do so is not the task of every commentator on school processes. But surely as sociologists our work must be informed by the theoretical concerns which we bring to bear on our findings which do not exist by themselves in a vacuum. However, a concern with theoretical principles alone can result in an extreme case of a lack of concern with the facts on the ground, as it were, The point is that we should aim for a middle course rather than adopt either extreme posture.

The second problem is that an exegesis on educational processes in India is rarely concerned with the human beings who participate in these processes. There are studies about teachers and their problems or about pupils but we do not hear their voices. Education, it would appear, is discussed without its own voice. We might ascribe other voices, such as.those of the prevailing influences from outside or of the internal dynamics of school organization, for example, but we do not let its own voice speak. Teachers and pupils remain largely silent participants in the educational process. It is only when their voice is heard, as that of the major participants in the process, that 'meaning' is introduced into any study of educational processes. This work is therefore also an attempt to restore the missing voices of teachers and pupils to the sociology of the school in India.

In this process, I seek to understand the 'subjective meanings' which teachers and pupils attach to or perceive in their actions in an effort to establish their meaningful behaviour patterns. These subjective meanings are individual and collective orientations based on varying motivations, interests, and intentions. These may include, on the part of the teachers, a commitment to the school's ideology and its implementation in the school or, alternatively, a desire for professional advancement, personal gain, status or power, or a combination of these. The pupils, on their part, may be oriented towards success, acquiring knowledge, or simply towards 'having fun' and enjoying life at school. These orientations would necessarily affect the nature and content of interactional processes. Pupil and teacher orientations towards each other and their roles are therefore significant in my understanding and interpretation of school processes.

In allowing the 'missing voices', as it were, to speak for themselves in studies of schools, for example, we are in fact imbuing educational studies with meaning that somehow gets lost in our descriptions and explanations of facts alone. The major problematic at this level then emerges as 'What does it mean to be a teacher or a pupil?' within a larger question on 'What really is life at school all about?'

It is important to point out here that the interpretive understanding of subjective meaning fulfils only one level of adequacy in sociological understanding, namely, 'adequacy on the level of meaning'. Sociological explanation must also be 'causally adequate'.[6] In this sense, I am concerned with adequacy at both individual and structural levels. I have tried to identify the structural conditions of both the internal and external orders of RVS which partly inhibit the execution of its particular educational programme but also provide the possibilities and opportunities for the effective functioning of its pedagogic process.

Two major points need to be made here. First, the school has an external reality in the sense that it is 'out there' as an observable social fact. It is located in a specific physical and social setting as well as in a particular ideological ambience which lends it a special character. The school's existence is legitimated by its function: it is engaged primarily in the task of the reproduction of knowledge and in the production of certain kinds of 'transformed' human beings as envisaged by one set of goals. Second, there is another aspect to the school's existence, namely, the processes of social interaction which give to it the quality of a living reality. The patterns of behaviour arising from the participants' relations to one another in fact constitute the social structure of the school. I am therefore also concerned with an explication of this structure through both the observation of processes of social interaction and an understanding of the participants' point of view.

The manner in which I seek to combine objective facticity with subjective meaning may be viewed as reinforcing the two apparently diverse perspectives in my analysis of the school. This appears possible if we take the view that 'society does indeed possess objective facticity. And society is indeed built up by activity that expresses subjective meaning . . . It is precisely the dual character of society in terms of objective facticity and subjective meaning that makes it "reality sui generis"' (Berger and Luckmann, 1967: 30).

Organization of the book

I begin with a discussion of ideology which is the school's *raison d'être* and provides the guidelines for action. I present Krishnamurti's world-view and, more specifically, his educational thought, as forming the ideological underpinnings of the school.

I then view RVS in terms of its historical background, physical setting and the organization of its material and human resources. In examining the roles of the key personnel in the school, such as the Principal and the Headmistress, and the processes of decision-making and communication, an attempt is made to identify the relations of power and the principles of control that operate in school processes.

This is followed by a discussion of the 'culture' of the school in terms of certain rituals and ceremonies that characterize the daily and yearly round of activities. These include the annual examinations and Krishnamurti's brief visit which are the high points of the academic year and constitute the critical elements in the school ethos. The culture of the school provides us with a backdrop which serves to evoke the atmosphere in which the activities of schooling and the processes of interaction take place.

In terms of the central function of the school, the pedagogic process itself, the two most important categories of participants are, of course, the teachers and the pupils. The rest of the work is therefore a discussion of their roles and relationships. I view the teacher's role in terms of social and situational expectations, institutional factors affecting it as well as teacher perspectives on the role. Their recruitment and commitment to the role and role performance are examined in order to identify and describe the different strands that constitute the teacher's experience in and out of the school.

Teacher–teacher interaction is an important aspect of social interaction in the school and is also discussed. The processes of institutionalized or formal interaction include the problems encountered by teachers *vis-à-vis* one another in the performance of their roles. Such interaction is viewed as being affected by, among other things, the ideology, institutional factors such as a teacher's position or status, and personal differences. The formation of friendship groups, cliques and factions, depending on various factors, such as the age, gender and institutional position of a teacher, are part of the process of informal interaction. Such processes as well as the flow of informal interaction among teachers is also discussed.

The nature and content of pupil culture is made up of the different aspects of pupil life and by the pupils' perspectives on life in the school. Beginning with pupil entry into the school, and identifying their social background, I consider the pupil at work or engaged in sport, co-curricular and leisuretime activities. Pupil–pupil interaction is also significant as it is a central part of the pupil's experience in the school. The pupils' career aspirations, their perception of school goals, and attitudes towards school processes are also examined.

Interaction between teachers and pupils is the central social process in the school. There is a discussion of teacher–pupil interaction in a junior and in a senior classroom, in other settings related to the classroom, and in informal settings, such as, the 'house' and the outdoor. The purpose is to describe the nature and identify the reasons for the kind of interaction that occurs between teachers and pupils. Further, the 'strategies' that are developed by the participants in the course of interaction are a major focus of study.

Finally, as assessment is made of the ideology in relation to the educational process. It is suggested that the accomplishment of ideological principles is constrained at the level of practice since the ideology itself is ultimately constrained by society at large and has to operate within the nexus of prevailing social norms and values. The work concludes with some comments on the lines of inquiry that seem to emerge from the present study.

CHAPTER TWO

Ideology and Education
Krishnamurti's World-View and
Educational Thought

Ideology and Education

In seeking to define the term 'ideology' I am not concerned with the conventional treatment of ideology as a social creed nor with its political connotations which are evident in most contemporary definitions of the term in sociological literature. My concern with ideology stems from what may be viewed as its major characteristic which is its call for the *'unity of theory and practice'* (Gouldner, 1976: 30). That is, through the medium of discourse, ideology seeks to transform the world by providing a vision of 'a positive alternative to the existing pattern of society and its culture . . .' (Shils, 1968: 60). It is therefore concerned with ideas and values and social transformation.

Although discourse is the main instrument through which an ideologue seeks to transform the world, the change has necessarily to be brought about through action. This action arises from an individual's perception and understanding of the ideology and of its attendant blueprint for action. Moreover, the key to the success of ideological implementation lies in the personal significance the ideology acquires for an individual and the extent to which it thereby becomes imperative for him or her to act on the basis of perceived ideological principles. In other words, ideology may be seen as a generative concept inasmuch as it is not only a description of a way of life but also generates action towards fulfilling it.

Two factors appear to be essential for individual internalization of an ideology before any action can take place. An individual has to be dissatisfied with the present state of affairs which leads to a search for external guidance in a quest for personal and social change. A second factor of considerable importance in this context is the 'charismatic authority' of the chief proponent of the ideology. The recognition of such authority derives from the 'surrender of the faithful to the extraordinary ... which arises from distress or enthusiasm' (Weber, 1978: 1115). Recognition of charismatic authority is also dependent upon the extent to which ideological discourse relates to an individual's own attempts to decipher social reality. Further, 'charismatic domination transforms all values and breaks all traditional and rational norms: "it has been written ..., but *I* say unto you" ' (Ibid.). The 'charisma'[1] of the proponent is therefore central to the process of individual transformation and results 'in a radical alteration of the central system of attitudes and directions of action with a completely new orientation of all attitudes toward the different problems and structures of the "world" ' (Weber, 1947: 363).[2] Apart from the importance of 'charismatic authority' in ideological discourse, it is evident that an ideology gets its significance and force from the meaning it acquires in the lives of individuals, from its application, by the way it affects what is said and done.

An ideology also applies moral and value prescriptions to social institutions and processes and the relationship between ideology and social institutions is always one of interaction leading to possible change. Education is one such social process permeated with ideology, explicitly or implicitly. We may thus expect to find ideological underpinnings in formal systems of education. Education in this work therefore refers to the formal process of schooling with its attendant influences such as those of the implicit or explicit ideology of the school and of the socio-cultural environment. It also includes the pedagogic process itself which implies both the transmission and acquisition of knowledge and modes of thought and the transmission and assimilation of values and codes of conduct.

More specifically, ideology refers to Krishnamurti's philosophy as contained in his writings and talks. Krishnamurti himself however repudiates the role of philosopher or representative 'of any system of conceptual thinking or ideology'. He stresses his distrust of ideology stating that 'all ideologies are idiotic, whether religious or political, for it is conceptual thinking, the conceptual word, which has ... divided man' (Krishnamurti, 1972: 8–9). Krishnamurti is not concerned with abstract formulations or arguments but with thought in praxis, as it were, insofar as he urges the individual to immediate action. Whilst I am aware that Krishnamurti does not consider himself as the proponent of an ideology, I am using the term with reference to his thought for the purpose of analysis.

It is important to state at the outset that Krishnamurti is not addressing himself to a particular set of people nor is he dealing with specific aspects or problems of life. Rather, he is concerned with the universal human predicament and in that sense the ideology is applicable to every aspect of life and to people across cultures. The most significant aspect of this ideological discourse is its rejection of the present social order (insofar as society is viewed as being corrupt and in a state of total disintegration) and its attempt to refocus the individual's orientation to society (insofar as social change is viewed as being a result of inner transformation and not, for example, of political revolution).

Krishnamurti's World-View: Some Essential Elements

THE TEACHING

While Krishnamurti may not consider himself a 'teacher' the fact remains that all over the world people seek him out and listen to him in an attempt to understand themselves and make sense of their lives. The most significant aspect of Krishnamurti's definition of his own role however is his complete disavowal of authority. The individual usually turns to an external agency—'God, an ideal, a guru, a teacher'—for a revelation of the 'right path' and for instructions for living. Krishnamurti questions whether such authority can actually initiate individual perception and change. According to Krishnamurti, authority in any form in fact breeds insecurity and fear because of the individual's dependence upon the source of authority. It is therefore necessary that the 'journey of understanding' has to be made by oneself which means that one has to discard every kind of authority: 'to be a light to ourselves we must be free of all tradition, all authority, including that of the speaker, so that our own minds can look and observe and learn' (Krishnamurti, 1972: 52).[3]

Krishnamurti sees himself as one who holds up the mirror to the individual in the process of self-discovery. He asks his audience to 'use the speaker to observe yourself . . . as a mirror in which you see yourself without any distortion and thereby learn what you actually are' (Ibid.: 43). He also suggests that the mirror can be thrown away once there is no use for it as attachment to the mirror is a form of bondage and that the act of perception itself is of primary importance.

On being asked what his teaching is, Krishnamurti has stated that it is a matter of partaking or sharing together rather than the giving or receiving of something. It is in the act of listening to him, without comparison or accumulation, and acting *immediately* on one's perception, that change occurs (1982a: 8–18). There is an emphasis on the instantaneous nature of the transformation: it is 'not something that is accomplished gradually through striving, seeking and bringing one's life, one's conduct and thought by degrees more in conformity with some ideal' (Holroyd, 1980: 35). There is therefore no state of 'becoming' or of 'being' but rather a sense of timelessness, as it were, in Krishnamurti's scheme of things.

Insofar as truth is an inward process of self-discovery, Krishnamurti has often said, 'the teachings are yourself' which would seem to be the crux of the teaching. There is however no culmination of this process and therefore there is no arrival at an aimed-at perfect state of being. If one undertakes Krishnamurti's challenge of understanding oneself, 'there is only the journey. There is no total knowing of oneself but rather an unending process of knowing oneself' (Jayakar, 1982: 28).

The Individual and Society

Krishnamurti's stress on self-discovery as the central tenet of his teaching may be viewed as an undue emphasis on the individual and a lack of concern with the social order. It would appear however that he sees individual change as being significantly related to social transformation.

Krishnamurti suggests that, historically, revolutions based on ideas have not wrought any meaningful change in society and have, in fact, brought about other forms of domination and repression. He is therefore emphatic that the only revolution that can transform society is the one that begins in the individual: 'We need to change completely, *that* is the greatest revolution . . . whether the mind can transform itself immediately and be entirely different tomorrow' (1972: 47). Recognizing the individual's relationship to society, he thus stresses 'the urgency of an inward revolution, which alone can bring about a radical transformation of the outer, of society' (1970a: 15).

In his assertion 'you are the world' Krishnamurti seeks to show the individual his responsibility to the social order. He suggests that the content of human consciousness—which is anxiety, hope, fear, joy, sorrow, pain, and so on—is the same everywhere. To this extent, there is no individual consciousness as such but rather a collective consciousness which implies that the world is not separate from the individual. One individual's action therefore affects another as 'to *be* is to be related' (1970a: 22). According to Krishnamurti, 'all relationship as it is now, is conflict' as it is based on 'images' that people build about themselves and others. Relationship means 'actual contact' and it is only when the mind is free of image-making that there is the right relationship (1972: 50).

Moreover, as society is 'the relationship that we establish or seek to establish with each other', the most important area where change is necessary is in this relationship itself (Krishnamurti, 1970a: 21). Thus it is in 'seeing oneself from moment to moment in the mirror of relationship—one's relationship to property, to things, to people, and to ideas', that change can occur (Ibid.: 27). Knowing oneself is therefore essential to establishing the right relationships: '. . . the first thing is to become aware of one's relationship to everything and everybody, and to see how in this relationship the "me" is born and acts. This "me" that is both the collective and the individual; it is the "me" that separates; . . . To be aware of this is to understand it. And the understanding of it is the ending of it' (1970b: 303).

While Krishnamurti perceives the individual's autonomy in taking the step towards transforming society through 'inward revolution', he also shows an awareness of the negative influences of society on the individual. That is, 'if the relationship between individuals . . . is not the outcome of an inward revolution, then the social structure, being static, absorbs the individual and therefore makes him equally static, repetitive' (1970a: 18). Thus without an inner change the individual will only perpetuate the disorder in society.

On Self-Knowing

The inward revolution that Krishnamurti sees as being essential for social transformation implies that 'we must begin with ourselves'. In this process of self-knowing the intention is very important. That is, 'the intention must be to understand ourselves and not to leave it to others to transform themselves or to bring about a modified change through revolution . . .' (1970a: 21). It is the individual's 'responsibility' to bring about an inner transformation which may then perhaps affect the world at large.

According to Krishnamurti, life is only 'what is'. An individual however, in not knowing how to dissolve or transcend 'what is', invents the 'what should be' and 'my invention then becomes a contradiction to what I am, to what is, and there is a battle between these two and that is my life' (1983: 10). It is therefore important to be aware of 'what is' rather than what has been or should be. This is not merely an injunction to be aware of the present instead of mulling over the past or thinking about the future. Being aware of 'what is' implies an awareness of reality: of what one really is, without accepting, condemning, rejecting or suppressing anything but exploring the working of one's mind, thoughts, feelings and action.

Such an awareness suggests a passive state of mind which is not however asleep but watching every movement and expression taking place within oneself. Krishnamurti is not advocating 'the cultivation of an unconscious state, but of what he calls the silent mind, which comes into being when the mind empties itself of its content, of the known, and which is not in a state of mindlessness but of intense and clear awareness of *"what is"* ' (Holroyd, 1980: 53). Further, Krishnamurti suggests that 'it needs an extraordinarily astute mind, an extraordinarily pliable heart, to be aware of and to follow what *is*; because what *is* is constantly moving, constantly undergoing a transformation, and if the mind is tethered to belief, to knowledge, it ceases to pursue, it ceases to follow the swift movement of what *is*' (1954: 21).

Krishnamurti says, in reading the 'book of life' which is oneself, awareness includes the 'art of listening' to what the book has to say without selection or interpretation (1981a: 3). In order to be able to really listen to oneself and others, 'one should abandon or put aside all prejudices, pre-formulations . . . and reaching beyond the verbal expression, to listen, so that we understand instantaneously' (1954: 20). Secondly, there is the 'art of seeing' which is the observation of oneself as one really is without distortion or separation from what one is observing. Krishnamurti questions whether there is an ' "observer—the centre from which you look, from which you see, from which you listen—a conceptual entity who has separated himself from the observed?' (1972: 12). It follows that if there is such a division, which is a result of the imagery that arises from one's accumulated knowledge or conditioning, conflict is inevitable in the process of understanding oneself and in relationship.

Krishnamurti suggests that the problem arises 'from our dualistic way of thinking, which makes us imagine that experiences are something we *have* rather than something we *are*, that there are two distinct entities, the experiencer and the experience, the observer and the observed' (Holroyd, 1980: 56). When the image intervenes between the observer and the observed the relationship is between images. One therefore has to break away from tradition, from the knowledge one has accumulated over the years which is one's conditioning, in order to observe what is real.

This brings us to Krishnamurti's definition of the 'art of learning' which is the third essential in understanding the 'book of life'. Conventionally, 'learning' implies a cyclical movement as described by Krishnamurti, 'we first experience, accumulate knowledge, store it in the brain, then thoughts as memory come into being and then action. From that action you learn. Thus learning is the accumulation of further knowledge . . . The mind is never free from the known. Our learning is always within the field of the known . . . [and] becomes mechanical' (1981a: 4, 5). By breaking this cycle, Krishnamurti shows that there is another kind of learning which is not based on thought or experience and is therefore not static. For this, 'the mind must be in a constant state of learning, therefore always in the active present, always fresh . . . To learn about myself there must be freedom to look and this freedom to look is denied when I look through the knowledge of yesterday' (1972: 15).

Awareness is therefore the art of seeing, the art of listening and the art of learning. Such an awareness implies that one is not 'caught in the same pattern or invent another pattern, but the constant breaking down of patterns, the norms, the values, which doesn't mean . . . that society is permissive' but that the mind is constantly aware of the pattern (1981a: 6). Moreover, this passive or 'choiceless' awareness implies that one is not caught in 'the movement of becoming or being'. That is, such an awareness does not flow from the 'centre'—which is 'the self, the "me", who is the very essence of fragmentation'—but is merely an observation of that whole movement (1978: 170, 171). Such an awareness is both an outward and inward process, a 'unitary process which brings about a total integration of human understanding' (1970a: 194).

Apart from emptying the mind of tradition and knowledge, Krishnamurti advocates the clearing out of psychological memories which do not allow one to meet life afresh. The ending of psychological memory is the beginning of non-attachment. 'When you end something, when you end attachment to your wife, to your people, to your gods, to your guru, to your concepts . . .—that tremendous burden of attachment with pain, anxiety, jealousy—. . . there is something totally new that takes place' (Krishnamurti, 1982b: 30). Living, according to Krishnamurti, is 'a process of continuity in which there is identification' (for example, 'me and my house, me and my wife, me and my bank account . . .') and its opposite is death which puts an end to all that. There is however a fear of death because 'we cannot experience the unknown while we are living'. Krishnamurti nonetheless asserts that death *can* be known while living: as that which has continuity has no renewal, it is only 'when we die each day to all that is old ["our experiences, our memories and misfortunes"] that there can be the new'. Thus, 'only in that dying, in that coming to an end, putting an end to continuity, is there renewal, that creation which is eternal' (1954: 235–7).

Krishnamurti's answer to the problem of overcoming sorrow and suffering is that with the knowing of oneself, sorrow comes to an end. A mind which has freed itself of the burden of attachment and sorrow and is in 'sensitive awareness of the totality of life . . . without choice and without being caught by any one of its issues' and flows with the whole of life is an 'intelligent' mind (as quoted by Holroyd, 1980: 59). Intelligence comes into being 'when the mind, the heart and the body are really harmonious' (Ibid.). As intelligence is born of harmony, 'actions governed by it bring harmony into the world. Morality and virtue, then, are not the observance of precepts or principles, but consist in the spontaneous functioning of intelligence in the world, which "naturally brings about order and the beauty of order". And this, concludes Krishnamurti, "is a religious life" ' (Ibid.).

FREEDOM AND THE RELIGIOUS MIND

Since 1929 when Krishnamurti declared that his only concern was to set man totally free, 'freedom' as a state of being has been central to his view of life.[4] Krishnamurti does not however advocate that freedom is something to be achieved, for 'in seeking to achieve something there is striving, . . . an element of time—the idea that something *is not* but *will be*—and there is dualism and conflict because the person conceives simultaneously an actual and an ideal state, and all these things negate true freedom' (Holroyd, 1980: 41). He views freedom as being possible when one is 'conscious and aware of the modes of bondage that circumscribe and delimit our lives' (Ibid.: 40). It is in this sense that 'freedom implies the total abnegation and denial of all inward psychological authority' insofar as dependence on someone or something is seen as breeding fear (Krishnamurti, 1978: 21, 26).

In urging the individual towards 'freedom from the known', Krishnamurti is really suggesting freedom from thought and knowledge which keep one bound to the past which then acts in the present and creates our future: 'memory, the past, expectation and thought are all involved in a form of human bondage . . . fear . . . and really to be free and to be without fear is not to be tyrannized by pleasure, desire and death' (Holroyd, 1980: 42–3). It is through understanding—by being choicelessly aware—of the nature of pleasure and desire, of how they arise and are perpetuated, that the individual can be liberated from them. It follows that if a mind is inwardly free there will be freedom of action outwardly. Such action will arise from a mind that is without conflict, and is clear and whole.

It may seem that Krishnamurti's emphasis on freedom may result in disorder or licentiousness in the individual and thereby in society. According to Krishnamurti, however, freedom and discipline go together. A disciplined mind is one 'that is learning, that is observing, seeing actually "what is", is not interpreting "what is" according to its own desires, its own conditioning, its own particular pleasures' and is therefore a free mind (1978: 24). Moreover a free mind will bear such action that arises from order and therefore will create order in relationship, in behaviour and thereby social order.

Finally, such a mind which has laid the 'foundation of freedom' is the religious mind. Religion, for Krishnamurti, does not mean devotion to a god or an idol, ritual, piety or prayer which are one form of gratification or another. Rather, 'religion— . . . where there is no kind of fear or belief—is the quality that makes for a life in which there is no fragmentation whatsoever,' (1978: 73) To be religious is to think and act out of the totality of one's being which means out of a quiet mind, an 'innocent mind' by which Krishnamurti means 'that whole in which are the body, the heart, the brain and the mind' (Ibid.: 79). Such a mind is the religious mind as it 'sees the whole of life as a unit, a unitary movement . . . [and] acts totally not fragmentarily' (as quoted by Holroyd, 1980: 69). Moreover, the religious mind is in a state of meditation which is not a method to be followed rigorously in order to attain something. Rather, it is the choiceless awareness of 'fear, of the implications and the structure and nature of pleasure, the understanding of oneself, and therefore the laying of the foundation of order, which is virtue, in which there is that quality of discipline which is not suppression, nor control nor imitation' (1972: 93). Such a conception of the religious mind and the religious way of life is therefore not in conflict with one's life in the world. 'It is a way of being in the world, of seeing and relating to the world and its phenomena. It is not a yearning after the superhuman or the supermundane, but . . . is a realization of full humanness and of the sacredness of the mundane world, of *what is*' (Holroyd, 1980: 70). The 'new human being' then is one who is 'passionate about the world and the necessity for change, . . . free from political activity, religious conformity and tradition—which means, free from the weight of time, free from the burden of the past, free from all the action of will' (1970b: 318).

Krishnamurti on Education: The Intention of the Krishnamurti Foundation Schools

In his exposition on 'right education' Krishnamurti is critical of the present systems of education as well as of the quality of education being imparted through them and therefore argues for an holistic approach as an alternative. He sees education as having emphasized only one aspect of life to the neglect of the other more significant aspect. Thus, 'education is today a movement of knowledge which conditions the mind. It is a movement, not only of the acquisition of knowledge during school, college and university, but throughout life' (1982c: 145).

Krishnamurti however identifies 'two vital movements' in an individual's life: 'One stream is that of the technological world, the world of computers, of knowledge, the physical world with all its complications. The other stream is the psychological world with its conflicts, miseries, confusion, opinions, beliefs, dogmas, religious

divisions, sorrows, pains, fear, a lack of integrity and so on. These
two rivers are . . . life' (1982c: 145). The contradiction between these
two worlds as a result of an undue emphasis on the physical over the
psychological world, results in conflict and disorder. And, 'order can
only come about when there is complete harmony between the two'
(Ibid.: 145–6).

Krishnamurti thus seeks the harmonious development of the
inner and the outer worlds insofar as 'what one is inwardly will
eventually bring about a good society or the gradual deterioration of
human relationship'. This harmony however 'cannot possibly come
about if our eyes are fixed only on the outer'. The inner world is the
'source and continuation of the disorder' and, for Krishnamurti,
education should be concerned with changing the source which is
the individual as it is 'human beings who create society, not some
gods in heaven' (1981b: 93–4).

In this sense, education 'is essentially the art of learning, not only
from books, but from the whole movement of life'. The knowledge
acquired from books is important as it is considered necessary for
understanding one aspect of life. Krishnamurti however argues that
'what is far more important is to learn the book, the story of yourself,
because you are all mankind. To read that book is the art of
learning' (1981b: 76–7). Thus 'education, in the true sense, is the
understanding of oneself, for it is within each one of us that the
whole of existence is gathered' (1973a: 17).

Krishnamurti also believes that such an education cannot be
based on a system of ideas or a blueprint for action as 'there is no
method by which to educate a child to be integrated and free'
(Ibid. 21). According to Krishnamurti, therefore, 'the right kind of
education is not concerned with any ideology, however much it may
promise a future Utopia: it is not based on any system, however
carefully thought out; nor is it a means of conditioning the
individual in some special manner' (Ibid.: 23).

It is in this sense that Krishnamurti therefore does not accept the
view that 'the teaching' (widely understood as his philosophy) is
something that has to be first studied and then translated into action
in the school. He says that 'the teaching asks you to "look at
yourself" ' and in that sense, 'it is you—it is your life. Not something
"out there" which has to be studied and translated into action'.
There is no doubt however that the bases for the Krishnamurti
Foundation schools are 'the teachings' inasmuch as Krishnamurti

has himself said that 'these schools are intended to bring about through education the application of the teachings. The implication of this is complex and can be carried out only when there is a group of teachers in every school who are concerned with these teachings' (1976: 1). It is to emphasize the notion that the teachings imply an inward search that Krishnamurti does not advocate an understanding of the teachings externally followed by their implementation in the school. It is a mutual process: that is, an understanding of the teachings and action derived from this understanding occurs simultaneously. He therefore argues that RVS was not founded for the teaching but was 'started out to bring about a good human being'. He places the origin of the school as lying in its beginnings: the 'coming together' of a 'community of people interested in this kind of education'.[5]

Krishnamurti has stated that the intention of all the Krishnamurti Foundation schools is that they 'are not only to be excellent academically but . . . are to be concerned with the cultivation of the total human being' (1981b: 7). Thus, 'these schools fundamentally exist to help both the student and the teacher to flower in goodness. This demands excellence in behaviour, in action and in relationship. This is our intent and why these schools have come into being; not to turn out mere careerists but to bring about the excellence of spirit' (Ibid.: 14–15).

Krishnamurti defines learning as the 'whole movement of life' as 'every action is a movement of learning and every relationship is learning' (Ibid: 22). This obviously implies that one learns not only from books but from life. His emphasis on relatedness—'to live is to be related'—suggests that one learns from one's relationship to people, nature, things and ideas. He describes the school as 'a place of leisure' as 'learning can only take place when there is no pressure of any kind . . . Leisure implies a mind which is not occupied . . . free observation is the movement of learning' (Ibid.: 23). The school, then, in Krishnamurti's scheme of things, is not merely a place for accumulating knowledge but also a place for learning.[6]

The schools are not viewed by Krishnamurti as mere centres of education: they are also places with 'religious' intent. It is in them that Krishnamurti hopes that human transformation will take place through the process of education. He describes the 'total responsibility' of these schools: 'Surely they must be centres for learning a way of life which is not based on pleasure, on self-centred activities, but on the understanding of correct action, the depth and beauty of relationship, and the sacredness of a religious life . . . these schools . . . must become places of light and wisdom . . . [they] exist for the enlightenment of man' (1981b: 84).

The Role of the Parent, Teacher and Pupil

Krishnamurti considers the role of the parent, the teacher and the pupil of equal importance in the education process. He urges parents to be aware of the disorderly situation in the world and to see that their children are brought up differently so that they are whole human beings. Thus, 'to love one's children is to be in complete communion with them; it is to see that they have the kind of education that will help them to be sensitive, intelligent and integrated' (Krishnamurti, 1973a: 104).

In the school Krishnamurti is concerned with first 'educating the educator'. He describes the teaching profession as the 'noblest' in the world and teaching as a 'holy act' if the teacher is aware of what is 'right education and of his important role in this process. Krishnamurti suggests that the first question a teacher must ask himself is 'What exactly he means by teaching? . . . Does he want to condition the child to become a cog in the social machine, or help him to be an integrated, creative human being. . .?' If the latter is the aim of teaching, 'the teacher himself must first begin to see. He must be constantly alert, intensely aware of his own thoughts and feelings, aware of the ways in which he is conditioned . . . of his activities and his responses; for out of this watchfulness comes intelligence, and with it a radical transformation in his relationship to people and to things' (1973a: 104, 105).

The highest function of the teacher is to bring about the 'psychological freedom' in the pupil and in himself. It is therefore 'the problem of the educator to investigate, and his creative capacity lies in observing very closely his deep-rooted conditioning and that of the student' (1981b: 41). This process of investigation is a 'mutual process' for psychologically the teacher cannot teach the pupil; each has to discover his inner world for himself. This does not mean that Krishnamurti denies the other significant aspect of the teacher's role: that of the transmission of knowledge. The teacher is also expected to bring about 'academic excellence' in the pupil through creative teaching and by establishing the right kind of relationship, and thereby, communication with him.

These aspects of the teacher's role are not necessarily contradictory. This depends on the teacher's perception of his role and on a view of education as not merely the acquisition of knowledge but as 'the awakening of intelligence which will then utilise knowledge' (Krishnamurti, 1981b: 16).

For the teacher to perform his role, it is first essential for him to perceive and feel his 'total responsibility . . . not only to the student but to the whole of mankind' (Krishnamurti, 1981b: 53). According to Krishnamurti, the origin of the word 'responsibility' is 'to respond not partially but wholly' and therefore implies that one is totally responsible 'for the whole, not for oneself, not for one's family, not for some concepts or beliefs, but for the whole of mankind'. In the school, then, 'responsibility to the earth, to nature and to each other is part of our education' (Ibid.: 19, 20). The teacher should however begin by feeling his complete responsibility for the pupil.

The most fundamental responsibility of the teacher in the school is that of bringing up 'a new generation of human beings who are psychologically, inwardly free . . .' (Krishnamurti, 1981b: 79). The sense of total responsibility gives rise to 'passion' in the teacher which is different from 'enthusiasm' and creativity is the result of this passion so that the teacher finds new ways of imparting information which do not make the mind mechanical. And such a creative process of teaching makes the teacher's mind 'always fresh, eager, discovering a wholly different approach to teaching (Ibid. 57).

The teacher's responsibility includes establishing a 'direct personal relationship' with the pupil. The relationship between the teacher and the pupil is in fact central to the process of bringing up a new generation of human beings as well as, more specifically, to the pedagogic process. In his dealings with pupils, the first thing the teacher has to be aware of is that there is no authority, status or power attached to his role. Krishnamurti considers authority as 'corruption . . . the breaking up of integrity, the whole . . . Authority basically denies freedom. It is the function of a true teacher to instruct, point out, inform, without the corrupting influence of authority' (Ibid.: 35).

The teacher's authority becomes evident in the act of comparison. By comparing one pupil with another, in terms of behaviour or skills, the teacher inculcates and perpetuates a sense of hurt and fear in the pupil. Pupils then begin to compete with one another in an attempt to excel in all aspects of school life. For Krishnamurti, comparison and competition are not the necessary tools for bringing about academic excellence. It is only when the teacher 'puts aside comparison and measurement, then he is concerned with the student as he is and his relationship with the student is direct and totally different' (Krishnamurti 1981b: 80). Such a relationship gives rise to communication which enables the pupil *to learn* and not merely acquire knowledge.

It is also the teacher's task to create such an atmosphere in the school that the pupil feels secure, protected, cared for and is happy and feels at home. It is only when the pupil experiences this sense of happiness at school that he will be capable of learning. The teacher therefore has to 'create this atmosphere of learning, a seriousness in which there is s sense of freedom and happiness' (Krishnamurti, 1981b: 32).

It would appear that the teacher's responsibility to the pupil takes the form of three tasks, as pointed out by Krishnamurti, which have to be performed together so that they make a harmonious whole. The first is his role in the awakening of the pupil's intelligence or insight which is a holistic way of looking at things. Secondly, the teacher is responsible for taking care of the details of pupil behaviour, the daily routine, and so on. Finally, there is the task of academic instruction (1975: 198, 199). If the performance of one of these tasks is emphasized over another, this gets reflected in the educational process itself which becomes fragmented and incomplete.

The teacher however is not the only participant in this educational process. Krishnamurti recognizes the role of the pupil as being complementary to that of the teacher in the pedagogic process. He points out the pupils' responsibility as being 'to study, to learn and to act' and that this is the main purpose of education. Krishnamurti explains 'responsibility' to the pupils as implying 'care and concern for our world' and that which has nothing to do with duty and is therefore free of the burden of guilt and tradition. He asks them to observe themselves with affection and attention and suggests that the study of the inner world requires greater diligence than that of the outer (1981b: 95–6).

Krishnamurti's emphasis on the psychological world stems from his explanation to the pupils, in discussion with him, of the function of education which is 'to give you freedom—complete freedom to grow and create a different society, a new world . . .' (1970a: 96). The first task of the pupil in this educational process is to question and examine the roots of fear so that 'you are not isolated by . . . [it] and are not enclosed in ideas, in traditions, in habits, but are a free human being with creative vitality' (Ibid.: 100). Rather than being moulded by parental or social expectations or by tradition, Krishnamurti asks them to find out what they would like to do and choose their careers accordingly: in this manner they would be acting as free human beings with a sense of responsibility towards themselves and the world.

He discusses the problem of freedom with the pupils and suggests that it does not imply doing whatever one wishes to do. On the contrary, 'to be free is to be intelligent' and intelligence 'comes into being only when you begin to understand your whole environment, the social, religious, parental and traditional influences that are continually closing in on you'. Freedom also lies in 'understanding what you are from moment to moment' which is only possible 'when you are in revolt against the whole tradition of trying to become something. That is the only revolution leading to extraordinary freedom. To cultivate this freedom is the real function of education' (Ibid.: 113–15).

In advocating resistance to social conditioning or rebellion to the established social order, Krishnamurti believes that the prevailing social order can indeed be transformed. This is indicative of the view that there is no inevitability of an unceasing reproduction of social values and norms. There is a difference however between the reproduction of values and that of material interests represented by one's position in society. Krishnamurti of course does not comment on this at all. It would nonetheless appear that while it may not be too difficult to resist or rebel against a particular culture, it is more difficult to change what is materially given in a particular culture.

On Co-operation and Living Together in the School

As Krishnamurti's definition of a school is that of 'a community of people working together' in which authority has no place, co-operation between the participants becomes essential for the school to function. Co-operation between the teacher and the pupil is only possible when 'they have a relationship which is essentially based on affection'. The importance of co-operation between them is necessary to enable free enquiry into ourselves without the barrier of the one who knows and the one who doesn't' (1981b: 99, 100).

Krishnamurti has stated that 'in laying the foundations of an environment in which our principal concern is to live together intelligently' what is required is freedom and 'self-critical awareness'. To establish the co-operation that living together entails, 'every form of prejudice . . . of conclusion' must come to an end (1975: 50). Thus working together 'implies the abnegation of the self without any motive. It is like learning together in which there is only function without any status' (Ibid.: 237).

Such a spirit of co-operation enables communication which is 'learning from each other, understanding each other'. It follows that, as the teacher and the pupil are both in a relationship of learning, discipline enters of its own accord. As Krishnamurti would have it, there is no need for the formation of rules as 'a mind that is learning is a free mind and freedom demands the responsibility of learning' (Krishnamurti, 1981b: 102).

Concluding Comments

It is obvious that one of the ways through which Krishnamurti seeks to realize his world-view is through the process of 'right education'. Education is his tool for change and the school is the institutional medium through which this change can be brought about. 'Right education' is holistic in nature and takes account of both 'academic excellence' and 'psychological freedom'. The onus rests on individuals—parents, teachers, and pupils—in their contribution towards the creation of a different social order through their behaviour and action. There is thus a synthesis between Krishnamurti's ideology for life and his attempt to realize this in practice. This unity of theory and practice is a significant aspect of the ideology; he does not himself dwell on abstract formulations but rather emphasizes the urgency for change and therefore the need for immediate action.

Krishnamurti's educational thought and practice may not be particularly original in the history of educational thought. It may be compared to progressivism which has emphasized a child-centred approach and considered the uses of freedom in the educational process. Such an approach was embraced by educators in revolt against the traditional methods prevalent in schools. The ideology of the 'progressive' child-centred educator, who believes in 'growth', cannot be attributed to any one central thinker. Rousseau was perhaps the first 'progressive' followed by Dewey, Neill, and others in the West.

Progressive education is characterized by a familiar core of tenets and arguments: education is the development from within of the potentialities rather than 'moulding' from without; the curriculum should arise from the needs and interests of the child rather than from the demands of the teachers; children should not be coerced or punished and should be allowed to learn from 'experience' rather than be told things (Peters, 1959: 88). The ideology of progressivism also challenges the right of the teacher to be anything more than a facilitator, responsive to the expressed desires of the learner. Whether one enriches the environment in the school (as Rousseau, Dewey, or Neill might suggest) or counsels deschooling the environment (Illich, Reimer), the intention is to leave the individual free to develop in any direction s/he chooses.

Among progressive Indian educators, Rabindranath Tagore may perhaps be considered nearest to Krishnamurti in terms of ideology. Education, for Tagore, is a process of 'creative joy' which would lead to the attainment of a life in harmony with the universe. This realization of harmony is specified by Tagore as the 'pursuit of fullness (*bhuma*), the pursuit of the whole man' (Cenkner, 1976: 46). This essentially means, on the one hand, an inner and individual perfection and, on the other, the realization of social awareness and relationships.

Tagore believed that education is the 'gradual and progressive' growth of an organism. Hence, the child must be left 'free' to do as he wishes. The school of Tagore's conception has therefore been described as 'open, free, abundant and spontaneous where young people could be free in spite of themselves' (Cenkner, 1976: 51–5). All this could be done in an environment that was natural, open and free, and his first school was modelled along the lines of an *asram* community which was also seen as necessary for the expression of 'religious power', as he defined it.

A more significant comparison could be made between Krishnamurti's educational thought and what are labelled the 'communitarian' elements in modern progressive education. These imply that a person is essentially a social rather than an individual being with an expected commitment to change society (see Skilbeck, 1976: 32). Insofar as Krishnamurti views the school as a community, and as most of the KFI schools *are* self-contained, rather isolated

communities established with a view towards eventually transforming the social order, one aspect of the ideology may be viewed as
being communitarian.

There is one fundamental point however that places Krishnamurti
apart from the progressive educators. He is concerned essentially
with bringing about a revolution in the *psyche of the individual* which
he is sure will transform society. This is sought to be done without
any form of indoctrination and is instead dependent on individual
perception and action. The school thus has to provide the ambience
for the 'awakening of intelligence', the teacher is allowed no
authority and the participants are in fact engaged in a process of
'mutual education'.[7]

It has been assumed, over the years, that progressive education is
over-permissive, irresponsible, and 'becoming a soft educational
option' resulting in a view of progressivism in education as
'reproducing rather than producing, transforming and anticipating
social systems' (Morrison, 1989). Morrison in fact suggests that it
has 'failed to address or challenge society and social movements at
large because of its conceptual confusion and because of the neglect
of its emancipatory potential—potential for changing society and
children in that society' (Ibid.). Krishnamurti has quite emphatically and clearly stated that education does indeed have a crucial role
to play in the transformation of society through generating a critical
consciousness, for example, among other things. For Krishnamurti,
however, the impetus for change has to begin in the individual
leading to social transformation; it can never be the other way
around. This is perhaps what worries certain critics of Krishnamurti: that he does not begin from the social but from the individual
to the social.

Krishnamurti has also been criticized for his 'Rousseauian
confidence in the innocent integrity of the individual' and in the
latter's ability to transform the world (Campbell, 1980: 149). While
the individual may be seen as creating society, the latter also acts on
the individual and the constraints that are imposed on individual
action by social values, norms and institutions are considerable. A
similar criticism views Krishnamurti's thought as impractical and
unrelated to the demands and pressures of modern society and
therefore difficult to internalize. Moreover, the integrity and
excellence in behaviour and action expressed by Krishnamurti are
viewed as being almost impossible to attain.

At another level, Krishnamurti dwells on questions or problems of inequality either at a personal or a very general level. He does not however directly address himself to the question of *social* inequality and the problems it generates. This is again due to a clear perception and firm belief that all problems as well as their solutions originate in the individual who has first to change before effecting social change of any kind. Such an approach has been considered a shortcoming to the extent that is appears to neglect an explicit discussion on problems of social inequality and justice in a work otherwise suffused with brilliance and compassion.[8]

CHAPTER THREE

School Organization
The 'transcendental' and the 'local' orders

The most significant aspect of school organization in RVS is the fundamental dichotomy in school processes between the 'transcendental' and the 'local' orders. The transcendental order is governed by Krishnamurti's world-view which is the school's *raison d' être* and provides guidelines on how the school *ought* to function as well as guides administrative policy and decision making. The local order constitutes the *actual* schooling process and tends to function independently of the transcendental order.

The transcendental order constitutes one strand and is concerned essentially with values and the production of a new kind of human being through the process of self-knowledge and transformation. The local order is based on the school as an institution and is mainly concerned with the reproduction of knowledge through the transmission of educational knowledge. RVS participates in an ongoing educational programme through its affiliation with the Council for the Indian School Certificate examinations in New Delhi and its academic programme adheres to the syllabi set by the Council. Thus the curriculum and the pedagogic process in the senior school are primarily geared to the accomplishment of Council goals. In this sense, learning is, among other things, the accumulation of knowledge in preparation for the examination to be taken at the end of the academic year. The local order in RVS is largely derived from the broad-based educational system and other social forces outside the school: notably, the demands of institutions of higher learning for pupils of a certain academic calibre and success judged in terms of examination grades and parental expectations regarding the academic progress and success of their children. The expectations of senior pupils, governed by their awareness of parental and social expectations, are indicative of competitive striving and of 'getting-on' in the world. It is evident that the local order is quite significantly different from the transcendental order in terms of motivations, aims and values—a difference which would inevitably be reflected in school activities and processes.

RVS as an organization exists at the level of both these orders. This is its paradox and in a certain sense, it is what lends it the quality of a 'different' kind of a school. There is in the school a continuous effort to achieve a certain balance between the two orders. This is what makes it a somewhat unusual school constantly in the process of becoming, as it were, rather than the more commonplace, well-defined, established schools.[1] In fact, RVS as an educational institution makes sense because of the bearing of one order, with its attendant form of discourse, upon the other and the relationship between the two orders.

History and Goals

The internal structure and character of RVS is created by the actors in it. I therefore attach paramount significance to their *individual intentions* and *collective goals* in the consequent construction of a particular social reality. It is the interaction between actors and the resultant configuration that give rise to what may be termed an organization. An organization, such as a school, is therefore created by the meanings and purposes an individual brings to it and through his or her relations with similar other individuals in the same setting. It is in this sense that organizations may be viewed processually as 'definitions of social reality', just as they may be viewed synchronically as structures of given goals and roles.

However, actors also encounter already existing intentions and meanings both within the organization and from the external world. Thus, there are certain internal conditions arising from a combination of the physical resources available and the institutional structure of the school itself which not only establish its concrete character but also influence the nature of activity and interaction. In the case of RVS, the ideological framework of education is an additional and critical factor. Besides, the actors' relations with the external world shape their goal orientations and activity pattern within the school. The goal orientation of the school as an institution therefore implies its interaction with society insofar as goals are influenced both by the actors' expectations of what they will give to society, through the medium of the school, and by society's expectations of the school as an institution of learning.

This does not, however, mean that all individuals have similar definitions of the task at hand. Variations in the actors' goal orientations—as a result of motivations or commitments—result in multiplex goals which may or may not conflict with one another. These variations also reveal one aspect of the relations of power and control in the school insofar as one group of actors formulates goals and takes decisions regarding the manner in which they are to be realized which may be contrary to the orientations of some other actors.

While variation in goal orientations appears to be central to life in an organization, there also is interaction between goals. Thus the school's official goals have been formulated in the light of its ideological aims; the school's 'operative goals' are conditioned by internal and external factors and the official goal orientation. Goals thus activate interaction between actors and, in that sense, they are not remote statements about intended action but are rather sought **to be realized** through activities.

The purpose for which the school was set up may be traced to its beginnings which take us back to 1918, when Dr Annie Besant, President of the Theosophical Society, formed the Society for the Promotion of National Education. A school was then started at Teynampet in Madras based on the principles of education enunciated by Besant.[2] This school, called the National Theosophical School, was shifted to Guindy (also in Madras) in June 1920. In 1922, the school was affiliated to the Theosophical Educational Trust as the Society for the Promotion of National Education had been wound up.

Meanwhile, several changes were taking place in the Theosophical Society, and the idea of developing an educational centre around Madanapalle—Krishnamurti's birthplace—was gathering momentum.[3] Around 1925, it is believed that Krishnamurti started surveying the land around Madanapalle for locating the educational centre. It is said that Krishnamurti selected the present location, viewing from a rock the vast panorama of the valley stretching to the west with Rishi Konda (literally, the hill of the Rishi) at its apex. The presence of a large banyan tree in the valley, believed to be about 300 years old, is said to have influenced Krishnamurti's decision.

The valley was locally known as Thettu Loya (literally, Thettu Valley) after the name of the village, Thettu, at the foot of Rishi

Konda. The traditional belief of the villagers in the area that two rishis were still living in the hill invisible to the human eye, resulted in the valley being renamed 'Rishi Valley'. Between 1926–9, 280 acres of land were acquired in the area for the proposed centre.

A new organization, the Rishi Valley Trust, was registered on 22 February 1928 to administer 'The School, Rishi Valley' (as it was called) as well as the sister institution at Rajghat, Benares. Between 1930–2 the necessary buildings were constructed and the development of the dairy and the estate took place at Rishi Valley. By 1931, when the minimum essential buildings had come up, the main effects of the Guindy school, which had been damaged by a cyclone the previous year, were gradually shifted to Rishi Valley, along with 93 pupils out of the nearly 300 enrolled.[4]

Meanwhile, Krishnamurti had stated his views on education at a camp in Benares in 1928–9 which became the basis for the new Krishnamurti schools. On 3 August 1929, he dissolved 'The Order of the Star', a major organization founded by G. Arundale, of which Krishnamurti had been designated the Head. In his speech on this occasion Krishnamurti made an important statement which gave a new direction to his world-view (see Krishnamurti, 1929). He resigned from the Theosophical Society in 1930. In the midst of the storm that was brewing in the Theosophical Society due to Krishnamurti's dissent and eventual departure, particularly as he had been proclaimed the World Teacher by Besant and other eminent Theosophists, RVS came into being.

The historical background of RVS identifies the specific goal orientation of the school. The formal aspect of goal orientation is the 'charter' of the organization defined as 'the system of values for the pursuit of which human beings organize' (Malinowski 1944: 52). In the case of RVS, this charter may be seen to exist in the form of Krishnamurti's writings on education in general and on the purpose and content of schooling in particular. The Krishnamurti Foundation (India), (KFI), in its task of running the school, also states its avowed aims which are derived from Krishnamurti's educational thought. The Foundation came into being in March 1970 as the successor to the Rishi Valley Trust which had been renamed the Foundation for New Education in 1953. In the 'Memorandum of Association' the Foundation lists fifteen objectives which include research projects in various areas, and the sponsorship of rural development, afforestation and agriculture schemes. The first objective, 'to promote educational, cultural and humanitarian activities in the light of Sri J. Krishnamurti's teachings' (1983: 1), however appears to be the main task of the Foundation. It is in this sense that the Foundation exists 'solely for the propagation of Krishnaji's teachings'. One way in which this is sought to be achieved is through its 'activities' in the five Krishnamurti schools in India which it 'owns and directs'.[5] In recent years, Krishnamurti has been known to say that 'the schools have taken over the Foundations' thus indicating the extent to which the KFI schools have grown and expanded (Jayakar, 1987).

The Foundation is therefore the major link between Krishnamurti and the schools in terms of being the main decision-making body which gives effect to Krishnamurti's directives for the schools. Krishnamurti has however clearly stated that 'the Foundations [the Indian, American and British] have no authority in the matter of the teachings. The truth lies in the teachings themselves . . . The Foundations have no authority to send out propagandists or interpreters of the teachings. . . I have no representatives who will carry on with these teachings in my name now or at any time in the future. . . . The Foundations will not give rise to any sectarian spirit in their activities . . . [and] will not create any kind or place of worship around the teachings or the person' (1973b: 2–3). While Krishnamurti defines and thereby curtails the authority of the Foundation *vis-à-vis* the teachings, the Foundation is apparently given full autonomy in its manner of functioning with respect to the schools.

The Foundation states the intention of the schools, based on Krishnamurti's educational thought, in an advertisement for teachers as the effort to 'awaken the intelligence of the child . . . the cultivation of a global outlook . . . [and] a religious spirit without any sectarian bias and a concern for man and his environment. . .'. This is to take place in an atmosphere of 'freedom and responsibility'.[6] These are the school's 'expressive' goals and provide its official goal orientation.[7] This is also stated in the school brochure, sent out to interested parents, which states the school's aim simply as 'to awaken the intelligence of the children and to help them to look, to listen and to learn' (1981).

The official aims of the school are thus clearly aligned to its ideological goals insofar as the Foundation and the Management take care to emphasize the latter in official statements on their aims. The ideology as a system of values therefore provides 'legitimacy' to the organization just as it justifies its activities and, in fact, its very existence. A distinction needs to be drawn between the official goals, located in the school's transcendental order, and the more immediate or 'active' goals of the schools, located in its local order, that are related to the actual situation in which the goals are sought to be realized.[8]

In one sense, the school's operative goals are derived from the official, ideological goals and, therefore, are 'abstractions made more concrete' (Hall, 1972: 84). This is evident in the school's attempts to incorporate ideological values and aims in its curriculum and daily round of activities. Operative goals, in this sense, are influenced by the school's internal environment or atmosphere derived from ideological aims. Operative goals, however, also include 'instrumental goals' which are a result of three main factors: (i) the external environment, which impinges on the school through the requirements of the Council for the Indian School Certificate Examinations (Council) and the school's affiliation with the Indian Public Schools Conference (IPSC); (ii) parental expectations *vis-à-vis* their child's academic performance; (iii) and pupil expectations in terms of their perception of their life after leaving school.

Instrumental goals may therefore be defined as being primarily concerned with 'the transmission of useful skills and information or the acquisition of qualifications' or, in other words, with the 'gaining of knowledge or of examination results' (Lambert *et al.* 1970: 56). Insofar as the pupils take the Indian Council of Secondary Education (ICSE) and the Indian School Certificate (ISC) examinations at the end of Standards (Stds.) 10 and 12, the school has to adhere to the prescribed syllabi in the senior classes. Learning, at this level, is therefore primarily directed towards a specific end, namely to prepare pupils for the examinations. As a result of its external order (i.e. relations with the Council), the school appears to fall short of its ideological goals.

The school is also a member of the IPSC which was formed in October 1939 by the headmasters of five public schools and which defined 'the essential character of the Indian Public School and gave it authoritative sanction' (De Souza, 1974: 24). While the Management are of the opinion that membership of the Conference in no way affects the school's functioning, apart from having to attend the IPSC's annual conferences, the IPSC has certain requirements for membership. These are in essence directed 'to the creation of a

structured internal environment conducive to the socialization of
boys in the norms and values of the public school code of conduct'
(De Souza, 1974: 31). Although the proposed norm is that of a
residential, 'all-male school', co-educational or girls' schools are not
excluded from membership.

To attain its objectives, the Conference holds a periodic 'inspection' of member schools after which a report is prepared on the
nature of the school's 'compliance with the essential requirements of
the rules and regulations' (Ibid.: 29). The 39th annual session of the
IPSC was held at RVS in 1978 and the comments by the editor on
the school in the IPSC Newsletter indicate the high esteem in which
the school is held by members of the IPSC.

While affiliation to the Council and the IPSC means that the
school has to fulfil the basic requirements, it is allowed some amount
of freedom in doing so. For example, although the Council
prescribes the syllabi and suggests the textbook requirement for
each subject, the school is given considerable freedom in using
textbooks of its choice. Similarly, according to the rules of the IPSC,
all power rests with the Principal in a public school, but RVS has its
own pattern of decision-making and does not strictly adhere to the
rules of the IPSC.

Apart from the external factors of the school's affiliation with the
Council and the IPSC, with only the former significantly influencing
its operative goals, there are parental expectations, that the Management and teachers have to cope with, particularly in relation to the
pupils' academic performance. The parents pressurize them to pay
special attention to their children: this really means that the school
should pressurize the pupils to work towards well-defined academic
goals. Parental interference in fact forces a compromise in the
school's functioning to the extent that a comparative element in the
evaluation of pupil competences is introduced.

Besides the pressures emanating from the school's relations with
external agencies there are certain internal factors—'organizational'
in nature—which also influence its operative goals. These goals are
concerned with 'ensuring that the organization has adequate
personnel, that its continuity is certain, that its reputation is
unsullied, that it operates in a smooth, orderly and efficient way,
and that its members are kept busy in ways which serve its other
goals, or at least do not threaten its "efficient running"' (Lambert *et
al.*, 1970: 56). The organizational aspect of the school's goal

orientation may therefore be viewed as being concerned with maintaining it as an 'ongoing system' (Ibid.).

The Management is entrusted with the task of achieving the school's official goals, directing activities, and taking decisions pertaining to school organization assisted by various committees concerned with the different aspects of school life. RVS also has an elaborate administrative system, under the authority of the Bursar, which deals with the recruitment of personnel, the procurement and distribution of its finances, the maintenance of school property and with the organization and efficient running of the school. A rationally planned and organized time schedule keeps the participants involved in school activities through the working day and the academic term. In short, the efficient management of time and resources combine to maintain and perpetuate the system.

The distinction between the official and operative goals is not merely analytical in nature and based on its internal structure or external relations but is also perceived by the participants themselves. The pupils, in particular, view ideological goals as being 'impractical' and unrelated to their lives after leaving school and their main concern is their success at the examination in order to secure admission to institutions of higher learning in relation to their perceived occupations.[9] Operative goals are thus a combination of the school's external order, its ideological goals, and equally important, the 'modifications and subversions' of these by the participants (Hall, 1972: 85).

The informal aspects of an organization, such as the participants' perceived goals and interaction between them, significantly affect its goal orientation. Thus 'organizations, once created, develop a "life of their own"' as the interests and aims of the participants alter the official specifications of the 'charter' (Davies, 1973: 255). Moreover, these interests and aims—what Davies calls 'motivational goals'—may be seen as changing over time thereby adding to the complexity of the school's goal orientation. For example, among the pupils, there is a distinct change in their goals as they move up from the junior to the senior school.

The participants' goals may also diverge from the official or the operative goals of the school. This is evident in the case of the professional teacher who is less concerned with the ideology and more with fulfilling her perceived operative goals. In contrast, the ideologue teacher is first committed to the ideology and experiences some amount of strain in the process of accomplishing the school's operative goals.[10]

Among the pupils, those at the junior level have unarticulated goals and take part in the activities organized by the school in the particular atmosphere prevalent in the junior school. The senior pupils, on the other hand, perceive their goals primarily in relation to school work and are not particularly concerned with ideological goals. There are some pupils who may be interested in the ideology but this is in no way more important than their interest in school work. The Management, in particular those members who are committed to the ideology, strive for an interweaving of official, ideological, and operative goals—of the transcendental and the local orders—but the distinctions survive in practice. It is evident that what different individuals are working towards may contain elements common to all participants, but may also vary in terms of their perception, modification, and re-creation of school goals.

The Key Functionaries

Following Bernstein, I would like to argue that there is in th school a 'structure of social relationships' which controls 'curriculum, pedagogy and evaluation' different from that structure of social relationships which controls 'the transmission of the moral order' (1977: 3, 4). In RVS, quite obviously, the former may be seen as being located in its local order, the latter in the school's transcendental order. Similarly, the school's 'instrumental' and 'expressive' dimensions are not merely extended as different aspects of role performance but, as pointed out by Bernstein, refer to 'structural relationships of control' (Ibid.). Different actors seek to effectively control the academic-instrumental dimension of school life, for example, while others control ideological dissemination in school processes (see Figure 1).

There are different categories of personnel in RVS organized around a division of functions and the distribution of duties and responsibilities. This is particularly true of the professional personnel. The principles of authority that play a significant role in the organization of personnel are muted in RVS to a considerable extent in apparent concurrence with its official framework. They are not, however, absent.

There are certain 'key functionaries' such as the Principal, the

Figure 1

ROLES OF KEY FUNCTIONARIES

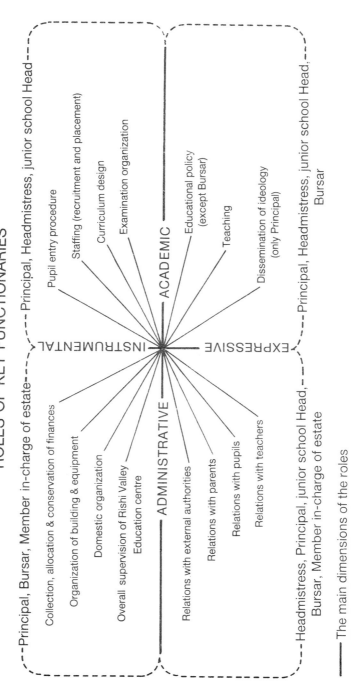

Note: *This figure has been adapted from Taylor, 1964, as given by Musgrave, 1968: 47.*

— The main dimensions of the roles
— The functions of the roles

Headmistress, the junior school Head, the Bursar, and the Member in-charge of the estate, who perform specific roles in addition to their other tasks. They are all members of the Managing Committee, including one other senior teacher, which shares the responsibility for running the school. I am here concerned with an analysis of the role of the key functionary and the meanings brought to it by such a person's role perception and performance. This will help us in understanding the somewhat complicated structure of social relationships in RVS which, through consensus and co-operation, effectively directs and controls life at school. I begin with the Principal and the Headmistress as they are central to school processes. Although the junior school Head is an important functionary, his role is discussed more appropriately in the next chapter in terms of his significant function as an ideologue teacher. The roles of the Bursar and the Member in-charge of the estate are considered briefly here as they perform specific functions concerned primarily with the maintenance of the school.

The Principal was appointed to his post in August 1977. His contact with Krishnamurti, who appointed him to his post, and his interest in the ideology indicate his special position in the school in terms of its transcendental order. This is apparent from the 'special function' he is expected to perform as Principal. As specified in his appointment letter, he is the Director of the Rishi Valley Education Centre (which includes the main school (RVS), the Rural Centre, the estate, and the dairy) and the Principal of RVS, and in effect, he is 'totally responsible for all that happens' at Rishi Valley. The Principal identifies his 'special function', arising out of the expectations of Krishnamurti and the Foundation, as the conveying of 'the range and significance of Krishnamurti's teachings' to the teachers and pupils. This function is 'special' to the school as he would not have been performing such a role in any other school.

He performs this function in an indirect manner with the pupils whom he meets in groups at least once a day. He also meets the teachers collectively at the weekly staff meeting, at which a definite attempt is made to bring about an awareness of the ideology and its implementation through an explicit discussion of Krishnamurti's works and the school's intention. At these meetings, the Principal experiences some resistance as the teachers demand discussion on the actual problems they face in the classroom and the school rather than on the ideology. This is one indication of the conflicting expectations of his role which create problems in performance.

While the dissemination of the ideology may be his special function, the Principal performs other roles which are academic and administrative in nature, both internal and external to school processes, and include formal and informal interaction with teachers, pupils and other staff at both the individual and collective levels. There are thus the two broad dimensions of the instrumental and the expressive to the Principal's role which is performed in conjunction with the other members of the Managing Committee in terms of the division of functions, duties and responsibilities amongst them (see Figure 1). The Headmistress and the Principal attend to the academic and educational administration. Administration relating to the physical organization and functioning of the school is conducted jointly by the Principal and the Bursar. A major administrative task for the Principal is the 'financial conservation' of the school to which he attends by sending out appeals for donations and collecting them from parents and patrons of the school. In his relations with external agencies, he sometimes attends the annual IPSC meeting, and meets members of the Council and government officials for discussion on work pertaining to the school.

The most significant aspect of the 'expressive' dimension of the Principal's role, shown in the lower portion of Figure 1, is the dissemination of the ideology and his relations with parents, teachers and pupils. In all areas of the expressive dimension, he functions both individually and collectively along with other members of the Managing Committee. He gives priority to the dissemination of the ideology and his relations with teachers and pupils in creating an 'educational atmosphere' of 'order, responsibility and co-operation' through discussion.

To the extent that the Principal expresses the strain of performing his role due to the pressure of work and lack of privacy and leisure, he experiences some amount of 'role strain' defined as the 'felt difficulty in fulfilling role obligations' when 'the individual's total role obligations are over-demanding' (Goode, 1960: 483–5). This is also a result of the conflicting expectations of, and demands on, his role by the Foundation and the teachers. Moreover, with the formation of the Managing Committee in 1980, there has been both a proliferation and differentiation of functions with members of the Committee jointly performing several functions as well as being specifically in charge of particular areas of activity. While' this reduces the obligations of the Principal, it also reduces his authority in all matters pertaining to the school. He therefore cannot act independently, without the requisite authority to take independent decisions, being bound by the Managing Committee and ultimately the Foundation in every area of functioning.

As a result of his authority having been eroded, the Principal adopts a restrained diffident manner with the teachers and other staff who tend to consult the other members of the Managing Committee, particularly the Headmistress, on important matters. Hughes' conclusion on the 'under-powered' secondary school head is apt at this point: 'The occupant of an executive position, who is granted little authority . . . tends to behave in relation to his subordinates in a cautious and defensive manner, which exposes him to as little risks as possible' (1976: 53).[11]

The Headmistress, on the other hand, appears to have more authority in matters pertaining to the functioning of the school and can therefore perform her role more independently than the Principal. For her, consultation with her colleagues, particularly the senior teachers, is of primary importance in taking a decision. She seeks the advice and co-operation of the staff and feels that they are 'a source of great strength' to her and that they are in fact 'working together as a body'. Her relations with the Principal therefore suggest that she has an equal, if not a more independent, status than he has. In a sense, she is able to exercise greater control than the Principal over all aspects of school life apart from the ideological domain—dissemination of the ideology remains the Principal's main task.

She was appointed Headmistress in January 1981, and has been teaching Biology to the senior classes in the school for 14 years. Although she works jointly with the Managing Committee in the task of running the school, she is in charge of four areas: the senior school, the hostels, the hospital, and the dining hall.

She recognizes the 'welfare of the child' as her principal task particularly as RVS is residential. That is, she considers the 'physical and psychological welfare' of the pupil as being more important than the organization and administration of academic work. The Headmistress would therefore like to 'project the right value of education as Krishnamurti propounds it', thus placing her role in an ideological perspective. Although she exhibits a keen awareness of the school's multiple goals, the Headmistress is engaged primarily in the administrative and organizational tasks of the school.

She also does some teaching and prefers her role as teacher to that of administrator which she thinks is a 'thankless job' and which she is doing only because Krishnamurti has asked her to do it. In her relations with the teachers, she has no problems with the senior teachers who help her a great deal in her work. She finds it difficult, however, to communicate with the teachers particularly when she has to sometimes restrain them in their behaviour.

The Headmistress emerges as an efficient administrator and committed professional teacher with sufficient authority vested in her role to enable her to act independently. She works closely with both the Managing Committee and with her colleagues in the school in the administrative, academic and expressive dimensions of performance (see Figure 1). She also plays a major role in maintaining order and discipline and is involved in almost every area of the school's functioning. Her dynamism is reflected in the changes she envisions for RVS; for example, she would like to raise the 'general standard of academic excellence' by admitting only those pupils who meet the school's academic standard. She would also like to send the staff members to attend various seminars and refresher courses which would broaden their perspectives and percolate through to their teaching.

To the extent that the Headmistress has no control over the ideological domain, she is not attuned to attempts at its dissemination. She is critical of the weekly staff meetings which become discussions at the level of 'mere ideas' because of the 'abstract philosophy' discussed and does not see the relevance of this to schooling processes. She would instead like to hold discussions on how to bring about 'awareness' and 'responsibility' amongst the teachers and the pupils. The decision to implement her suggestions does not however lie with her but with the Managing Committee and, ultimately, the Foundation. She nonetheless remains a major functionary in the efficient maintenance of the school.

The junior school Head, who is also the Convenor of the Managing Committee, housemaster and teacher, is in complete charge of the junior school and is 'independent and autonomous' with regard to its functioning. He, however, feels that he shares the 'responsibility and function' with all the teachers in the junior school. He therefore does not perceive any special authority attached to his role by virtue of his being the Head and views his responsibilities as being shared by other teachers in the junior school.

An engineer by profession, he joined RVS in 1981 (after having worked at another Krishnamurti school for five years) and spent most of his first year trying to implement certain changes he saw as being necessary. For example, he changed the curriculum in the Preparatory (Prep.) Section with a view towards eventually changing the entire curriculum for the junior school. He also introduced team teaching in some classes in order to give more individual attention to the pupils and make teaching an easier task. The junior school Head perceives his role primarily along the expressive dimension as he is totally committed to the ideology. The urgency with which he seeks to implement it is the major cause of his disharmonious relationship with the teachers. Attempts to exercise control through discourse on the ideology does not cut any ice with either teachers or students. It is only because he has sufficient authority, vested in him by Krishnamurti and the Foundation, that he is able to perform at all, and cope with resistance even from senior teachers and the Managing Committee.

The Bursar, appointed in 1981, is in charge of the financial as well as the ancillary administration of all the four units in the RVEC (see Figure 1). He has spent 14 years in RVS teaching Accounts and Commerce to the senior classes. A member of the Managing Committee, he works closely with the member in-charge of the estate and consults the Principal occasionally, appearing to perform his role quite independently. The member in-charge of the estate was appointed to his post in 1978. He oversees the entire functioning of the estate and performs his role working closely with all the other members of the Managing Committee, particularly the Bursar.

There are variations among these functionaries in terms of, among other reasons, their commitment to the ideology and control over its dissemination, which is evident from their perception of their roles. Thus while the Principal and the junior school Head view their roles primarily in relation to the implementation of the ideology, the Headmistress obviously does not. Although this does not create serious problems in their mutual interaction, there is a definite difference in their relations with other teachers. The Principal and the junior school Head, for example, encounter problems in interaction with teachers which the Headmistress does not. In fact, it is precisely because the Headmistress is not particularly associated with the school's transcendental order that she faces no problems in interaction. To this extent, the ideology appears to be a source of antipathy between some key functionaries and the teachers in the school. In our understanding of the teacher culture, it becomes clear that this is largely a result of the teachers' inability to comprehend the ideology and, more importantly, their prior commitment to their task as 'professional' teachers. The hiatus between the transcendental and local orders once again appears as a site for potential disorder in school organization. This is however contained by the absent presence, as it were, of Krishnamurti which does not allow any major dissension in school processes. This is further heightened into a strong sense of communitarian unity during his annual visit to the school.

Amongst the key functionaries themselves, the pattern of interaction that emerges is one of collective leadership in consultation with the Foundation and, ultimately, in deference to Krishnamurti's directives. Some functionaries however consult members of the teaching staff in decision-making and, in that sense, the latter are included in the task of running the school. The picture that emerges is that of collective governance and control through mutual co-operation except in matters pertaining to the ideology. However, a clear hierarchical pattern of exercising control emerges in our analysis of decision-making in the school.

Decision-Making and Authority

The meanings and intentions that the actors bring to the school are to some extent influenced by the processes of day-to-day administration. Decision-making is one such critical process. An examination of its reveals the patterns of authority and control operative in RVS.

We have seen that the key functionaries share joint responsibility in running the school and work together in collective leadership. The process of decision-making is similar as, apart from Krishnamurti, no single individual normally takes decisions in RVS. These are usually taken jointly after discussion and consultation by various groups of individuals. The Foundation however is the highest decision-making body as it gives effect to Krishnamurti's directives and also has sufficient autonomy in taking decisions on school matters (see Figure 2).

Decisions may be taken on (i) utilitarian or instrumental premises in order to attain specific goals; or (ii) expressive or value premises, which attain a primacy in terms of the ideology, insofar as they are concerned with bringing about a desired state of affairs rather than merely with performing specific administrative or academic tasks. In both areas it is the Foundation that plays the most important role in decision-making. It is the main link between the school and Krishnamurti to whom it reports on school activities. He takes specific decisions that range very broadly from directions regarding routine school activities to the appointment of the Principal, initiation of special houses for certain groups of pupils in the school, acquisition of land, and advice on school architecture, administrative planning, and staff appointments. He is the single most important person taking decisions; although he may discuss matters with the Foundation or the Managing Committee, he may finally take a decision independently.

The Foundation takes policy decisions, for example, on appointments and dismissals of teachers, or admission of pupils, and functions through the Executive Committee which consists of seven Foundation Members and the six members of the Managing Committee. In terms of its function, the Executive Committee is viewed, by a Foundation Member, as primarily providing a link between the Foundation and the school.

The Executive Committee meets occasionally, depending on the presence of Foundation Members in RVS, and takes decisions relating directly to the functioning of the school and to the roles of the key functionaries. At the Executive Committee meeting held in December 1980, a major decision was taken regarding the establishment of the Managing Committee. At the meeting, the Vice-President of the Foundation stated that Krishnamurti had expressed the need for the Principal 'to be concerned mainly with the communication of the "teachings" [the ideology] to the students and teachers at Rishi Valley and to see that the teachings were introduced at all levels of the working of the school'. Moreover, to provide the Principal with 'competent assistance and help to free him from the responsibility of managing the school, the Estate, the Dairy and the Rural Centre', Krishnamurti had 'felt that a

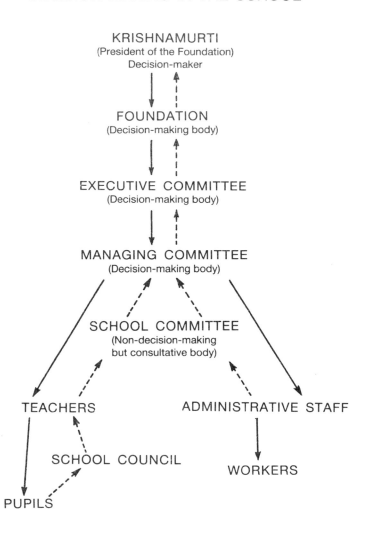

Figure 2

DECISION-MAKING IN THE SCHOOL

KRISHNAMURTI
(President of the Foundation)
Decision-maker

FOUNDATION
(Decision-making body)

EXECUTIVE COMMITTEE
(Decision-making body)

MANAGING COMMITTEE
(Decision-making body)

SCHOOL COMMITTEE
(Non-decision-making
but consultative body)

TEACHERS

ADMINISTRATIVE STAFF

SCHOOL COUNCIL

WORKERS

PUPILS

Upward flow of information and communication
Downward flow of authority

Managing Committee should be responsible for running the Rishi Valley Education Centre'.[12]

It is clear that Krishnamurti plays a pivotal role, directly and through the Foundation, in decision-making pertaining to important policy·matters. Although the Executive Committee agreed to the appointment of the Managing Committee, it was explicitly pointed out that the decision had been taken on Krishnamurti's advice. This was said, it would appear, primarily to establish the correct procedure, namely a directive from Krishnamurti, as well as to avoid total responsibility for the decision taken. Krishnamurti's influence on school matters is obvious. To some extent, such influence can be justified: he is after all the founder of the school that exists for the explicit purpose of implementing his world-view. It is important, however, to examine the ramifications of this influence. It would seem that the tasks of the 'key functionaries', for example, are decided by Krishnamurti—in the case of the Principal, the dissemination of the ideology; control over administration and the academic system for the Headmistress; and so on. One could conclude that in fact the transcendental order is in complete control and that this should ensure the subservience of the local order. This is not however the case.

The Managing Committee consists entirely of school staff—there are six members of whom three are also Foundation Members—and meets at least once a week. It shares 'executive power' inasmuch as it takes decisions on matters pertaining to finance, appointments, dismissals and the general functioning of the school. Although the Principal, Headmistress and the junior school Head are members of this Committee, all decisions are taken after joint discussion and consultation. No authority is therefore vested in any single office. In an emergency, when all members of the Managing Committee may not be present, decisions are taken by individual members of the Committee who always however consult at least some senior teachers. This procedure is different from that in other public schools in terms of the rules of the IPSC which clearly state that in all school matters, the Principal's authority is paramount. However, the Managing Committee cannot take some decisions without the final approval of the Foundation. For example, it can recommend the appointments of certain teachers but the Foundation takes the decision to actually do so. Its function appears to be twofold: formally establishing a democratic procedure of decision-making, and ensuring that no single person is held responsible for any instance of malfunctioning in the school. Some members of the Management thus consciously pursue consultative decision-making to ensure joint responsibility.

Six senior teachers and the six members of the Managing Committee constitute the School Committee; some other teachers may also be nominated to it by the Executive Committee. This Committee discusses various matters on which it provides information and makes recommendations to the Managing Committee for decisions to be taken. There are also other types of committees, such as, the Dinning Hall Committee, the Finance Committee, the houseparents' group, and so on, which deal with specific issues.

The meetings of these committees are usually attended by some members of the Managing Committee as well, which is thus able to keep in touch with what is going on, and is able to pick up important issues for its own consideration. There is thus an upward flow of information from the teachers, through the various committees and finally, through the Foundation, to Krishnamurti on all crucial matters. The Executive Committee is clearly the most powerful decision-making body in the school insofar as it is the final authority on all important matters.

The pupils present their problems through their representatives on the School Council which meets the senior teachers and members of the Managing Committee at least twice a term. The pupils therefore have a forum where they can discuss their problems and state their opinions. It is the teachers, however, who finally take decisions after having consulted the pupils' representatives and obtained their assent.

While the existence of the various committees and the manner of joint decision-making may suggest a democratic mode of functioning, based on consensus and co-operation, the authority of the Foundation is all-pervasive and is granted legitimacy by Krishnamurti's approval and support. Its decisions are implemented and their efficacy is usually unquestioned by the teachers and the Management. Control, however, never remains unquestioned in any situation: the Foundation's role in school affairs is viewed as interference by some members of the Management and teachers who feel that they should have some independence in taking decisions. Moreover, the Foundation Members' visit to the school, which takes place only once in the year (usually during Krishnamurti's visit), suggests to the critics that the former cannot be adequately aware of school problems to take decisions regarding them. They also resent the constant critical scrutiny of their performance by the Foundation.

On their part, the Foundation Members not only consult the Managing Committee but also communicate with other teachers on their visits to the school and such consultation plays an important part in their decision-making. An inherent tension is however present in this apparently consensual and democratic mode of decision-making, inasmuch as school staff are in effect coerced into making certain decisions, or accepting them, by virtue of the authority vested in the Foundation. This coercion may be viewed as emanating from the ideology itself since RVS has been established for a particular purpose and the Foundation has been entrusted with the task of accomplishing this purpose.

It is therefore apparent that RVS is held together and in fact sustained by the operating modalities of both co-operation and coercion or of consensus and control. Co-operation is viewed as a positive value in terms of the ideology for achieving the school's purpose, and is therefore the prevalent mode of functioning insofar as there is no sharp hierarchical division of roles but rather a joint responsibility for accomplishing the tasks in hand. As we have seen, however, certain coercive measures are also in operation. These may be viewed as arising from two sources. There is an inner constraint arising from the collective consciousness of the community. That is, the ideology creates an ethos in which living together necessitates co-operation between participants. There is also the constraint exercised by centres of authority, such as the Foundation, which is internal to the system but external to the individual actor. This external constraint exists in the form of rules and regulations and the established norms of the system.[13]

The Academic System: Differentiation through Specialization

Activities depict the real state of an organization as different from the desired or ideal state of its goals. The activity pattern of RVS, and the procedures and rules used to regulate it, are the means used to fulfil the ends for which the school has been organized, as also to accomplish individual and institutional goals. My primary concern here is with outlining the organization of activities which relate to the participation of teachers and pupils in school life. These may be said to constitute the core activity pattern insofar as teachers and pupils spend most of day in the classroom and its related settings—in the house, on the sportsfield, and elsewhere—in pursuit of official, common or individual goals according to a formally structured time schedule.

Of these activities, the pedagogic process is, of course, central to school processes. The organization of the academic system into the junior and senior schools is important in this context.[14] The pupils are further divided in a vertical arrangement of 12 classes according to the pupil's age and level of academic ability. There are about 24 pupils in each class except in Standards (Stds.) Seven, Eight, Nine and Ten where they are divided into two sections per class. Pupils of each class move up to the next annually in the conventional manner. In the junior school, pupil ability is assessed by the teachers who keep a subject-wise record of each pupil's progress. The pupils are given revision exercises at the end of each teaching unit. RVS is however considering awarding grades at the junior level due to pressure from parents who find the reports on pupil performance inadequate.

In the reports, the teachers comment on the 'Achievement' and 'Effort' of the pupil in each subject, apart from making general remarks. The report card on pupils in the senior school contains their grades, remarks by subject teachers on the pupil's perform-ance, remarks on activities, health and house behaviour, and a general remark by the Principal or the Headmistress. The pupil and class teacher also make a joint estimate of the pupil's behaviour in the report card. This elaborate system of reporting, which inevitably entails an evaluation of pupils in terms of their ability to meet a certain standard fixed by the teacher, is explained as being the result of parental demand rather than school policy. Nonetheless, this practice deviates from the goals of the transcendental order, as I have already pointed out.

In a conscious effort to avoid comparison between pupils, however, there is no streaming within a particular class. Although Standards Seven, Eight, Nine and Ten are divided into two sections each, both have pupils of mixed ability. Streaming of pupils according to ability was tried in the teaching of English Language in the senior school as an experimental measure but given up. While teaching was made easier, the pupils apparently 'set their goals too low' as they were aware of their position in the streaming and this resulted in the failure of the system.

In the organization of the curriculum, there are five academic faculties: Science, Mathematics, Social Studies, English and the Languages (Hindi, Telugu, Tamil and Sanskrit). The Head of each faculty is appointed on the basis of her seniority for the entire duration of her stay in the school. The major task that the Head is expected to perform is that of curriculum development: that is, to bring the latest teaching methods, books, etc. to the notice of the other teachers on the faculty. The Head is also responsible for the general supervision and organization of co-curricular activities in the particular department. General co-ordination of the work done by the department is the joint task of all the members on the faculty.

The main instrument in terms of which the curriculum is activated, and instruction in the classroom and other settings organized, is that grand routinizer, the timetable. It lays down the number of periods, each lasting 40 minutes, that are to be devoted to teaching a subject or other activities. The relative emphasis on various subjects and activities is reflected in the number of periods allotted to each. Thus, in Standards Eight, Nine and Ten, basic skills such as English, Mathematics and the Languages are each allotted six to seven periods while the other subjects are given three periods a week per class. At this level, basic skills are considered more important than other subjects. The importance given to these subjects is also reflected in the fact that there are more full-time teachers in these departments than in any other.

In an attempt to incorporate the ideology in the curriculum, 'Culture', 'Tape' and 'Discussion' get one period each a week per class. At these classes, either a taped talk by Krishnamurti is played to the pupils or they discuss social issues, current affairs, their problems at school, and other things. Pupil attendance at the tape meeting is optional but compulsory at the Culture and Discussion classes.

In the junior school, the weekly period allotment includes six subjects and two co-curricular activities. English and Arithmetic get the maximum period allotment (six each), followed by Second and Third Languages (five and threë respectively), Arts and Crafts (four), General Science (three), Social Studies (two) and Music (one). The inclusion of Arts and Crafts and Music in the curriculum is part of the school's policy to develop the creative and aesthetic elements in the pupil. In the senior school, Arts and Crafts is offered as an optional co-curricular activity and is the most popular choice with the pupils. Music in the junior school curriculum includes teaching the pupils the songs and chants which are part of the morning assembly collection of music. An important aspect of the curriculum are projects in which the pupils in each class take up a particular topic, from any subject, for study. The curriculum for the Prep. section (the junior-most class in the school) includes social, physical, intellectual, emotional, and aesthetic blocks of learning.

While the syllabus for the senior school is prescribed by the Council with the school being given some leeway in the choice of textbooks, the junior school is more independent in this respect, and the syllabus is constructed by the staff in consultation with senior school teachers. Each faculty decides on the textbooks to be used for a particular class. Textbooks used in the senior school partly become the basis for the selection of textbooks at the junior level. For General Science and Social Studies no textbooks are used. Books on these subjects are placed in the library and the pupils are expected to make use of them.

A significant distinction is made between the Arts or Humanities and Science subjects in the organization of the academic system. While subjects of both streams are taught, there is a definite stress on the Science stream in Standards 11 and 12 reflected in the weekly period allotment. The school's explanation for this emphasis is that most pupils choose Science subjects. RVS however offers only three streams of subjects for pupil choice in Standard 11, thereby restricting choice to one of the streams. These are:

I	II	III
Mathematics	Physics	Commerce
Physics	Chemistry	Economics
Chemistry	Biology	Accountancy
Fourth Elective:		
Economics	Mathematics	Mathematics

History and Special English Literature are two other subjects offered but most pupils choose one of the main streams. One reason for low pupil choice of the other subjects is, perhaps, their awareness of the secondary status of the Humanities stream. For example, Special English Literature has no period allotment in the prescribed timetable, and the subject teacher has to hold the lesson during the evening prep. (homework) hour or utilize some other free time. Similarly, History is allotted only two periods in the week. The present curriculum is justified on the grounds that the school is not large enough to offer the range of subjects in the prescribed syllabi and is constructed primarily in accordance with pupils' demands.

This perceived influence of pupil choice has certain implications for the organization of the school's academic programme. It suggests that the latter, rather than being directed by school policies, is largely shaped by the demands of the pupils, and thus by pressures external to the school. It would appear that the pupil who is expected to become an agent of social transformation is in fact a restraining factor inhibiting this process. This contradiction between the transcendental and the local orders is however not merely a result of external pressures but may also be seen as arising from organizational factors within the school itself.

The emphasis on subject specialization in RVS has a major consequence, namely increasing differentiation between pupils according to their choices and competences. Such differentiation engenders evaluation or what the ideology refers to as 'comparison' and pupil identification in terms of subject-choice. The Science stream pupils are therefore the 'elite' who seek admission into the prestigious Institutes of Technology and Medical Colleges in the country and abroad. The few who opt for the 'soft' subjects of History or English Literature are considered somewhat 'different' and not particularly bright by the Science teachers as well as by other pupils. The differentiation that is created by excessive specialization is an obvious departure from the goals of the transcendental order.

It appears that the structure of the syllabus in RVS has a double logic: it is intended to direct the upward mobility of pupils from one class to another as well as to produce a particular kind of pupil. To achieve the latter aim, a holistic approach to education would imply exposing the pupil to both the 'instrumental' and 'expressive' dimensions of school work. The instrumental dimension may be seen as being intended to prepare the pupil for the demands and activities of the technological and 'material' external world, as it were, while an expressive dimension is viewed as being necessary to assert 'the reality and importance of the inward world—the world of imagination, of feeling, of fantasy, dream, aspiration and vision'

(Abbs, 1979: vii). It is in the failure to sufficiently incorporate this dimension in its curriculum for Standards 11 and 12, due to the presence of already existing arrangements, the inability to employ teachers in other subject areas, the lack of time and resources, that the school is constrained by internal factors resulting in a crucial contradiction between the transcendental and the local orders.

CHAPTER FOUR

School Culture
Rituals and Ceremonies

School culture may be understood in terms of certain fundamental values and norms, which are its basis, as well as the configuration of activities through which these are expressed. In RVS, these values and norms are derived from two kinds of practice that are constitutive of school life; first, *organizational practice* which consists of vertical and horizontal boundaries constructed on the basis of time (age relations), space (home and community relations) and gender, and realized through reward and punishment. Here, positions are significant and are based on specialization in relation to individuals and groups giving rise to a form of explicit hierarchy. And second, *discursive practice* which consists of the discourse that is transmitted in the classroom and evaluated through the rituals of tests and examinations. Transmission is an important process and deals with relations between teachers and pupils wherein there is an implicit or explicit hierarchy. The important point is that evaluation is crucial to both kinds of practice inasmuch as there are elements of specialization and differentiation in them. Organizational and discursive practice are common to most schools but in RVS, there is a third element, that of *value*, enshrined in Krishnamurti's philosophy—the school's ideology—which is realized through organizational features and practice as well as through rituals of challenge and effervescence; and evaluation is central here as well in terms of certain practices and competences. In RVS therefore all three fields operate together resulting in different activities including the performance of certain kinds of rituals and ceremonies.

If we define rituals as an expression and an affirmation of the school's ultimate values, we need to understand these in terms of the two differing orders in the school. At one level, the school's ultimate values may be located in its transcendental order concerned as they are with essentialism and are participatory and collective in nature. As I have already pointed out, these values are expounded by

Krishnamurti and, as he is the founder of the school, they represent the most fundamental and revered values of the school. This transcendental order has organizational features and practices (for example, the recruitment of certain kinds of teachers—the ideologues—to the school) and rituals of challenge and effervescence (for example, Krishnamurti's visit to the school when there is both a rejuvenation in his presence as well as the evaluation of practices and competences). Evaluation in this order generates implicit hierarchy. There are also those other rituals of ultimate values which are grounded in the local order, i.e. the social order, and are concerned with the legitimacy of educational knowledge through tests of performance. These tests are rituals of preferment and humiliation based on individual performance and achievement, deriving from the local order which encourages both specialization and differentiation. Thus we find that as specialization increases, differentiation is greater and therefore these rituals generate explicit hierarchy. It is important to note that both kinds of rituals are representative of the school's ultimate values. Rituals therefore signify not only the collective celebration of certain ultimate values but also individual performance to legitimize and maintain other ultimate values. Such a view of ritual brings together the collective and individual as well as the expressive and instrumental or the affective and cognitive elements of institutional activities. Thus the 'practical and the mundane' and 'how these domains become sanctified inside schools' (McLaren, 1986: 35) become as important as the domain of the transcendental and the sacred in the analysis of ritual. It would appear that conventional definitions of ritual need to break away 'from the strait-jacket of "ritual-sacred-symbolic" versus "practical-profane-instrumental"', and the contortions to which this simple-minded opposition leads' (Skorupski, 1976: 173) in order to incorporate, understand and thus explain what is an important ritual element in school processes, namely the legitimizing of educational knowledge through tests of performance.

In RVS I distinguish between rituals and ceremonies in terms of the affective meaning they hold for the participants. Ceremonies may therefore be distinguished from rituals inasmuch as they are not performed as an expression or affirmation of the school's values but in accordance with official regulations to commemorate certain events, for example, hoisting the national flag on the Independence and Republic Days. Such ceremonial occasions are then used for alternative events that are more meaningful to the participants such as the Sports Day. Finally, I would like to distinguish between routine rituals and dramatizations of the routine in an effort to highlight the importance of both ordinary everyday activities and unusual periodic events in the school routine.

Teachers in RVS both participate in and conduct certain rituals and ceremonies which are both consensual and differentiating in their function but whose main feature may be seen as that of integrating or binding together participants into a 'moral community'.[1] Waller has suggested, in what is perhaps the earliest and most perceptive study of school life, that 'the school is . . . marked off from the world that surrounds it by the spirit which pervades it' and, further, that this '*we*-feeling of the school is in part a spontaneous creation in the minds of those who identify themselves with the school and in part a carefully nurtured and sensitive growth' (1938: 13). It is in the latter sense that control enters the situation and the function of ritual is viewed as that of relating the individual

> through ritualistic acts to a social order, to heighten respect for that order, to revivify that order within the individual and, in particular, to deepen acceptance of the procedures which are used to maintain continuity, order and boundary and which control ambivalence towards the social order (Bernstein, 1977: 54).

Needless to add, this view of ritual is derived from Durkheim:

> There can be no society which does not feel the need of upholding and reaffirming at regular intervals the collective sentiments and the collective ideas which make its unity and its personality . . . this moral remaking cannot be achieved except by the means of reunions, assemblies and meetings where the individuals, being closely united to one another, reaffirm in common their common sentiments (1961: 474f).

In defining rituals in institutions, such as a school, as collective activities that are essentially an expression and affirmation of the values of the institution, there should be an emphasis on the subjective meaning that such rituals acquire for the participants. These rituals are, in the first place, concerned with the routine ongoing life of the school and are therefore part of the daily round of activities; in this sense, they are 'closer to *ritus* as a daily custom than to a rite as a periodical ceremony . . .' (Erikson, 1977: 79), and are predictable elements of the school culture. In RVS, these include activities, notably the morning assembly, the evening *asthāchal* (literally, 'the hill where the sun sets' but the word has acquired a special meaning in the school, namely 'watching the sunset'), and in the senior classroom, the weekly rite of tests and the announcements of test results. Second, there are other rituals, such as Krishnamurti's annual visit to the school and examinations, which do not take place every day but are a part of the routine inasmuch as Krishnamurti's visit is an anticipated event and preparations for it begin months in advance. However, such a ritual occasion partakes of the dramatic by highlighting what is overshadowed by other activities during the rest of the year and by its significant role in the creation of an ethos special to the school. Moreover, the affective components of such rituals—which are dramatizations of the routine—are shortlived as they are enacted infrequently. This is in contrast to routine rituals to which certain meanings that are attached to them by the participants remain consistent over a period of time as a result of their daily enactment.

Routinized rituals and ceremonies

Rituals and ceremonies primarily perform an integrative function, particularly if they are incorporated into the routine of an institution. Such rituals are called 'consensual' by Bernstein who suggests that 'they assist in the integration of the various goals of the school, within a coherent set of shared values, so that the values of the school can become internalised and experienced as a unity' (1977: 60). He distinguishes these from 'differentiating rituals' which 'tend to mark out specific groups in terms of age, sex, age relations, and house' in the school and 'deepen local attachment to, and detachment behaviour from, specific groups; they also deepen respect behaviour to those in various positions of authority, and create order in time' (Bernstein, 1977: 58, 56). Rather than suggest a difference between consensual and differentiating rituals, except as analytical categories, I would like to argue that consensual rituals themselves contain elements of differentiating rituals and are often a good cover for discrimination and differentiation between pupils. Thus the morning assembly, for example, which is a celebration of the school as a community, also serves to differentiate between the participants in terms of age, gender and authority relations.

Routinized rituals are based on and take place in both the local and transcendental orders in RVS. The latter is present in the morning assembly and the *asthāchal*. The assembly at the beginning of the day may be seen as a ritualistic commencement of the daily routine and a coming together of the participants to celebrate, as it were, the intention and existence of the school. The *asthāchal* may be reviewed as signifying the end of the day and is the time for introspection and meditation after the completion of the day's tasks. The importance of the two rituals lies in the role each plays in the daily routine—that of announcing a new day and that of bringing to a close another day of work and activity.[2] In between these two rituals there is the daily enactment of the pedagogic process which, in the senior section of the school, consists of testing pupils in different subjects twice or thrice a week. These tests are obviously an attempt to ensure the pupils' competence at a particular level set by the teacher each time, indicating the authoritarian and differentiating character of such rituals. Rituals located in the transcendental order, like assembly and *asthāchal* are, on the other hand, indicative of their participatory nature, bringing participants together in collective celebration of the community and its surroundings.

The morning assembly is a daily event lasting for about twenty minutes. Both junior and senior pupils meet together for singing and chanting thrice a week and there are separate assemblies for talks and discussions on the remaining three days. The setting is fixed: the school auditorium is used by the seniors and for all the joint assemblies and a smaller auditorium in the junior school is used for their assemblies. The assembly always begins at the stipulated time and is never excluded from the daily routine except when Krishnamurti speaks to the school.

The physical organization of the assembly, in terms of the seating arrangement, is strictly structured as in other settings such as the classroom and the dining-room where girls and boys, junior and senior pupils, all sit separately. The teachers sometimes mix with the pupils but usually sit at the back of the auditorium. Thus, demarcating lines are clearly drawn, separating boys from girls, juniors from seniors and teachers from pupils. In accordance with the transcendental order, the purpose of the musical component of the assembly is to develop in the pupils an interest in, and an appreciation of, the elements of music such as rhythm and tone and the correct method of chanting. The teachers say that the meaning of the songs and chants is not important and they therefore do not explain their thematic content to the pupils. This viewpoint is based on Krishnamurti's argument that singing and chanting as an act of religious devotion or worship is meaningless and that it is far more important to cultivate a sensitivity to the music itself.

A reading of the songs and chants used by the school, however, indicates that thematically they fall into two categories. Most of them are devotional songs from within the *bhakti* tradition in Hinduism expressing the love of the devotee for a personal deity. In devotional songs, a great deal of emphasis is laid on the singing, the *bhajan*, as a way of expressing devotion to the deity. The school's collection thus includes songs of such outstanding medieval *bhakti* poets as Tulsidas and Meera. There are also famous hymns, such as the classic 'Bhajagovindam', by the Adi Shankaracharya, and other popular *bhajans*. A second group of songs and chants is more abstract or metaphysical in nature. These are derived from such sources as the *Vedas* and the *Upanishads* and from mystic poets like Kabir.

The songs are mainly in Hindi and Sanskrit but some are in Telugu and Tamil and a few in Bengali, Punjabi and Marathi. The pupils would thus understand most of the songs despite the official emphasis on the intent and not the content of this component of the assembly. Moreover, as a result of their experience at home, the pupils and the teachers may associate these songs with religious devotion. This is clearly evident in the case of the senior boys who join in the singing only during the examinations, obviously in the hope of gaining something from their participation! The official version of the intention underlying the song-music items notwithstanding, the selection of songs and chants from religious texts with an emphasis on their devotional content in itself suggests a bias towards a particular kind of music. Further, the songs and chants are exclusively Hindu in content and the exclusion of other religious texts such as the Koran and the Bible indicates the non-secular character of the selected music.

The assembly also contributes towards the integration of teachers and pupils in the joint performance of a daily ritual and in creating an atmosphere of harmony and mutual goodwill between them in the routine of the school day. The relationship between teachers and pupils is thus characterized primarily by informality and freedom, not so much at music assemblies where teachers and pupils are both passive participants, but more so at the talks and lectures and joint presentations when they are active participants. The spoken component of the assembly is wide-ranging in scope and may consist of talks by visitors, teachers or pupils, the performance of short plays and skits by pupils and teachers, and the playing of taped music occasionally. These assemblies are held separately in the junior and senior schools and their content therefore differs. Their intention is, however, the same; apart from the plays that are staged primarily for entertainment, they are intended to inform and instruct the audience on a variety of topics.

The talks in the senior school vary every day but the emphasis is on different aspects of science and religion. An effort is also made, by most speakers, to discuss Krishnamurti's world-view without any explicit reference being made to it. Some teachers and visitors, however, speak explicitly on it. This aspect of the assembly, with its implicit and explicit references to Krishnamurti and his thought, is an attempt to bring about an awareness of the special nature of the school in the pupils. As they participate in the discussion, the pupils are at least exploring these subjects which is what the school expects of them. Thus the assembly serves the purpose of not only bringing people together through music or the spoken word but collectively reaffirms the ultimate values and beliefs of the school through talk and discussion.

The local order is, however, not entirely neglected and in fact it may be argued that the discussion of science, in the context of Krishnamurti's world-view is an effort to locate the transcendental order within what is currently considered the more important subject stream in the school's local order. Moreover, there are other talks on particular subjects, such as mathematics, travel, adventure, and also on other Krishnamurti schools. The talks thus seek to integrate the pupils in a number of collectivities apart from that of the school: the other KFI schools in India and abroad, the wider school system, and the socio-political environment.

In the junior school, the talks are suited to the age-group of the pupils, and teachers and pupils usually give informative talks on various subjects. An important element of the junior assembly, in terms of pupil participation are the plays that are staged by pupils with the help of teachers. There is however a disparity between boys and girls in pupil participation in the plays as a larger number of boys generally take part in them. The selection of pupils for participation usually depends on the teachers helping them. For example, men teachers tend to work with boys and women teachers with girls because of the tendency for boys and girls to quarrel amongst themselves in the junior school. The problem appears to be accentuated by the teachers who not only disapprove of free and close interaction among them but also tend to create differences by often supporting and encouraging activities within gender groups.[3] The assembly is one such activity as a result of which there is very little interaction. This is evident not only in the kind of pupil participation but, as earlier stated, in the physical organization of the assembly as well.

While the assembly is a morning ritual, the *asthāchal* is an evening ritual routinized in RVS's daily flow of events. Every evening, all the pupils and house-parents are expected to watch the sunset for about twenty minutes from an appointed place, located at a slight elevation with a clear view of the sun setting behind three hills, from one of which, Rishi Konda, the school takes its name. Pupils and teachers sit on the ground, or the rocks surrounding the area, facing the hills. A bell is rung to announce the commencement of the event. Most pupils rivet their gaze on the three hills in the distance in complete silence. The juniors get somewhat restless, after a while, but the seniors watch the sunset for the stipulated period with some staying back after it is over to sit quietly for a little longer. The juniors leave for dinner and the seniors for an hour of prep. before dinner.

The purpose of *asthāchal* is formally stated to be aesthetic in content, that is, to develop an appreciation of nature in the pupils. This is in accordance with Krishnamurti's world-view which stresses the importance of the close observation of nature, as well as an appreciation of music, as indicated in the assembly, in the learning process. The response of the pupils from the three senior-most classes in the school indicates that about half of them considered their experience of *asthāchal* in terms of the relaxation they derived from it using such terms as peace, calm, silence and expressing their ability to sort out their problems and worries, to understand their thoughts and to quieten and rest their minds at the end of a long day. Some of them expressed their appreciation of nature in terms of the 'beautiful' sunset, the setting and the surroundings. Others mentioned the joy and happiness they experience at *asthāchal* though a few referred to it as a dull routine activity. Moreover, the setting itself acquires a sacred value for the pupils as it is only used for this ritual: it is literally sacred, i.e. set apart. In their spare time, many of them visit the '*asthāchal* place' to be alone and quiet. The setting is therefore associated with their positive experience at *asthāchal* which they seek to renew at other times. The subjective significance the event acquires for the pupils is in keeping with the intention and perhaps surpasses it in that they not only observe and appreciate nature but also experience a sense of joy and renewal.

As Eliade has pointed out, a 'sacred' space is 'strong' and 'significant' and, if a mountain (or hill), may even symbolize 'the Centre of the World', the '*axis mundi*': it thus 'opens communication between the cosmic planes (between earth and heaven) and makes possible ontological passage from one mode of being to another' (1959: 20, 37, 35, 63). Rishi Konda obviously is such a place. Insofar as it is an element of the school's transcendental order, the ritual of *asthāchal* implicitly reinforces this order among the pupils. Further, its contribution to the culture of the school lies in its creation of a particular kind of atmosphere by the very nature of its performance.[4] This is in fact one of the factors which bestows on RVS a differentiating quality in its ambience thus lending it its 'special' character.

While *asthāchal* may be viewed as being essentially located in the school's transcendental order, the assembly is an expression of both the transcendental and local orders, although it often deviates from both, tending to take elements from the wider system, such as the Hindu religious system. There is a third ritual however, which, resulting from the educational order, is crucial to the schooling process in the senior school and is located in the classroom: the weekly test. Upward movement in the senior school is dependent on the pupils' academic ability which is assessed through regular tests in various subjects and classroom and preparatory work. Conducting tests becomes imperative as the pupils take the public examinations in Standards 10 and 12 and have to be adequately prepared for them. Thus, about four tests per subject are conducted every term. There is no organized test programme but after the completion of each teaching unit, a test is generally conducted in which pupils are awarded grades as well as remarks (such as 'Good', 'Fair', 'Satisfactory'). The use of grades establishes a distinct reward system in the senior school in conformity with the examination system but is contrary to Krishnamurti's world-view which stresses the undesirability of comparison and competition in school processes.

The pupils take these tests very seriously and prepare for them, often surreptitiously during other lessons, during the prep hour and in their houses after dinner. The test situation is similar to that of the examination except that the latter takes place in the school auditorium and not in the more familiar setting of the classroom. At the test, the pupils are tense when the questions are distributed or written out on the blackboard and the rules do not allow them to converse amongst themselves or look into one another's notebooks. Taking a test remains an individual activity for the pupil, albeit in a collective situation. The pupils also exhibit an anxiety about their performance in the tests which is evident when the teacher announces the results or distributes the answer sheets or notebooks in the classroom. Once again, the pupils tend to function at an individual level as they prefer not to share their grades with one another and in fact tend to look at their papers very privately. The test is therefore a differentiating ritual inasmuch as it creates differences between pupils primarily in terms of competence through a process of preferment and humiliation. This is in marked contrast to *asthāchal* which is consensual in character bringing teachers and pupils together in silent and harmonious communion with themselves and nature.

So far we have examined the major rituals that constitute critical elements in the everyday routine of RVS. All routine is not ritual but rituals may be routinized, which is why they become *critical elements* of the routine. There are also those ceremonies that take place on special days, or are special events or occasions in the school calendar. These are some of the national holidays, such as, the Republic and Independence Days which the school is expected to observe in adherence with government regulations. They are distinctive occasions only because of the nature of activities that take place as no subjective meaning is attached to them. On such days, pupils and teachers are expected to dress in white and gather at the flag-pole in the morning. The Principal, aided by a teacher, hoists the national flag after which the national anthem and other national songs are sung. There is not much enthusiasm exhibited in the singing which is of a poor, lacklustre quality. The ceremony is over in a few minutes with a minimum of fuss and the rest of the day is like any other holiday in school. This ceremony is of no consequence to school processes as Krishnamurti's world-view does not empha-size the significance of such occasions and in fact attempts to positively devalue commemorative events in terms of their narrowly defined national character. The participants therefore attach no affective importance to them and they are special events only insofar as they are not a daily occurrence.

RVS holds its annual Sports Day on one of these ceremonial days: the school does not intend the event to be an occasion for the celebration or fulfilment of conventional school values, such as, achievement and success. For the pupils, however, it is a special occasion with a strong element of competition as they strive to succeed in every area of sports activity during the day. The competitive spirit is therefore an important component of the school culture evident in pupil attitudes to sport and school work. This goes against Krishnamurti's world-view but assumes an importance due to the perceptions and attitudes of teachers and pupils and the structure and nature of the activities themselves. It is also another example of the conflict between the transcendental and local orders in the school.

Other events and occasions contribute to the overall configuration of the culture of the school. Thus some special occasions within the routine of the school day bring the teachers and pupils together informally at periodic intervals: for example, the 'moonlight dinners' organized once or twice a term. There is not, however, any particular kind of interaction between teachers and pupils on these occasions. The larger number of pupils compared to that of teachers makes the event a festivity for them and they take over the occasion, as it were, while the teachers recede into the background. The occasion therefore assumes an importance primarily because of its enlivenment of the routine. The same may be said of the faculty dinners and farewells for teachers and pupils. Such occasions are nonetheless symbolic expressions and affirmations of the school as a community in the very nature of their performance which is an informal coming together of the participants in the school.

It is evident that the ceremonies and other events discussed above contribute to an overall school culture. The three major rituals of assembly, *asthāchal* and the weekly test are high in affective meaning for the participants and can be distinguished not only in terms of the different orders to which they belong but the implications this has for the culture of the school. The tests, located as they are in the school's local order, create an atmosphere of fear and even terror for the pupils as they symbolize success or failure for them. The pupils consider it very important to succeed at these tests as they view their results as an indication of their performance in the public examinations. The teachers, on their part, reprimand pupils for their poor performance and encourage those who have done well in the tests.[5] The ritual of conducting and taking tests therefore creates differences between pupils and brings the authoritarian role of the teacher into play. The pupils are evaluated depending on their individual performance in relation to other individual performances.

This can be contrasted with the assembly and *asthāchal* which are based on collective pupil and teacher participation and are therefore participatory, as opposed to differentiating, in nature. The performance of *asthāchal* in fact tends to create feelings of love and joy in the pupils who are relaxed and experience a renewal as opposed to the fear and competition of the tests. The sense of the collective is maintained by the teachers who do not differentiate between pupils on this occasion. The assembly however has a more ambiguous character as it cannot be sharply located in either order. It contains elements of both orders as well as those of the wider system; bringing participants together but also differentiating between them in terms of age, gender, and authority relations; exposing them to the aesthetics of music but also to the content which does not coincide with Krishnamurti's (i.e. transcendental) values; celebrating the school as a community but also creating an awareness of the external socio-political and cultural reality. This is perhaps the only occasion in the school when there is a merger of the two opposing orders. The opposition and the resulting differences are however highlighted when certain other activities take place. It is in the performance of certain rituals that are *dramatizations* of the routine that the culture of the school becomes sharply established as the delineation between the transcendental and the local orders.

Rituals as dramatizations of the routine

The highlights of the RVS academic year—beginning in June and ending in March–April the following year—are the examinations and Krishnamurti's annual visit. The school year is in fact structured around these events; for example, the duration and timing of the autumn break is dependent on Krishnamurti's forthcoming visit. Examinations are the culmination of the academic year in the senior school and their importance is evident in the school's activities of preparation for them. These events are dramatizations of the routine as they create significant changes in the ambience by highlighting at different times such opposing elements as collective responsibility and goodwill, and individual preparations and competition: one concerned with bringing about an internal effervescence in the individual, the other creating a sense of fear and trepidation in the individual in relation to an external situation.

Krishnamurti visits RVS for a period of about three weeks in November or December every year. Prior to his arrival, members of the Management plan and prepare for the numerous activities that are to take place during his visit. Both pupils and teachers are involved in these preparatory activities, for example, special dance and music programmes, drama etc., sometimes with the help of professionals from outside the school. the physical layout and organization of the school including the gardens and the estate are also sought to be improved. This is at the surface level of practical preparation for an obviously very important event in the school. There is however an undercurrent of tension associated with Krishnamurti's impending visit and, in particular, his critical reactions to school processes which engender preparations at another level. The Management and the ideologues experience this anxiety the most as they feel responsible, and personally committed, to Krishnamurti. That Krishnamurti should not find fault with the work they are doing in the school becomes an overriding concern as the time for his visit approaches. There is thus an effort to improve the situation as best they can by attempting to either rectify existing practices or introducing new activities. For example, a tutor system was begun in 1981, without adequate planning, by which each teacher had about ten senior pupils in his or her care and was expected to attend to their problems. This proved to be an unsuccessful venture as some teacher–pupil combinations were incompatible. Moreover, the pupils themselves reacted unfavourably viewing it as a strategy to win Krishnamurti's approval. There is also a fear among members of the Management of being unable to present the school in the right perspective to visitors, some of whom may be distinguished educationists (as in 1983).[2]

It is obvious that these anxieties and apprehensions reflect the importance attached to Krishnamurti's visit in terms of the school's performance *vis-à-vis* his world-view. That Krishnamurti does not attach any authority to his own role—in fact he appreciates spontaneity and joy in relationships—may be understood by the teachers and the Management at a personal (individual) level, and is reflected in their informal interaction with him. Institutional activity however creates strains and tensions in performance which, in this case, appear to be the result of the felt difficulty in transferring individual perception onto the collective plane of working together in the school. The fear and anxieties experienced by teachers prior to the visit are also indicative of a form of social control that operates through the invisible pedagogy of the transcendental order. That is, while Krishnamurti appreciates spontaneity and freedom in relationships, he sets very high standards for performance in the school and tends to question teachers about their lack of perception of transcendental goals and the means of their fulfilment. The teacher is therefore not really 'free' to interpret the world-view and act accordingly: he or she is expected to perform according to Krishnamurti's expectations which tend to be axiomatic in nature.

Krishnamurti's arrival in RVS is a special event with teachers and pupils gathered to greet him. It is here that another aspect of the differentiating nature of essentially consensual rituals is apparent. While his visit in general is conducive to generating feelings of collective co-operation and friendliness, the Management discriminates among pupils in selecting those who should present bouquets of flowers to Krishnamurti on his arrival. While this may appear an apparently trivial matter, it is significant inasmuch as Krishnamurti is central to the school ethos and greeting him would be considered special—whether in terms of privilege and honour or duty—by both pupils and teachers.

An important aspect of his visit is that Krishnamurti's presence in RVS enriches the atmosphere and lends a special mystical quality to it. There is an inexplicable aura associated with Krishnamurti which is experienced by those who come into contact with him and which pervades the atmosphere during his visit. A stillness and a sense of calm descends on RVS, temporarily removing the differences between people and uniting them in a commonly shared task.

Foundation Members and ideologue teachers, in particular, treat Krishnamurti with considerable veneration and look to him for guidance in implementing his world-view. Moreover, as a result of their contact with Krishnamurti and his teachings, they are committed to the task of fulfilling his vision—which they have internalized as their own—having renounced other occupations and careers. They are apparently dependent, for a personal sense of well-being, on their contact with Krishnamurti on his visit to India. Some of them view this period of their interaction with him as providing them with the necessary sustenance to go back to their difficult and generally unrewarding jobs (as viewed by one ideologue due to the constraints involved in performance). Thus one teacher told Krishnamurti that in his presence they experience a 'widening of horizons and sensitivity', which does not however remain once he leaves, and they turn back to the 'narrow challenge' of their daily work. This is indicative of the charismatic quality of Krishnamurti's presence which has a transforming effect on some teachers that however diminishes after he leaves RVS.

The charisma is communicated in part through his contact with pupils and teachers which takes place in the talks and discussions he has with them. He holds two talks with the pupils at which pupil attendance is compulsory as it is considered 'good' if they are exposed to Krishnamurti's presence—a suggestion apparently made by Krishnamurti himself. It is hoped that some of the ideology may percolate through to them simply by their having listened to Krishnamurti over the years. Teachers and visitors also attend these talks at which some senior pupils participate keenly in the discussion and exhibit no fear or restraint in their questions which often express their dissatisfaction with the school and the teachers. Krishnamurti however does not answer any questions and instead goads pupils into thinking and discovering things for themselves. In fact, he often rhetorically poses the question 'What kind of a school is this?' to the audience when he finds the pupils' views steeped in convention and tradition. He emphasizes the responsibility of the pupils towards the change they expect in the school's educational processes and demands excellence from them in their adherence to the values which they themselves perceive as being right. These are the moral imperatives to which he expects adherence. Krishnamurti's public contact with the pupils culminates with his asking them to sit quietly with their eyes closed for a few minutes. This emphasis on introspection and inwardness, as in the music assemblies and *asthāchal*, is an effort to highlight their inner life in contrast to their external life in the school which is more easily perceived as it were.

In his contact with teachers, Krishnamurti's task seems to be that of shaking them out of their apathy and complacence by expressing his dissatisfaction with school processes and their own performance. When he asks them to explain the causes of a particular problem, the teachers tend to be evasive by blaming the pupils' home background or other factors external to the school, thus shirking their own responsibilities. Krishnamurti however throws them a challenge, where they have to contend with social pressures, in accomplishing which their creativity plays a major role. Thus Krishnamurti's contact with teachers, in which he reiterates the importance of transcendental goals and seeks to relate the teachers' performance to achieving them, serves to reinforce the transcendental order, albeit briefly, in the teachers' role definitions. Krishnamurti however does not neglect the local order and questions the quality of teaching which he views as resulting in the lack of brilliant performances by pupils in the classroom. He therefore demands excellence from the teachers in the specific area of their function in the classroom as well as in their more diffuse but important role in the house and other settings. Moreover, the extent to which teachers and pupils are dependent on Krishnamurti's presence is evident in their seeking from him guidance, solutions, and methods by which his world-view can be implemented in their personal lives and in the school. This is indicative of the control that operates from the transcendental order through the person of Krishnamurti on the lives of teachers and pupils in the school and on school processes themselves. Not only are teachers and pupils asked to define their roles in a particular manner within an overall transcendental order but they become dependent on Krishnamurti who is viewed as the authoritative voice of that order. The pedagogues or professional teachers also experience this control but their essentially weak or limited commitment to Krishnamurti and his world-view prevents them from operating to the tune of this order. They seek instead to fulfil the demands of the local order which are paramount to the proper functioning of the school, as they view it.

In one sense, Krishnamurti's visit serves to strengthen his influence on RVS, so that he can be spoken of as a constant presence in the school. This feeling is heightened by the many taped talks that are played to teachers and pupils, the video recordings that are screened, and the talks and discussions on the ideology that take place regularly. Through these means an attempt is made by the Management to keep Krishnamurti's presence alive in his absence.

His brief presence in RVS is a reaffirmation of the purpose of the
school and a reminder of what he stands for, and by creating
effervescence tends to reorient the participants into action in relation
to his world-view. When Krishnamurti departs from RVS he leaves
behind a certain intensity in the atmosphere which results in a surge
of activity such as an increasing number of staff meetings, both in
the junior and the senior schools, where the Management and the
teachers discuss his world-view, the educational process and the
ways and means by which they can attempt to solve some of their
problems.

While this collective questioning and sharing of a joint endeavour
may continue in the junior school until the end of term, it evaporates
rather quickly in the senior school as the examinations take place
only a couple of months after Krishnamurti leaves. The teachers and
pupils are once again preoccupied with preparation for the
examinations as they have been during the rest of the year. Thus in
the senior classes, teachers and pupils discuss school work with
constant reference to the examinations. The teachers talk about and
plan for them in the class and staff-room while the senior pupils'
anxieties and fears centre around the examinations most of the
time.[7] The weekly test in different subjects is not only an assessment
of the pupils' abilities but also an effort to expose and prepare them
for the examination situation. The value attached to examinations is
also apparent in their setting: the school auditorium is a special
place set apart for them; and there is an atmosphere of utter gravity
and silence when the examinations are in progress thus imposing
their importance on other pupils in the school.

The school's affiliation to the Council and parental expectations
are the major factors responsible for the importance of examinations
in RVS. The pupils as a result are also very examination-conscious
and achievement-oriented in their aspirations. In a sense, therefore,
examinations embody the school's local order in the extreme and are
a counterpoint to the transcendental order highlighting the dramatic
event of Krisnamurti's visit to RVS which is the ultimate
embodiment of that order. The differences between the two
situations, which are both dramatic in their occurrence, can be
distinguished at different levels: the most apparent is in terms of
participation, i.e. examinations, like tests, imply a concern with
individual performance among pupils and are concerned with
individual anxieties and fears. Krishnamurti's visit, on the other

hand, implies a collective responsibility, sharing and coming together of participants in a celebration of the school's dominant values. At another level, the examinations are an affirmation of the pedagogic process, legitimizing individual success and failure and establishing a particular path for the school's educational order. Krishnamurti's visit, on the other hand, is an act of regeneration, a renewal which implies 'a new birth' of the community as a whole through a return to the origins of the school. It is thus the 'archetypal act', the repetition of which at periodic intervals ensures the regeneration of the community (Eliade, 1955). It is indicative of constant striving and symbolic of the hope that the new school, the new man, the new society will arrive.

The culture of RVS is thus a configuration of rituals and ceremonies which are located in both the transcendental and local orders constituting the school. A distinction has been made between rituals and ceremonies and between routine rituals and rituals as dramatizations of the routine. The routine or everyday life of an institution has a uniformity and regularity about it; thus the assembly, *asthāchal*, and the weekly tests capture—each quite differently—the rhythm of life in RVS and indicate its participation in different cultural and social universes. Certain other rituals which, although a part of the routine inasmuch as they are regular annual events, dramatize the routine by sharply emphasizing and highlighting the essential characteristics of the two differing orders which otherwise remain embedded in the routine of the school calendar. The rhythm of routine activities may have no reference or meaning beyond the functions that are performed or the immediate satisfactions that they afford. The significance of rituals, however, lies in their links to ultimate values of some kind. In RVS these have been identified as deriving essentially from the two differing orders.

The local order is exceedingly demanding due to the temporal factor involved in the giving and taking of examinations. Preparing the pupils for the examination becomes the major task to accomplish in the senior school, as no risks may be undertaken in this venture. To the extent that examinations are a crucial element of this order, to which most classroom activity is oriented, we can conclude that it is primarily a *credentialist* order in nature. The concern with credentials results in rituals which are authoritarian and discriminatory, create fear and anxieties, and, above all, isolate participants from one another. They may also be seen as being related to the 'outer', i.e. to an expression and affirmation of external values. The external life of the individuals in a social setting of an institution is of paramount importance. Rituals in this category are therefore a metaphor of the entire structure, values, function and relations of the pedagogic process and in that sense, they are external to the individual.

Rituals in the category of the transcendental order are non-academic and participatory in nature bringing participants together in love and joy in the creation and celebration of communitas in the sense of an experience 'that goes to the root of each person's being and finds in that root something profoundly communal and shared' (Turner, 1969: 138). Such rituals are therefore related to the inner life of the individual inasmuch as an internal effervescence is sought in order to create a transcendental being who, through immediate perception and action, will bring about social transformation. In that sense, these rituals are *essentialist* in nature concerned as they are with the essence of life.

In this affirmation and legitimation of the institution—in both transcendental and local terms—there is the crucial factor of evaluation which operates through the rules of the different kinds of practice, identified at the beginning of this chapter (and implicitly present throughout the discussion), namely, organizational practice, discursive practice, and the element of value. Implicit or explicit forms of hierarchy are created by differentiation through age, gender and authority relations as well as through specific academic and other practices and competences. This is linked with elements of social control that operate to condition participants towards expected appropriate behaviour patterns. Control operates through the transcendental order's concern with the production of a transformed human being and through the local order's concern with the reproduction of knowledge. In one case, there is an implicit hierarchy inasmuch as everything appears equal due to the stress on freedom and equality but the ideologue teachers and members of the Management seek to direct and control participant attitudes and behaviour in terms of Krishnamurti's world-view. In the other case, there is an explicit form of hierarchy inasmuch as teachers obviously monitor and control pupil performance in the classroom in a particular direction. This does not, however, imply that there is no scope for resistance to, or withdrawal from, both kinds of situations which does take place in the form of pupil and teacher rebellion to the transcendental order and pupil withdrawal from the local order.[8]

This analysis of the forms of ritual and the resultant forms of control in RVS moves away from the conventional view of ritual as that which binds groups and society together creating a kind of primordial unity to one which considers the differentiating character of ritual equally important as its participatory nature. It is by broadening the concept of ritual in institutions, such as schools, to include the locally (i.e. socially) sanctified practices of tests and examinations as well as what is conventionally considered ritual behaviour (e.g. the collective affirmation and celebration of communitas), that we are able to establish the characteristic, albeit divergent, elements of the culture of a particular kind of school.

CHAPTER FIVE

Teacher Culture
Professional and Ideologue Teachers

The teacher's role: definitions and expectations

We have so far examined the world inhabited by teachers and pupils in RVS in terms of the school's ideological underpinnings, its organization, and its culture. The voices of teachers and pupils have however only been partially heard in the construction of the social reality of the school. But teachers and pupils make significant contributions to this process and have views and identities of their own, in relation to their environment. This results in the construction of a particular culture or many cultures in the school that exist in interaction but nonetheless tend to be specific to themselves— little worlds, as it were, encapsulated within the larger world of the school.

What is the world of the teacher, or teacher culture, all about? In RVS, it is made up of several strands: the teacher's role as perceived by the school and their recruitment to this role; their orientations and commitments to this role and the forms these take in terms of their perceived identities.

There were 36 teachers (in 1981) of whom 15 were women. Most teachers belonged to a south-Indian upper caste, middle class, urban background. The majority of teachers in RVS fall within the 18–39 age group and while this may suggest the preponderance of younger teachers in the school, such teachers in fact tend to change jobs more frequently than older teachers.

The school's expectations of the teacher are shaped explicitly by the ideology and other institutional and organizational factors and, more implicitly, by the historical and social situation in which RVS is located. The Management, on its part, makes an effort to realize these expectations by seeking to ensure teacher compliance to them through various means. A teacher's role is however not merely influenced by an external definition of it in terms of the expectations of the role but also by the teacher's own response to the situation. Such a response entails the teacher's perception of the different elements of the situation—the other participants with whom she is in interaction, the specific contexts in which such interaction occurs, and the overall ideological orientation of the school—and her adaptation to these elements in relation to her own orientations to the process.

Intersubjectivity is central to the process of perceiving and enacting one's role insofar as 'my life-world is not my private world but, rather, is intersubjective; the fundamental structure of its reality is that it is shared by us' (Schutz and Luckmann as quoted by Hammersley, 1977: 11). It is in this sense that 'all roles . . . involve the actor in constructing and/or adopting a distinctive perspective on the world, but . . . it is a perspective shared with fellow occupation members and provides the unspoken grounds for communication between colleagues' (Ibid.). An understanding of teacher perspectives is therefore essential to an understanding of the teacher culture in the school.

Such a view of the teacher's role suggests that rather than merely enacting a role, the teacher engages in a process of 'role-taking' whereby 'roles are identified and given content on shifting axes as the interaction proceeds' (Turner, 1962: 27). However, teachers interact not only with colleagues and pupils but also with the Foundation Members and the Management and are participants in a school system organized for a specific purpose. This results in 'a compromise between the role-taking process and the simple conformity behaviour demanded by organizational prescriptions' (Ibid.).

The teacher's location in a particular social setting is thus an important factor by which her specific role may be identified; it also directs her role performance in a particular direction. Every school may be seen as functioning within a proximate setting of values which is important to understand in order to identify the more explicit bases of the school's functioning. The specific ideology on which RVS is grounded stresses the teacher's role in bringing about academic excellence in the school through creative teaching. Krishnamurti also emphasizes the responsibility of the teacher in helping the pupil to understand his or her psychological processes. He expects the teacher to establish a close personal relationship with the pupil based on affection and co-operation. By helping to bring about the psychological freedom of the pupil in her relationship with him, the teacher would fulfil what is considered her main function in the school.

Although the school's transcendental order provides the under-lying guidelines for action in RVS there are other institutional and external factors which influence school processes. Expectations of the teacher's role are in fact influenced by a combination of these factors.

The demands of the local order

The teacher's performance is influenced in part by the allocation of various responsibilities by the school's local order. The structure of the timetable specifies the teaching load of each teacher in terms of the number of periods per week she is expected to take in one or several subjects depending on her subject specialization. For example, a teacher may have anything between 9–28 teaching periods a week depending on whether she is involved in other activities, such as administration, or whether she devotes her time to teaching exclusively.

In addition to their teaching load, teachers are also allotted games duties and afternoon activity periods. They may also be required to perform certain administrative tasks such as drawing up the timetable, conducting examinations, and so on. Their most import-ant function, however, apart from teaching, is that of house-parentship. Out of a total of 36, at least 16 teachers are houseparents. Most single teachers are expected to take charge of a house (of about 24 pupils) when they join the school. Houseparents take up residence in the house and are totally responsible for the pupils in their care in terms of their health, dress, behaviour, relations with other pupils and general well-being.[1]

These five areas of the teacher's formal school life explicitly define her role in the school. This structural definition of the role lends it a multiplexity in performance: a teacher is expected to be several persons in the school. While the teacher's role may be viewed as being multiplex, the prevailing structural arrangements bring together two very important aspects of it. These are the 'demanding' or teaching and the 'caring' or 'pastoral' aspects of the role (Blackburn, 1980: 59). The dimension of 'pastoral care' which is a necessary feature of residential schools is incorporated into the teacher's role as the school does not employ special persons for the post of houseparent. The multiplex character of the teacher's role may be beneficial in the sense that pupils interact with the same set of teachers in different situations and contexts and, in the process, both are likely to achieve a high density in their interrelations. However this may also lead to stress and strain in the teacher's mind who feels that she is too preoccupied with the performance of her allotted tasks and, thus, has no time or energy to contribute to her relationship with pupils outside school hours.

The multiplex character of the teacher's role also suggests that the role has to be defined in relation to other roles. It is evident that once a teacher is recruited, she is required to interact with several others over a period of time. Thus, the role of the teacher forms part of the following 'role set':[2] teacher, pupil, parent, colleagues, Management, and Krishnamurti. This defines the range of teacher relationships within the formal structure of the school. However, while interacting with all others, the teacher performs her role in relationship primarily with some 'significant' others. These are those who are seen by the teacher as having a direct relationship to her role, for example, pupils, colleagues and the Management.

Social institutions also play a part in shaping the teacher's role in the school. Prominent among these are the pressures imposed by the Council and by institutions of higher learning. The teacher is constrained in her task of teaching by the syllabus set by the Council and by the pressure of having to complete the syllabus before the scheduled examination. Teachers are also aware of the expectations institutions of higher learning have of pupils who apply for entrance to them, which directs their task towards a particular goal in the senior school. Moreover, pupils tend to accept these expectations and therefore the demand on the teacher to help them to acquire the requisite qualifications is greater. This leads to some strain in the teacher's performance as she is also aware of school expectations, located in its transcendental order, which contradict these other expectations.

Parental concern with pupil performance in the classroom results in pressure on the teachers to improve pupil performance. Insofar as an excessive concern with the pupil's academic life is contradictory to the school's official goals and teacher expectations, the teacher once again faces a dilemma in performance. The pressures of one set of expectations are therefore not seen as being necessarily related to the other which leads to some confusion in the teacher's performance, and in her definition of her role and to a sense of dissatisfaction with her work.[3] The teachers cope with the strain resulting from conflicting expectations by evolving 'strategies'[4] and techniques which enable them to handle particular situations, achieve their goals, and meet the expectations of others to some extent within the overall framework of the school and its wider setting.[5]

Recruitment of teachers at the school

There are two avenues through which the teacher is recruited to RVS. In the first mode of recruitment, the Foundation advertises the vacancies for all the KFI schools in India. Ideological aims are prominently stated;[6] educational qualifications are specified as those of 'bright graduate and postgraduate teachers' in various disciplines. Those who may be 'interested and dedicated' are invited to apply to the principals of the respective schools.

Applications are screened at RVS by the Headmistress and the heads of different faculties. The interviewees are asked to spend a couple of days at the school, interact with teachers and pupils and also take a class which is attended by members of the Management. The manner in which she handles the subject and the pupils influences the prospective teacher's selection.

School expectations, in this context, are therefore related to certain minimum qualifications, the competence to teach particular subjects on the basis of the acquisition of a specific content of knowledge, and the ability to conduct a lesson presumably as a result of either professional training or occupational experience, as the case may be. The committee also takes into consideration factors such as appearance ('smart turnout'), social background, fluency in conversation, an ability for good communication, and an interest in co-curricular activities (such as hiking, music, sport, etc.) A teacher is also expected to have a 'certain quality of deeper intelligence' which is viewed as being necessary for the accomplishment of ideological goals. It is however evident that the qualities sought in the teacher are mainly related to the task of teaching and her interest in other school activities rather than any specific commitment either to the ideology or the wider aims of the school. They are obviously stated in the advertisement to acquaint prospective teachers with the school's special character.

Apart from recruitment through the advertisement, teachers come to RVS by hearing about the school through friends, Foundation Members and others. For example, a Foundation Member who had earlier been the Principal of a college of education suggested to student-teachers that they apply to KFI schools on the completion of their training. Two teachers are in RVS as a result of this connection. Two others heard about the school through friends teaching there and then applied for posts. For example, the music teacher had applied for a post after it was offered to her by an eminent musician who was then on the faculty. Such teachers go through an informal interview and are recruited if they meet school expectations.

Teachers recruited through the first mode, which includes the procedures of the advertisement and personal contact, join the school for a variety of reasons. RVS is known to be one of the better schools in south India with good academic results and an established reputation. Lakshmi and Asha, on their first job, said that they would like to have a 'good start' to their careers by teaching in a 'good school' which would ensure their recruitment to other schools later. Some join for personal convenience and then stay on for several years. For example, Devaki had been a teacher abroad and wished to return to India. In order to enrol her son in the school, and be with him, she and her husband applied for posts at RVS. In his previous job, Ranjan felt as if he was 'in a cage' and opted for RVS because he wanted a 'life of leisure'. Similarly, Chaturvedi came to the school because he was tired of city life and wanted to live in the country. A couple of older teachers, who have retired from jobs elsewhere, sought temporary refuge in RVS. Others find RVS a comfortable and quiet place with low living expenses due to its secluded location. Apart from all such considerations, they are nonetheless qualified teachers—in the school to teach.

The second mode of recruitment follows a different pattern. In the KFI's task of the dissemination of the ideology, Foundation Members visit universities and other institutions of higher learning, with a view to spreading Krishnamurti's thought and also to suggest, to interested people, the idea of working at one of the Krishnamurti schools in a teaching or non-teaching capacity. Such people are recruited to the school after they have been interviewed by Foundation Members.

In the second mode, teachers are also recruited during Krishnamurti's public talks on his annual visit to India. Announcements for teachers are made before the talk, and later, interested people may approach the Management. All such people may either be directly recruited if they have made a firm decision to work at RVS or they may be invited to visit the school, find out what they would like to do and then take a decision.

It is apparent that there is no formal procedure for recruitment as there is in the first case. Interviews are however conducted at different places inasmuch as informal discussions are held between prospective teachers, the Foundation and the Management. The attributes sought in these teachers are an appreciation and understanding of the ideology and commitment to it. Educational qualifications are never specified; most teachers recruited in this manner are usually over-qualified for school teaching holding doctorates or with specialized technical training.

The ideological commitment of the teacher recruited through the second mode is viewed as compensating for her lack of subject specialization, professional training, and teaching experience. Giving up a job, a successful career or a way of life is a form of renunciation for this teacher and is considered indicative of her commitment to her new assignment.[7] For example, three teachers gave up what are socially viewed as lucrative careers: the Indian Administrative Service, a professional engineering career, and a teaching assignment at a university abroad. The renunciation of these careers, and of a way of life associated with a particular class of people, was a strong indicator of their commitment.

This teacher's initial commitment to the ideology is indicated in different ways: Jai was 'intoxicated' with Krishnamurti for two years before he met him and it was his 'total surrender' to Krishnamurti that determined his decision to give up an engineering career for teaching in a school. In fact, Jai says there was really no decision to take as he had surrendered his life to Krishnamurti and will work for him wherever he is directed to.

Desai, another such teacher, was teaching at a university when he decided to switch to teaching at RVS. In 1971–2, a particular book by Krishnamurti had 'a tremendous impact' on him and he started corresponding with Krishnamurti. Finally in 1979, after meeting him and the Principal, Desai came to RVS. Vandana's husband was closely associated with Krishnamurti for several years. She was drawn to Krishnamurti because she perceived the truth of his philosophy and took up 'the challenge' of working at RVS as she wants to 'understand the child' and to see whether 'the child's mind can really be transformed'. David resigned a well-paid job in telecommunications, trained as a teacher and worked in other Krishnamurti schools before coming to RVS. His interest in teaching, and commitment to it, arose out of his interest in Krishnamurti after having read his works.[8]

Once recruited, this kind of teacher acquires the status of the 'twice-born', as it were, by the renunciation of a successful career and choice of a second career, which is qualitatively superior to the first, and is therefore on a higher plane. In addition to performing other tasks such as teaching, she devotes herself to the discussion, elucidation, clarification and propagation of the ideology. Her legitimacy is therefore acquired from the ideology as she is not only a teacher but also an ideologue. Moreover, as a result of her ability to interpret and disseminate ideological discourse, power derived from the ideology is bestowed on her.[9]

The teacher recruited through the first mode, on the other hand, may be viewed primarily as the transmitter of educational discourse and her power lies in the processes of transmitting it. She is also expected to understand the ideology and acquire a commitment to the same. However, in the area of ideological discourse, she is secondary to the other teacher and no power is bestowed on her by that discourse. Instead, her legitimacy rests in being like most other teachers inasmuch as there were 31 teachers recruited through this mode in the school. These teachers in fact have more influence in directing and shaping the character of everyday life in the school due to their larger numbers. The other teachers, five in number, can therefore function effectively—in terms of the ideology—only if some official authority is vested in them by Krishnamurti and the Foundation. It is only with reference to the ideology that this teacher is seen as being imbued with a special character.

It is obvious that the two modes of recruitment are broadly associated with two different kinds of teachers in the school. I will refer to teachers recruited through the mainly formal and impersonal mode of recruitment as 'professional teachers or pedagogues insofar as they look upon teaching as an occupation or career and are in the school in response to a demand for teachers and not because of any prior commitment to the ideology. The second category comprises the 'ideologue teachers' who have been recruited through a more personal and informal mode of recruitment and have taken on the job because of an explicit commitment to the ideology (see Table 5.1).

Movement across the two categories is rare; though professional teachers may develop an interest in the ideology, they rarely acquire the same kind of commitment as the ideologue. The two categories however are not mutually exclusive as teachers in one category may share some attributes and aspirations of the other. Thus many professional teachers exhibit an intellectual interest in questions raised at staff meetings about the ideology and their performance in relation to it. There are also some teachers who are deeply interested, in a personal sense, in the ideology but may not be explicitly committed to its implementation in the school. Although such factors lend an inclusive character to these two broad categories of teachers, the actual lack of movement from one category to another suggests the validity of the typology.

TABLE 5.1

Modes of recruitment and a typology of teachers (N = 36)

Modes of recruitment	Professional teachers	Ideologue teachers
Advertisement/formal interview	20	1
Personal contact/informal interview	9	4
No response	2	–
Total	31	5

Note: On visiting the school again, in 1983, I found the number of teachers had increased but, more importantly, while the proportion of professional teachers recruited through the formal procedure remained the same as before, in the case of ideologue teachers those who had come through personal contact now numbered 16 compared to 1 who had come through the formal interview. I do not of course suggest that this establishes a trend.

Commitment and role perception

In defining the different kinds of teacher commitment, I would like to draw upon the model presented by Woods (1984). He has suggested that such a model includes a 'vocational "calling" to teach or dedication to a set of ideals about education; a professional commitment to subject based teaching, to teaching as an art or craft, and to the institution such as the school; and an instrumental commitment to the teacher career purely as a useful career to be in' (Woods, 1984: 18). Woods also suggests that a teacher's commitment may vary across the three types at different times in 'intensity of commitment from core to peripheral'.

While this model takes account of three general forms of teacher commitment, there may also be situations when commitment diverges from these forms. This divergence is dependent on a fourth factor, which is quite obvious at RVS, namely, commitment to a world-view, only part of which may be educational, specific to a particular kind of school, and which may be distinguished from Woods' definition of vocational commitment inasmuch as it is commitment to a *specific* ideology about life and education and not a *general* set of ideals about education. Further, as we have seen, such commitment and its distinction from professional and instrumental commitment arises from a situation in the school which is defined by two orders—the transcendental and the local—which also give rise to two forms of discourse—the ideological and the educational. Moreover, these forms of discourse result in two modes of teacher recruitment and in the presence of two types of teachers. It follows that these two types of teachers would have differing kinds of commitment deriving essentially from the differing orders and through their performance, perpetuate the same in the school.

In the typology of teacher commitment, presented in Table 5.2, the teachers' role perceptions are viewed as indicators of their commitment. In the first category, professional teachers appear to have a superficial form of ideological commitment. Though their views suggest that they might have internalized the ideology, they are in fact conforming to an expected role, an ideal or standard set by Krishnamurti himself, in order to survive in the system which attributes a superior value to the ideology. This is evident particularly in the case of those teachers who have been in the school for a longer period of time and have therefore had a prolonged

TABLE 5.2

A typology of teacher commitment in RVS (based on the teachers' role perceptions)

I Superficial Ideological Commitment[1]	II Vocational and Professional Commitment[2]	III Ideological Commitment[3]	IV Indifference and Scepticism towards the Ideology[4]
1. Professional Teacher (15 years):* To see that pupils do not leave RVS thinking 'a career, money, success, etc. are the be-all and end-all of education'.	1. Professional Teacher (6 months): To help pupils 'acquaint themselves with the discipline concerned in the required manner'.	1. Ideologue Teacher (about 7 years): To establish the right relationship with the pupil as a 'fellow human being'.	1. Professional Teacher (15 years): To help 'the child to grow and adjust itself to society'.
2. Professional Teacher (10 years): To see that pupils 'have the strength to fight the injustice, inequalities and irresponsibilities of the present day world'.	2. Professional Teacher (6 months): To 'awaken an interest in knowledge in the pupils'.	2. Ideologue Teacher (6 months): Is unable to make a comment as 'deep down' he is aware that the educational process in a Krishnamurti school means the 'ending of the self'.	2. Professional Teacher (10 years): 'Krishnamurti and all that is OK outside the classroom but here I have to complete the course and prepare pupils for the examination'.
3. Professional Teacher (6 months): To 'develop a mind that is receptive to life as a whole'.	3. Professional Teacher (20 years): To give 'as much information as possible in the subject and prepare pupils		3. Professional Teacher (a few months): 'There is no Krishnamurti educational process. There is only the

educational process; the education of the masses. I shall be contributing to education if and *when* I become a *barefoot teacher*. At present, I am contributing nothing.

for the public examination'; to see that their 'behaviour is good' and that they understand Krishnamurti's philosophy and 'flower in goodness'.

4. Professional Teacher (20 years): Not to turn out 'mere careerists' but to 'produce the excellence of spirit' in a new generation who will then 'flower in goodness and intelligence'.

4. Professional Teacher (8 years): To remove the pressures of the learning situation by making learning 'fun' for the pupils.

5. Professional Teacher (28 years): To create the right kind of atmosphere in the learning situation leading to 'a sense of freedom through order, to an awareness in the pupil of the world around him and to good behaviour'.

---

[1] Teachers who exhibit an apparent interest in the ideology in order to survive in the school system which attributes a superior value to ideological principles.

[2] Teachers who perceive their role in terms of imparting knowledge, technical skills, and their subject specialization, and in creating a particular kind of atmosphere in the learning situation.

[3] Teachers who view their role essentially in terms of the ideology.

[4] Teachers who are generally indifferent, sceptical or reject the ideology totally.

* The period of time spent in the school by the teachers is stated in parentheses in each case.

exposure to the ideology which enables them to define their roles in terms of ideological expectations.

There are some other teachers, however, who have also been in the school for a long time and contradict ideological expectations in their role perceptions. For example, one teacher perceives her role in terms of helping the child to 'adjust' to society (see case 1, category IV, Table 5.2). The ideology in fact stresses the importance of the pupil's role in the *transformation* of society and does not at all advocate *adjustment* to it. This suggests that a teacher's understanding of the ideology, rather than being determined by 'external' factors, such as length of stay which may however help in formulating role perceptions, is actually dependent on a 'deeper' perception or an 'inner' conviction. This is also evident among the ideologue teachers whose perception of the ideology is not based on the period of time spent in the school.

Teachers who have spent a long time in the school may also have become indifferent or sceptical about the ideology, in actual situations, because of the practical tasks of running a school (see case 2, category IV, Table 5.2). They do not however give explicit expression to any feeling of distance or alienation from the ideology out of a personal sense of loyalty to Krishnamurti or a fear of losing their jobs, as the case may be. Their criticism is thus generally directed at the Management and school processes. Such teachers include those who are disenchanted with the lack of implementation of ideological principles in school processes and with the behaviour and attitudes of some ideologue teachers and Foundation Members which they see as being contrary to ideological expectations. Thus the lack of communication among teachers and between Krishnamurti and the teachers is viewed, by a senior professional teacher, as a serious shortcoming in the implementation of the ideology. An over-enthusiastic ideologue is criticised for his aggressive approach towards bringing about 'consensus' among teachers regarding ideological and individual aims and how these are to be implemented. An ideologue teacher did not find the 'atmosphere' conducive to the implementation of the ideology; what was lacking, he said, was 'warmth and affection' while the presence of a 'psychological hierarchy' (i.e. the implicit authority of Foundation Members and senior members of the Management) tended to create fear among the teachers and pupils. Several teachers, both professional and ideologue, are critical of the authoritarian role of

Foundation Members whose power is viewed as deriving legitimacy from the ideology.

A complete rejection of the ideology embodies the professional teacher in the extreme (see case 3, category IV, Table 5.2). Reputed to have earlier subscribed to Marxist ideology, this teacher finds the school's ideology 'foolish' inasmuch as it is based on 'one man's concept' which is never questioned. However, while he rejects the ideology, he is deeply committed to communicating his subject in a creative manner thus indicating his professional commitment. There are several professional teachers who exhibit a professional and vocational commitment in their concern with imparting knowledge, technical skills and their subject specialization, and in creating a particular atmosphere in the learning situation (for example, see category II, Table 5.2).

The ideologue teacher's commitment to her role is quite different and more complicated than that of the professional teacher. As a result of her personal commitment to the ideology, the ideologue is emotionally committed to her role and to others whom she sees as being participants in that process (for example, see case 2, category III, Table 5.2). By accepting and attempting to live in accordance with the school's ideological principles which order and give meaning to her life, the ideologue has given her total (both intellectual and emotional) commitment to it and has thus surrendered to it. Such a view suggests that role 'embracement' has occurred inasmuch as 'to embrace a role is to disappear completely into the virtual self available in the situation, to be fully seen in terms of the image, and to confirm expressively one's acceptance of it. To embrace a role is to be embraced by it' (Goffman, 1961: 106).

It is therefore clear that different teachers, within the two broad categories of the professional and the ideologue, may be committed in very different ways to one, a few or several aspects of their role depending primarily on their perception of the role and the ideology in relation to this role. Although the responses of professional teachers in category I in Table 5.2 and those of ideologue teachers in category III appear similar due to the stress on ideological principles, there is a difference based on the fact that they are essentially two *different* kinds of teachers as a result of the distinct modes of recruitment and the dissimilar forms of commitment to the ideology. It has been earlier suggested that movement from the category of the professional teacher to that of the ideologue teacher or *vice versa* is rare. To that extent, and keeping in mind the professional teacher's commitment to her career *and* need for survival in a school dominated by ideological discourse in its overall scheme, the professional teacher sees it to her advantage to define her role in terms of ideological principles. The ideologue teacher on the other hand defines her role in similar terms because of an initial commitment to the ideology inasmuch as she is in the school for the prime purpose of fulfilling the ideology.

As the commitment of several teachers is not essentially based on the ideology, they do not meet the wider ideological expectations of the school but are nonetheless indispensable in terms of the tasks they perform in the school. Consider the case of Vishwanathan who taught senior pupils, supervised and took an active interest in sports; he was also a senior house-master and assisted in administrative work. He was popular with some pupils who were known to be his favourites and generally disliked by the rest. By and large, he was popular with his colleagues and appreciated by the Management, in particular, for his efficient teaching and his ability to control pupils in the classroom and maintain discipline in the house. Although he participated in discussions on the ideology at staff meetings, he was privately cynical of it and often made derogatory comments on the activities of Krishnamurti and ideologue teachers to senior boys. After eight years at RVS, Vishwanathan decided to leave for a teaching assignment abroad. News of his departure astounded his colleagues especially the Headmistress who was not only concerned about the completion of the course that Vishwanathan taught but also felt that RVS was losing a 'good worker'.

This teacher had made himself valuable to the school by conforming to a particular kind of role that was essential to the school. His lack of interest and commitment to the ideology did not in any way affect the esteem in which his performance was held. It is obvious that the school performs not only the important function of attempting to accomplish ideological principles in education, but more significantly, in its daily life, the organization and transmission of educational knowledge. It is in the performance of this and other administrative and organizational tasks that reliance on teachers like Vishwanathan becomes necessary for its continuance in the overall school system.

Insofar as the school is dependent on such teachers, the Management has evolved a system of norms and rules apropos teacher conduct to ensure an expected level of competence and conformity. Newly recruited professional teachers are on probation for a year during which their work is assessed and their retention is dependent upon their performance.

A new teacher's performance in the classroom is under observation by senior teachers and reports of poor performance, determined by the level of noise in the classroom, the teacher's style of teaching (e.g. the dictation of notes is frowned upon), the use of reward and punishment, and so on, are discussed with the Headmistress. Thus one unsuccessful teacher was found 'too mild' and wanting in her ability to control the pupils and was asked to leave. As a result, the central concern of most newly recruited teachers is the control they are able to establish over the pupils in the classroom.[10] During the morning tea-break, such teachers may be found discussing the merits and demerits of a particular class depending on whether the pupils are 'noisy', 'rowdy' or generally 'quiet'. They are also very concerned about presenting a stern image to the pupils as they fear that pupils would otherwise 'take advantage' of them.[11]

Teacher assimilation into the formal system is controlled by assigning each new teacher as an understudy to a senior teacher on the same faculty who guides and directs the former. It is a relationship of both training and control: the senior teachers help, advise and direct the new teachers in the classroom and the house as well as control their performance by defining its limits and the shape it ought to take. Junior teachers are often reprimanded by senior teachers if, for example, they have not dealt with a situation in the appropriate manner. The teacher however has some amount of individual autonomy in the classroom, in interaction with pupils and in the implementation of the ideology. In the classroom, the teacher is relatively free to adopt a teaching technique that may be dependent on external factors but is largely of her own making. Similarly, a teacher can adopt or evolve an independent strategy or method for interacting with pupils that may adhere to school expectations but is also a result of her own perception. As the ideology provides no concrete guidelines for action, implementation is dependent, to a large extent, on individual understanding of the ideology. Certain areas where the teacher has no choice nonetheless remain, such as, in meting out grades and punishment, in methods of dealing with pupil misbehaviour, and so on.

Apart from the training the newly recruited teacher receives, there is a list of 15 rules for the 'guidance of staff'. These rules are not punitive but supportive, serve as guidelines and broadly refer to the teacher's relationship with the pupils as well as permitted methods of dealing with them; her responsibilities and duties and explicit advice on method, punctuality and attendance; her lifestyle on the campus; and the purpose of the school in terms of the ideology. It is obvious that these rules are primarily meant for professional teachers as ideologue teachers are expected to have understood ideological expectations and conform accordingly. The institution thus employs different methods of controlling teacher conduct in order to ensure compatibility with methods of implementation regarding educational discourse governed by ideological principles. Consequently, security for the professional teacher lies, as one teacher put it, in 'doing your job sincerely and fitting in with the place'. Such teachers have exhibited professional and instrumental commitment but also a superficial ideological commitment in an attempt to 'fit in with the place'. Similarly, the concern of junior teachers to establish control over pupils is a search for security as they know their survival depends on their acquiring that ability.

To the extent that commitment is related to continuance in the system, Kanter suggests the involvement of 'cognitive orientations'. That is, the individual finds that 'what is profitable to him is bound up with his position in the organisation, is contingent on his participating in the system—he commits himself to a role' (Kanter, 1974: 132). The professional teacher (e.g. in category I, Table 5.2) thus shapes his role within the boundaries defined by the institution primarily through 'matching one's interests with the demands of the situation'—in effect, through 'strategic compromise' (Woods, 1984: 17).

While the professional teacher's role is externally defined and controlled largely by the local order and educational discourse, and the school's intentions of meeting the requirements of that discourse, the ideologue teachers experience an external control on their conduct and activities primarily through the medium of ideological discourse and the transcendental order. Thus the insecurity experienced by them is the fear of being questioned on their performance by Krishnamurti and the Foundation. For example, Jai meted out stringent punishment to some errant boys who were having a detrimental effect on general discipline. For the rest of the term however Jai wondered whether he had taken the right decision.

That is, he was aware that a temporary course of action (such as, expulsion of the boys) only solves the immediate need for order whereas the order that Krishnamurti is talking about (namely an inner sense of order that inevitably creates discipline) can never come about through an authoritarian action. Jai was therefore afraid that he would be 'on the mat' before Krishnamurti and the Foundation for the decision taken by him.

Vandana, another ideologue teacher, admitted that she was personally afraid of the opinions of Foundation Members regarding her performance. The fear, however, in both cases, is of being found wanting by Krishnamurti and the Foundation rather than that of losing a job. The ideologue teacher's insecurity, unlike that of the professional teacher, is therefore not related to 'career-continuance' as such but to the judgement that may be passed by 'people who matter' (a term used by a teacher with reference to Foundation Members). As a result of strong commitment to the ideology, there are expectations of the ideologue teacher's performance which do not apply to the professional teacher. One ideologue teacher suggested that those who are in the school for a job, and do their job well, are secure. Their survival is only related to their conforming to the system. To the extent that the ideologue teacher has renounced an earlier career and surrendered to Krishnamurti and the ideology, everything is at stake; she faces 'career bankruptcy' (Woods, 1979: 145). That is, if the ideologue teacher is regarded a failure by Krishnamurti, there is no way in which she can continue as a teacher either at RVS or in any other school due to the high value she attaches to this judgement. Success in the organization, in terms of ideological approval, is essential for the ideologue's self-esteem, status and identity in the system as she has made the maximum investment in the organization. Kanter's observation is pertinent on this point: 'the more it "costs" a person to do something, the more "valuable" he will have to consider it, in order to justify the psychic "expense" and remain internally consistent' (1974: 133).

In her commitment to a profession and to a career, which she sees as being related to one or the other aspect of her task in the school, the professional teacher is concerned with the occupational and instrumental aspects of her role. The ideology and commitment to it is not of particular significance to such a teacher. Moreover, the commitment to the development of her personal career involves some amount of self-interest. Insofar as the ideologue teacher is primarily committed to the ideology, the point of reference is external to her and her commitment may be viewed as a value commitment devoid of self-interest. To the extent, however, that the ideology gives meaning and direction to both her inner and outer life, commitment to it may be viewed as arising from an interest in preserving the sustenance derived from it as well as in fulfilling an inner need for expression based on an internalization of the ideology.

The professional teacher's commitment to her role, however, cannot be belittled in spite of her concern for the advancement of her own career. Such a teacher is deeply committed to the correct performance of her role as she sees it, which may vary from ideological expectations but which nonetheless is evidence of the sense of responsibility she perceives in relation to her role. Further, the professional teacher is committed to her profession, as she views it, in much the same way as the ideologue teacher is committed to her vocation, as it is perceived by her. The difference lies in their commitment to the ideology and thus their varying perspectives on the role.

Case Study 1: The Professional Teacher

Ranjan came to RVS when he was 29 years old and has spent 10 years there. He teaches in the senior school and is responsible for conducting the examinations, compiling the timetable, house allotment work, etc. He is also a housemaster of 17 boys of the age-group of 10–11 years.

Ranjan went to a Hindi medium school run by a local south Indian association. He read for his postgraduation after which he tried his hand at a variety of jobs, ranging from a supervisor in a factory to a teacher in a college. He applied for a job at RVS after seeing an advertisement in a newspaper. At that time he was a trainee with a private company in a city and applied for a job at the school because he felt he was 'in a cage' and wanted a quiet, peaceful life. He was not 'after money' and wanted a 'life of leisure', an atmosphere similar to that of the college in which he had earlier taught.

His wife works as a part-time teacher and his children are pupils in the school. He has a good relationship with all his colleagues and is popular with pupils. Ranjan has a heavy workload: he takes 23 teaching periods a week and has games supervision duties, in addition to his other responsibilities mentioned earlier. The Management depends on him for the performance of administrative chores in particular which he has a reputation of carrying out to perfection. He is thus an important functionary in the school.

He is aware that his place in the system is dependent on his performance of certain specific, narrowly defined, roles. His commitment is, therefore, directed towards the performance of an occupational role in keeping with the many demands made on him by the school and his own perception of his role. However, he is not particularly satisfied with the school's performance as an educational institution, and with its efforts at ideological implementation.

His dissatisfaction with the present Management is apparent when he says that there has been a 'total collapse of the administration' in RVS. He in fact does not see administration and philosophy (in particular, the school's ideology) as being mutually beneficial for the efficient running of any school. With the decentralization of authority, decisions take a long time in being made and things move very slowly. The result of this 'democratic' mode of functioning, as he sees it, is that problems that can be handled by one person are discussed by several people and take longer in being solved. This upsets Ranjan's personal sense of efficiency as well as his own performance in the school as he feels 'frustrated' at times and does not quite know what to do in certain situations.

Insofar as the school's ideology is concerned, Ranjan thinks that one cause of the hiatus between ideological discourse and the school's implementation of it is that there is no real communication between Krishnamurti and the teachers. A teacher rarely speaks at the discussions with Krishnamurti and he feels that this is so partly out of fear of losing the job (if he or she is outspoken in criticism of the school), or because teachers have spoken before and no change has taken place. He feels that these meetings with Krishnamurti have become 'merely repetitions', as everything has been said before, and for himself, he has stopped participating in the discussion and prefers to just listen.

Ranjan had not heard of Krishnamurti until he came to RVS. Although he had always been 'God-abiding', he had never been 'superstitious' but believed in 'worshipping' the family idol. After coming to the school, he realized that his behaviour 'was not very intelligent' and that he was merely following his parents. However, while the school has helped him to become independent to a certain extent, he finds that he is unable to break away from his cultural and traditional background much as he would like to. He is very certain that in a school of the kind that RVS is, in order to implement any ideology, it is necessary 'to change ourselves'. He thinks that pupils looking at a teacher know at once whether that teacher is any different from the others. Therefore, it is very important to question oneself, one's beliefs and actions, in order to change. His incisive understanding of the ideology and his suggestions for change notwithstanding, he remains committed only to the correct perform-ance of his professional role. Although he feels frustrated at times and would like to leave the school, he feels he has to consider his responsibilities to his wife and children. He would, therefore, only leave the school if 'better prospects' were implied elsewhere.

Ranjan's major concern now in the school is to do his work well so that 'no one can find fault with it'. His commitment to his professional role is such that he does not brook any interference in its performance. For example, he was responsible for making the arrangements for screening Krishnamurti's video-taped talks. At a staff meeting, the Principal requested him to make additional screening arrangements. In the presence of several colleagues, Ranjan turned down his request on the ground that he would have to put aside his teaching and correction-work if he was to take on any more assignments. The Principal hastily dropped his suggestion. The professional teacher tends to give first priority to his teaching role, subordinating the propagation of the ideology to it and in such cases the Management has to be content with what it might consider a partial response to its expectations as it is dependent on such teachers for the performance of functional tasks.

Ranjan is aware of this dependence on his services as at any moment, during the course of formal or informal staff meetings, whenever the Principal or Headmistress require administrative assistance, they readily turn to him. His position being secure, he has stopped offering to help in any area because of his heavy workload and, as he says, if he makes any suggestions for improvement or change, he is immediately asked to do the job himself. He is however totally committed to his professional task of teaching and fulfilling his other responsibilities, for example, that of houseparent, as he perceives the accomplishment of these being his major function in the school.

Case Study 2: The Ideologue Teacher

In the case of the ideologue teacher, we find the most important point is the charismatic impact of Krishnamurti and his philosophy on the teacher and his response to it in his commitment to the ideology and his task as a teacher in RVS. As a 19 year old student Jai came across a book on Krishnamurti. After reading books on and by Krishnamurti for the following two years, he visited a KFI school to listen to Krishnamurti's public talks. On the first day, he met 'all the right people', that is, the Foundation Members and Krishnamurti, who invited him to stay at the school for a week. He later returned to that school as a teacher.

When Jai heard Krishnamurti for the first time, his image of Krishnamurti as a very 'compassionate' man was shattered because he was very 'abrupt and harsh' in his speech. Jai then asked himself whether he had decided to teach in the school for the image or for the ideology and realized that it was for the latter. In a very personal sense, his life became Krishnamurti's from the moment he decided to give up his career for teaching in a KFI school. After Jai had worked at the other school for five years, Krishnamurti asked him to go to RVS and take over a teaching-cum-administrative responsibility.

At the other school, Jai faced several problems in his relations with other teachers. These were primarily a result of his success as a teacher, increasing importance in the school's hierarchical structure, cordial relations with Krishnamurti and the Foundation Members, and zeal for bringing about change.

When he came to RVS, on the very first day, he experienced a 'terrible feeling of insecurity' as he felt that his colleagues and the Management seemed to be 'against' him and his presence in the school. The pressures of working in such an atmosphere appeared to obstruct the performance of his perceived role. With time, however, he was free of this feeling of insecurity and was able to organize his work largely in terms of the changes he saw as being necessary for the school. While the insecurity experienced by him was perhaps a personal feeling in reaction to a new place and different people, he has continued to face problems in his relations with colleagues and the Management. This is apparent in his relations with teachers some of whom talk in derogatory terms about him when he is not in their presence, dislike sitting with him at the dining table because he talks intensely about school matters and seeks their participation, and avoid him and his invitations to his room for discussions. Jai is aware of the teachers' negative attitude towards him and says he 'feels bad' about it at times but this does not deter him from his work which he will not give up under any circumstances.

Despite the difficulties he generally faces with his colleagues, Jai nevertheless has a good working relationship with them and faces no major problems of communication in matters of organization and administration. On the other hand, at other meetings when he brings up issues, such as the intention of the school or the role of the teacher in RVS, which, for him, are of central importance to the running of the school, he faces resistance from the teachers. It would appear that the ideologue teacher is also the strongest threat to the Principal's security because such a teacher is constantly examining existing school processes and suggesting alternatives for change. The Principal, defending his place and such authority as he has in the system, seeks to suppress the more active protagonists for change. This comes through at several meetings where he may refuse to discuss a point raised by an ideologue teacher and continue discussion on relatively safe topics. Moreover, the ideologue teacher cannot function effectively in the school unless some authority is vested in him by the Management, in particular, the Foundation. While Jai, in view of the responsibilities allotted to him, has sufficient autonomy and authority to enable him to perform effectively, two other very committed ideologue teachers play no role in the decision-making process as there is no authority vested in them.

The ideologue teacher also experiences a sense of loneliness, as perceived by Jai, who is aware that he alone is responsible for each decision that he makes and that there is no certainity as to whether his actions will be viewed as 'right action' by Krishnamurti and the Foundation. Jai feels that ultimately the opinions of the Foundation on his work are not as important as is the questioning by Krishnamurti. His apprehensions are related to the kind of 'demand' that might be made by Krishnamurti, 'being the tough person he is', and Krishnamurti's disapproval of his actions appears to be very painful, in a personal sense, to Jai.

Another aspect of his role that is disturbing to Jai is his continuous preoccupation with activity in RVS in terms of teaching and administrative chores. He feels that if he does not get completely involved with such activity, he would not be doing justice to his role. At the same time, he feels he does not have sufficient time for the pupils in his care in the house because of the other responsibilities alloted to him by the school. His dissatisfaction with his performance, and the negative attitude of some of his colleagues towards him has often made him feel 'disgusted' and at one point he even considered leaving the school. But he thinks that would be the 'easy way out' and that it is far more difficult to stay and face the challenge posed by Krishnamurti. He has accepted the challenge, the 'impossible challenge' as he calls it (because of the difficulties associated with meeting it), and while it is difficult to implement the ideology, the task has to be performed and his role is to work harder towards meeting it.

Jai is confident that he can bring about the 'intelligence' that Krishnamurti is talking about. It can be done if the teachers realize the fact of the necessity of the 'right kind of intelligence'. The thing to guard against, to his mind, is 'complacency': to join the 'stream of complacency would be death' for him.

The double-stranded situation in the school, identified in terms of its transcendental order/ideological discourse and the local order/ educational discourse, is borne out by our discussion on the difference in role perception of the two types of teachers and their commitment to it. The differing functions ensuing from the two orders and forms of discourse are not performed jointly but get differentiated into the roles of two different kinds of teachers. A dilemma in functioning is evident at staff meetings where there is often no consensus between professional and ideologue teachers and the latter are criticized for their constant review of school processes and attempts to bring about change. In fact, some teachers (in the junior school) clearly objected to discussion on the ideology being held during school hours as they were losing a teaching period on this account. In general, the attitude of professional teachers indicates a familiarity with educational discourse and thereby an identification with the school's local order whereas the inability to comprehend ideological discourse (as admitted by some) leads to a rejection of the school's transcendental order.

The ideologue teacher experiences a sense of isolation from the rest of the teaching community both in her formal and informal interaction with them. It is the ideologue's annual contact with Krishnamurti that removes the pressures of working in the school, and as one teacher put it, restores his 'sanity' and provides him with renewed energy to go back to 'nine months of hard work with no rewards'.

A fourth dimension to teacher commitment, adding to Wood's model, is ideological commitment identified in terms of a particular ideology to which the school subscribes. Although it is generally present in one form or another in all schools, it is highlighted when the ideology is articulated more explicitly, as in RVS. There are other schools however in which the ideology governing their functioning may be hidden or muted in expression or simply does not exist. But when it is explicitly stated, it gives rise to a special commitment in some teachers. Its contents would however vary from school to school depending on the nature of the school, for example, whether it is a private school founded on the world-view of a particular educator or one that is aided with government funds which would necessarily alter the ideological perspective.

While this chapter broadly establishes the culture of the teacher at RVS, it remains incomplete without a study of teacher interaction which is taken up in the following chapter.

CHAPTER SIX

Teacher Interaction:
Formal and Informal

Teachers interact with one another in both formal and informal settings. My analysis will focus on teachers not merely as teachers but as people who are more than merely performing a professional role. A study of teacher interaction is important for two reasons: first, it will enable us to describe the social processes through and in which the teachers live as members of the RVS community; second, it will help us to delineate the configuration of what I have called the teacher culture. This culture is activated through interaction and in the process reaffirmed or re-modulated or simply lived in. In this sense, culture and the social process are, for the purpose of my analysis, two sides of the same coin—namely the life of the teacher in the school—and therefore inseparable.

Interaction between teachers is affected by several factors such as the organization of the school, divided as it is into the transcendental and local orders, the structural position of a teacher—in the junior or the senior school, the ideology and commitment of a teacher, i.e. whether she is an ideologue or professional teacher, and so on. The school's ideology in fact emerges as a major determining factor in such interaction. Teachers' perception of the ideology and its axiomatic character, as well as their commitment to it, or lack of it, shape interaction in a certain manner. It also serves to be a source of dissension between teachers in their informal interaction with one another.

Teachers relate to each other in different contexts, at different times and on different occasions throughout the day. The range of interaction may extend from the classroom onto the sportsfield and into other non-curricular activities and events in the school. Formal or institutionalized interaction occurs between teachers in the course of the performance of their assigned tasks in the setting of their workplace. Informal interaction, on the other hand, occurs outside the performance of formally assigned duties, between teachers relating to each other as people. The opportunities and influences that shape both these kinds of interaction and the processes through which they are articulated are other important factors.

Formal or Institutionalized Interaction

Institutionalized interaction between teachers is affected by, and gives rise to, a number of situations. The organization of RVS into junior and senior schools, for example, has an impact on the community of teachers inasmuch as it creates a division between them. Thus senior school teachers have very little to do with teachers in the junior school except on an informal basis. A certain hierarchy in their relationship is in fact implied to the extent that the senior school teachers consider themselves somewhat superior to junior school teachers.

The teachers interact formally in different settings which provide the forum for discussion on matters primarily related to school life. In one sense, then, teacher interaction in the workplace is articulated through discussion and the teachers themselves highlight the use of talking as a strategy. Apart from having a functional utility, the discussions serve the psychological purpose of bringing the teachers together in their sharing of the many problems they experience in the school. This is not to say that their interaction is without the stresses and strains that are inherent in such relationships.

Interaction in formal settings between teachers at RVS takes place largely at faculty meetings, special staff meetings held in the junior school twice a week, and at the 20–minute morning tea-break. The staffroom is the 'arena'[1] in which teachers interact during the working day. While the junior school has a separate staffroom, the senior school staffroom is used by teachers of both schools throughout the day. It is located in the senior school building, flanked on one side by the offices of the Headmistress and the Principal, and on the other, by classrooms. The teachers however have very little privacy in this area as it is open to anyone in the school: the Management, pupils, visitors and parents.

For teachers, the staffroom is a place where they can relax in their 'free' periods, marking notebooks, reading, talking to one another largely about school matters such as the behaviour or academic progress of certain pupils, teaching methods (for example, şenior teachers may advise newly recruited teachers on how to handle subject matter or the pupils in the classroom), decisions to be taken on various issues, and so on. Teachers also meet informally at the 20–minute tea-break in between the morning classes.

There is a fundamental difference however in the interaction that occurs at such meetings in the junior and senior schools. At the senior school tea-breaks, the atmosphere is formal and restrained. The Headmistress, Principal or senior teachers may make announcements regarding other meetings to be held, tests to be conducted, reports to be written, impending excursions, and so on. The problems of individual pupils and teachers' responsibilities are also discussed at these meetings. It is significant that only senior teachers offer suggestions and make comments while junior teachers do not participate until they are asked to.

At the junior school tea-breaks, on the other hand, the atmosphere is quite different. It is apparent that the teachers are, in fact, taking a break from work and although they spend almost all the time discussing their work, there is an informal atmosphere. They however seriously discuss several aspects of school life such as the problems faced by newly admitted pupils, grading pupils in tests, and so on.

Apart from the informal tea-breaks, there are other settings in which teacher interaction takes place. Of these, the most important are the faculty and the staff meetings which are usually held once a week. The significance of such interaction lies in their content: the faculty meetings for particular subjects, such as English or Mathematics, are concerned essentially with the local order while the staff meetings are concerned with the transcendental order.

The faculty meeting takes place for 40 minutes every week when the teachers of a particular subject meet and discuss problems and issues related to the subject. Although such meetings may have an indirect effect on performance, their primary purpose appears to be the provision of an opportunity to the teachers for sharing and attempting to solve their problems in the teaching of specific subjects.

Another kind of staff meeting is held jointly once a week for teachers from the junior and senior schools for 60 minutes during the evening prep. hour in the senior school staffroom.[2] At the beginning of the academic term in 1981, the Principal opened the first meeting by clarifying the intention of such meetings. The discussion of administrative and other school matters was to be restricted to the faculty, school and Managing Committee meetings. These staff meetings were instead to be used mainly for teachers to acquaint themselves with the ideology through reading and discussion. This decision was apparently taken at Krishnamurti's request as he felt that the teachers should be familiar with his thought. Teacher attendance at these meetings is compulsory and the Principal specified that if a teacher wished to absent herself, she would have to seek prior permission from him. It is therefore considered important for the teacher to take part in the clarification of the ideological discourse as it is viewed as constituting the main reason for the school's existence. It does however impose a restriction on the teacher's autonomy insofar as she has no choice in the matter.

The teachers' lack of enthusiasm for such meetings is reflected in the limited extent of their participation in the discussion. Thus professional teachers by and large remain silent except for some newly recruited teachers, senior teachers and members of the Management. It is the ideologue teachers who primarily conduct the discussion.

One aspect of the role of such teachers at these meetings appears to be that of questioning school organization; for example, they once expressed their disapproval of the number of pupils (about 24) in each classroom which constrains their performance and thereby the implementation of the ideology as they perceive it. They are also critical of school processes, for example, of certain forms of punishment that may be meted out to errant pupils, of the content of the staff meetings, and the like. These teachers often suggest alternatives but existing methods and activities are stoutly defended by the Principal and other members of the Management and the Principal controls the discussion by holding the floor most of the time.

Ideologue teachers also tend to be concerned about the nature of communication, and thereby of interaction, between teachers and raise this issue often. They view the value of good communication, leading to a better understanding between colleagues, as being central to the implementation of the ideology. The problem of communication is viewed by them in two contexts. The first context is that of the meeting itself. The question raised by both teachers and Foundation Members is whether a teacher attends a meeting with set opinions and after an intellectual discussion goes away without any real sharing, communication or change having taken place. Or, it is asked, whether there is any communication at a 'deeper level'. This implies a more meaningful relationship in terms of a shared understanding of the ideology and a commitment to it.

The problem as perceived in the second context is whether teachers view one another and, therefore, relate only in terms of the role they are performing or at a more personal, human level as well. This issue is particularly relevant to ideologue teachers who are generally not accepted at a personal level by their colleagues.

This is not however to say that professional teachers are unaware of the lack of communication at the 'deeper level'. One such teacher, who had been in the school for 10 years, argued that, while teachers appeared to be communicating perfectly well on day-to-day issues, there seemed to be a lack of communication between them in relation to the ideology. He had observed that while teachers listen to Krishnamurti very carefully, they continue to function according to their own ideas and opinions. He feels that the situation could be rectified if the teachers could evolve a consensual definition of their role *vis-à-vis* the ideology. This, in turn, is dependent upon the quality of communication between them. However, as the teachers themselves suggested, a 'fragmentation' in their performance as educators occurs as a result of the poor communication between them. A professional teacher, for example, senses a certain aloofness in the teachers' attitudes to one another as he commented, 'Here, people are really short of time whether they are busy or not.'

This lacuna in communication is also evident in the 'poor relationships' between them, as noted by an ideologue teacher. For example, they do not visit each others' classrooms, nor is there 'a sense of community in working together', and friendly, personal relations between teachers scarcely exist. In order to improve communication at the meetings, he suggested bringing out the 'dirty linen' and helping each other in the solution of their problems. The teachers are however aware that while one may question or demand a relationship around the performance of a certain function, 'deep' relationships can only come from inner conviction. The professional teachers also suggest that the present structure of the school, institutionalized as it is, appears to demand functionaries and it is therefore necessary for them to relate to one another in that role. However, they are aware that with time, a 'binding relationship' of sharing and understanding amongst themselves and between them and the school is created.

Ideologue teachers, in general, are however insistent that relationships in RVS are only linked to the function a person performs because the school as an institution has taken precedence over the human beings in it. On one occasion, the junior school Head asked the teachers of the junior school if they could work together in the same sense as the Buddha's *sangha*.[3] That is, if they could *together* face the reality of daily living as well as the truth of the Buddha's (here Krishnamurti's) word. This would imply their discussing their problems frankly and helping one another 'with great feeling' and understanding.

It is apparent that the teachers view communication and interaction among themselves in three inter-related contexts: the functional, the more personal or human, and the 'deeper' relationship which is linked to the ideology. This would result in the creation of the 'right relationship' between themselves, which is viewed as being essential to working and living together in the school. While both kinds of teachers are conscious of the three contexts of interaction, it is primarily the ideologue teacher who attempts to bring them together in an integrated whole. Their assessment of the situation is based on two considerations. One is their perception of the teacher culture, as it is articulated through interaction, as being too superficial insofar as relationships are function-centred. Secondly, the ideology influences their perception: Krishnamurti has commented in discussion with some members of the Management that each teacher is in a closed circle and operates from within the circle. He suggested that it was only by bringing about a free flow of communication that the circles could be broken and meaningful relationships established which would then improve their performance. In a preliminary attempt to cultivate communication, it was decided by the Principal that the weekly staff meeting would be held in two groups to enable 'more conversation' and participation and that teachers would meet jointly once a month. This *did* serve the purpose of allowing greater participation as teachers felt that they were able to communicate more meaningfully in smaller numbers.

There is a clear disjunction between the junior and senior schools in terms of teacher interaction. Prior to 1981, senior school teachers would rarely visit the junior school for the purpose of teaching or attending morning assembly. It was only when the new junior school Head perceived an asymmetrical relationship between teachers from the two sections, as well as between senior teachers and junior pupils, that a change was brought about. Some of these teachers then began to take a few lessons in the junior school. Several junior school teachers also teach in the senior school as a matter of course.

While informal relations between teachers of the two schools are cordial, junior school teachers perceive a 'lack of faith' in their performance by senior school teachers. For example, there were complaints about the lack of academic rigour and discipline among the pupils of Standard Eight who until 1983 used to enter the senior school straight from the junior level. The senior teachers view this as a failure on the part of their junior colleagues to generate in pupils the school's 'ideal' in terms of various factors of which specific mention was made of 'sharp thinking ability and good manners'. Junior school teachers viewed this as an unfair criticism of their work based on the personal value judgements of some senior teachers. In turn, they were critical of the behaviour of senior pupils who 'set the tone' for junior pupils who 'hero worship' them and emulate their behaviour to a certain extent.

Junior school teachers also feel that their role is viewed by their colleagues in the senior school as being less important than their own primarily because of the difference in the level of educational knowledge being imparted by them. The junior teachers' perception of their lower status in the latent hierarchy of the teachers' 'occupational culture' does not however affect their relations with their senior colleagues.[4] It is nevertheless suggestive of a disparity in the teachers' perception of their functional roles which is in contradiction to the ideology according to which no status may be attached to any role.

Staff meetings held in the junior school differ from those held in the senior school. One factor contributing to freer communication in the junior school is the relatively younger age of the Head whose presence does not intimidate the participants.[5] When he took charge of his post in 1981, he decided after consultation with his colleagues to hold meetings alternately on the ideology and on educational matters. A committed ideologue, he felt that it was first necessary to be clear about the ideological foundations of their work and only then deal with specific educational issues.

An important issue that arose at one such meeting was based on the Head's concern for the teacher's neutrality in role performance. As an example he suggested that a teacher's identification with a particular class, or with a group of pupils in the house, could create 'disorder' in both the pupil and teacher communities as it created exclusive loyalties among them. The teachers, however, objected to the use of the word 'disorder' and argued that a class teacher's identification with a particular class in fact implied a concern for it. The Head's concern however stems from the cultural ethos of the school which frowns on the favouring of some pupils over others and is based on the ideology according to which all pupils are to be treated alike.[6] The teachers obviously do not always accept the ideology's prescriptions and tend to interpret them differently.

Teachers in the junior school moreover tend to favour discussion on issues emerging from the local order rather than on the ideology. They objected to the latter on the ground that no provision was made for such discussions in the timetable and, at present, they were losing one teaching period on this account. It is evident that the professional teacher's commitment to her teaching task is of paramount importance even though it may subvert the Management's attempts to implement the ideology.

The Head therefore perceived a lack of interest in the teachers for discussion on issues such as how they could help the pupils to apply their minds, to be attentive and sensitive, or whether it was sufficient that they concentrate on their main task which is teaching. Hence, when he announced that staff meetings in the junior school would no longer be used for such discussion but for problems of organization and matters directly related to the functioning of the junior school as these needed to be resolved immediately, he received an enthusiastic response.

Their enthusiasm and co-operation in coping with organizational and other tasks related to their teaching work is an expression of their commitment to high pedagogic standards. It appears that their hesitancy in approaching matters related to the ideology is an expression of their inability to completely understand the ideology and its expectations of them. This was clearly stated by a senior teacher who argued that as the ideology provides no 'guidelines' for action, there is 'no clarity' in his daily life as a teacher and that this is perhaps also a result of his not having fathomed it. The teachers' attitude indicates a dichotomy in their minds between educational and ideological discourse, as most of them are more familiar with the former and therefore identify with it.

Teachers also come together for the performance of a precise task such as drawing up the timetable and the examination schedule, preparing reports on pupils, and the like. Insofar as relations between *individual* teachers in the functional context are concerned, there appear to be some problems in the work situation itself rather than in the planning or organization of activities. For example, the authority that is associated with experience in the transmission of knowledge is vested in the senior and older teachers who guide and instruct junior teachers. At times, however, junior teachers are unable to relate to their senior colleagues and either evolve their own methodology or seek guidance from another member of the department or a related department. Similarly, some junior school teachers found the Head's mode of functioning too dynamic, pushy and overbearing to allow them adequate autonomy. As this was leading to some amount of conflict between them and creating problems in their performance, they began to consult the Headmistress.

Another problem in the actual work situation has to do with the teacher's need for individual autonomy in the classroom which gives rise to conflict when there is more than one teacher there. An illustration is taken from a study of the Prep. Section—the most junior class—in the school. This class contains 16 pupils whose ages range between six to eight years. Three teachers take care of all teaching periods with two or three other teachers coming in occasionally. The Head had prepared a new curriculum for this class catering largely to the needs of the pupil and a well-qualified younger teacher had been appointed as the class teacher as he felt that she would be able to understand the new approach and implement it successfully. The older class teacher was retained as a teacher as she was seen as having 'functional' value and would be able to help the younger teacher who lacked sufficient experience but had the necessary qualifications. A third, very young, teacher with no experience of working with children was to assist both these teachers. This arrangement did not, however, work out satisfactorily for several reasons. The older teacher, nearing retirement, was sensitive to the others' judgements of her professional competence. She complained to her colleagues that while her teaching work-load had been reduced, and her autonomy in the classroom removed, the Head was still dissatisfied with the manner in which the class was being handled.

The younger teacher now in charge of the class, however, found it difficult to relate to the older teacher who, she thought, was unwilling to adapt to change. While earlier the older teacher had the choice of following the new curriculum in her own manner, she was now being told what to do by the younger teacher and the Head. This led to a clash between the two teachers and to a breakdown of communication between them. The Head held discussions with both teachers, with a view to improving the situation and realized that the older teacher was so insecure about her position and reduced status that she was unable to perform effectively in the classroom. The younger teacher, he felt, had not understood the new curriculum, was not committed to it and was, therefore, incapable of implementing it. The young assistant teacher was caught in this conflict between the two teachers and her performance was limited by their conflicting approaches.

The result was lack of co-ordination in the work of the three teachers as no one knew what the other was doing in the classroom. The teachers filled in a weekly work chart for each period taken by them *after* the class was over but were unaware, at the beginning of the week, as to what was to be done during the week by each of them. The assistant teacher was aware of this confusion in their teaching methods and suggested that they meet weekly to plan their work schedule for the following week.

Only one such meeting actually took place where they primarily discussed the need for more co-ordination amongst themselves, to organize the class more systematically, and the general problems of discipline they faced in the classroom. They also decided that they would have a subject theme each week so that there was a link in the teaching activities of the teachers and the learning processes of the pupil. This was not, however, followed in practice.

This deteriorating situation led to the Head's intervention who met the three teachers concerned and questioned them on several issues related primarily to their teaching methodology and the pupils' behaviour and performance. He suggested that the class teacher's indifference to the discussion implied a lack of serious responsibility and care towards her class and her role. She finally opted out of her assignment with this class altogether.

The other teachers' sympathies lay with the older teacher and they were critical of her younger colleague who was seen as being disrespectful towards the former and uncooperative in her approach. The assistant teacher was leaving RVS at the end of term and the result of all this was that the class finally reverted to the care of the older teacher. The new curriculum was dissolved and the Head decided to start all over again in the following term.

This episode also created problems for the Head in terms of being in conflict with his perceptions of his role performance. He was particularly perturbed by these events as, for him, the Prep. Section was at the centre of what he had been trying to achieve in the junior school in terms of educational innovation. If this had been a failure, he felt he was unable to justify his presence in the junior school or in any area where he was attempting to bring about change.

This incident clearly suggests that the lack of an amiable working relationship affects the teacher's performance in the classroom and disrupts the pedagogic process. In this particular situation, the Head's commitment to his role and to the quality of education in the junior school prompted him to intervene and change the structure, which had been of his making in the first place. This may not be the case in other situations where change might have wider repercussions which may give rise to further disequilibrium in the larger system of the school. Thus, to ensure harmony and continuity, the Management may ignore functional incompatibilities amongst teachers.

The main factor responsible for this disharmony in working relationships, as noted earlier, is the teacher's need for autonomy in the classroom. A colleague's presence, as well as directions from outside (e.g. from the Head) on how to conduct the lesson or criticism of their teaching methodology restricts this autonomy which then gives rise to strain and conflict in their interaction. The assertion of the teacher's individuality in the workplace does not however appear to interfere with their informal interaction which is influenced by factors other than those obtaining in the functional arena of the teacher's life.

Finally, the teachers' relations with the Management appear to be governed by their definitions of their roles and by personal connections with Foundation Members. It is not possible to clearly identify the many elements of such interactions as they fluctuate from situation to situation and from person to person. In other words, their precise definition is restricted by contingency.

On issues where the teachers can take a stand, they tend to support the Headmistress and other members of the Management rather than the Principal. This could be due to the fact that the Headmistress had been a teacher in RVS for 15 years before she was appointed to her present post and is therefore well-acquainted with the teachers. The Principal, on the other hand, was brought in from outside although he had earlier taught at RVS. It would appear that any community would close its ranks against an outsider particularly if there are additional aggravating circumstances as in this case: for example, the Principal's inability to interact informally with his colleagues and his lack of identification with all aspects of his role.[7]

Disagreement often occurs at staff meetings between the Principal and the junior school Head and on such occasions, the teachers tend to support the Principal. This is in spite of the fact that the junior school Head is closely associated with Krishnamurti and all the Foundation Members. One factor that accounts for teacher support of the Principal in this case is that although both the Principal and the junior school Head are ideologue teachers, the latter is critical of school processes and an agressive proponent of change.

At one meeting, for example, the Principal suggested that in order to curb noise in the dining hall, some of the more noisy pupils should be sent out and asked to eat separately. The junior school Head was obviously not happy with this form of punishment and argued that sending pupils out of the dining hall should not become a habit with the teachers. Although he was aware of the 'objective necessity' of this form of action, he suggested that they should realize that a punitive measure 'shows us our own failure and we must be aware of that'. The teachers immediately reacted in protest: the Headmistress insisted that the suggestion for a punitive measure had come from the pupils' representatives; another teacher argued that the pupils themselves had 'created' authority in the teachers by not responding to their appeals for order. The Principal obtained the teachers' approval by suggesting that the pupils cannot organize their lives sometimes and need guidance which is what was being done in this case.

This discussion indicates that when the teacher's performance *vis-à-vis* the ideology is questioned, they turn hostile to the person making the observation, and whom they may support in other situations. Although most of them have a poor working relationship with the Principal, they tend to throw their weight behind him when he is supportive about their performance and school processes in general.

Informal Interaction

Teacher interaction that occurs outside teaching hours and the formal setting of the workplace varies from one context or occasion to another. Besides, such factors as seniority or juniority in service, one's being an ideologue or professional teacher, and one's gender, also influence the form and content of informal interaction. It would appear that there is an interplay of the various factors that influence the overall pattern of teachers' relations and, thereby, the ethos of the teacher culture in the school.

As all the teachers live on the campus, their evening schedule is dependent on the school's programme. Most teachers supervise pupils during the evening prep. hour, in the houses and the dining hall, attend meetings, and so on. Teachers relate to one another informally either in friendship groups or individually. However, the latter kind of interaction is rare and occurs only among men, particularly the ideologue teachers. Teachers rarely mix across gender groups but there are definite friendship groups within a single gender group. It is however evident that in the very nature of organizations of this kind, characterized by sharply patterned forms of interaction, it is to be expected that participants will evolve different kinds of informal patterns of social relationships to restore a balance in their everyday life.

I was able to observe closely a friendship group among junior women teachers. The moving spirit of this group was a very young teacher who had been in RVS for only a year. She was considered a rebel by her friends as she was opposed to the school's transcendental order and cynical about the possibility of the ideology being ever implemented. This group was made up of four young women teachers, all single, and one or two young men teachers joined in occasionally. Their relations were characterized by loud *bonhomie* which however was never exhibited in the staffroom. Most of their conversation was gossip that centred around the activities and personalities of other teachers in the school.

The high point for this group was the faculty play that was staged in the second term in 1981. All the members of the group participated in the play and did not encourage the inclusion of other teachers. For example, one teacher, considered by them to be close to the Management, was treated with goodwill but was excluded from the close association and the particular humorous idiom that was characteristic of this group. Another teacher taking part in the play faced hostility from them as they had earlier sought her companionship to which she had not responded. Participation in the play led to the group's acquiring an air of exclusiveness and distinctiveness from the other teachers which was not appreciated by some members of the teaching community, particularly the ideologue teachers. Such activity is viewed as setting people apart which militates against and thereby threatens the sense of community.

The exclusion of other teachers from this group, and therefore their closed circle of friendship, was primarily due to the content of their conversation, which they considered confidential. They were aware that any outward expression of rejection or dissatisfaction in relation to the ideology would not be appreciated and might jeopardize their position in the school. One teacher was in fact reprimanded for airing her negative views on the ideology and the school's efforts at its implementation. This group however remained one of the most closely knit and stable friendship groups in the school.[8]

The ideologue teachers are excluded from the teachers' friendship groups in general and do not form a group of their own. They do not come together as a group as they are very few in number and are ideologically not given to that way of acting: they are committed to the sense of community and to the broadening of human relations rather than narrowing them.[9] Their exclusion from other groups is primarily due to their strong association with, and deep commitment, to the ideology. For example, an ideologue teacher, initially acting in the faculty play, withdrew once rehearsals began, saying that he did not have sufficient time for this activity. This, in the others' eyes, confirmed their earlier reservations about ideologue teachers whom they view with a certain degree of suspicion. In informal groups, an ideologue teacher's presence has the effect of being a damper on group activities. This is mainly because he or she is associated with a sense of seriousness, even self-righteousness and, above all, with Krishnamurti, and is therefore viewed as being exclusive.

Ideologue teachers are aware of their inability to communicate with others as a result of their isolation from the larger teaching community. For example, one of them admitted being unable to share his observations about the school with other teachers at a personal, individual level, and felt disappointed and 'alone' in his task of implementing the ideology. This teacher was also the object of ridicule for some of the junior teachers who openly sneered at him even at staff meetings. Their disparaging attitude however was not a serious objection to what he has to say (which reveals his intense commitment to the ideology and his attempt to define the teacher's role in terms of it) but rather a personal rejection because he takes himself too seriously. Besides, he faces antagonism from his colleagues as his views and presence are seen as a threat to the status quo and he may succeed in bringing about changes which, for example, might increase the teachers' workload. His relations with his colleagues in the formal setting therefore appear to affect the nature of his informal interaction with them. Another ideologue teacher said that although he is able to relate to his colleagues to some extent, he is not interested in gossip or discussion on 'superficial' matters. His interaction with his colleagues, is, therefore, limited as he can have 'meaningful' discussions with only a few of them. Another such teacher feels threatened by professional teachers for she is quite sure that although she is very co-operative with her colleagues in the functional context, she is not going to let herself be 'bullied' by them and, therefore, keeps her distance from others socially.

This situation makes an important comment on the teacher culture in the school. There is clearly a division between the pedagogues or professional teachers and the ideologues and insofar as the culture is dominated by the former, the ideologue teacher experiences strained informal relations with his colleagues. It is significant that while the ideologue teacher's presence in the school is a result of her commitment to the ideology (which is not the case with the professional teacher), her place in the teacher culture is devalued by the professional teacher.

The professional teachers also view an excessive interest in the ideology on the part of a newly recruited teacher with distrust because they consider such enthusiasm a passing interest. While this appears to be the surface formulation of their attitude, they also experience a deeper anxiety insofar as they feel inadequate *vis-à-vis* the ideology and therefore threatened by it. Most new teachers are accepted into the teaching community as long as they do not deviate too sharply from a latent though well-established code of conduct. This includes an exhibition of professional competence and the ability to control pupils in the classroom. A limited interest in Krishnamurti and the ideology is appreciated and encouraged.

The professional teachers' attitude towards the ideology is influential in shaping the teacher culture as they are in a strong majority. The Management, ideologue teachers, visiting Foundation Members and Krishnamurti himself, however, make a sustained effort to restore the balance although they are unable to orient every teacher to the school's official and ideological goals. It is obvious that this inevitably influences the nature of teacher interaction in both formal and informal settings.

Senior teachers in the school also tend to dominate the teacher culture and having established the existent culture, maintain its closed structure which is based on professionalism and status dependent on the teachers' longer association with the school. In not being grounded in the school's ideology, it fails to completely incorporate the ideologue teachers who remain, more or less, outside the dominant teacher culture. This implies that the ideology itself is excluded from the prevailing teacher culture insofar as the ideologue teacher does not belong to it in spite of being in it.

There are two factors that inhibit teacher interaction across gender groups among single teachers. For most professional teachers, the fear of gossip among their colleagues and pupils appears to be a dominant factor. Among ideologue teachers, there are closer friendships but excessive interaction across gender groups is viewed by them as an interference with their primary task in the school.[10]

Another factor that inhibits close friendships across gender groups appears to be the structural positions of the teachers involved. Thus, in one such relationship, where a senior faculty member was involved, his friendship with a lady teacher was the centre of gossip among teachers for the two terms I spent in the school. With all this gossip, the 'scandal' (as it was referred to by the teachers) soon reached Krishnamurti's ears, and he had the lady teacher removed from the school as she was generally considered responsible for the situation. According to the teachers, this was done primarily because such a relationship did not conform to the expected behaviour associated with such a senior member of the Management who had been appointed to his post by Krishnamurti himself. This relationship was also viewed as not setting the right kind of example for pupil behaviour in the school.

For teachers, 'social occasions' are events that they look forward to in the school. One such event is the 'moonlight dinner' held twice a term where teachers meet informally with pupils. During these dinners, however, married teachers freely communicate with each other whilst single teachers tend to remain either within their gender groups or interact only with married teachers and pupils. Similarly, at special staff dinners or farewells, the extent of teacher interaction across gender groups remains the same. On such occasions, their behaviour is a result of the fear of disapproval for breaching what is generally considered proper social behaviour rather than the fear of forming close emotional relationships.[11]

Single teachers' relations with each other, however, seem to change substantially when they interact informally with pupils. It is apparent that outside the confines of the school, for example, on hikes, their whole attitude towards one another and the school changes. It is as if the constraints experienced by the teacher in RVS are completely removed which results in an opening of communication between them. This closely shared relationship outside the school exists only between the younger teachers; senior teachers maintain very correct, though informal, relations on excursions and rarely interact among themselves, other than in their roles as teachers on duty. Their inability to be completely relaxed is perhaps associated with their sense of responsibility or duty which arises out of their status as senior teachers in the school.

We have examined teacher culture in RVS in its many forms and aspects both from the participants' points of view and in terms of the interface between the different elements constituting it. These include not only the institutional and social factors but also the personal and interpersonal considerations that contribute to the creation and perpetuation of teacher culture. Teachers have been viewed in a dialogue not only with one another and the pupils but also with the ethos that is special to RVS through the medium of interaction. They are seen conforming, dissenting, changing, innovating, and constructing not only the content but also the forms of interaction. They therefore appear to be engaged in a continuous process of a twofold activity: the dismantling and reconstruction, as it were, of the social structure as they perceive it and the understanding, interpretation and transmission of teacher culture itself.

CHAPTER SEVEN

Pupil Culture
An Ensemble of Relations

We now examine the life of the pupil in terms of school-generated experiences and activities in order to understand what it means to be a pupil at RVS. Pupils' social background, attitudes, and general experiences; their perceptions and expectations of the school and the teachers; their encounters with one another; their hopes and fears for the future—all these contribute towards establishing a pupil culture in the school. Pupil culture is therefore made up of the pupil and his private world in interaction with the school environment in its manifold character including people, events and situations of the pedagogic process. People include the Management, teachers, and other pupils, administrative staff, school workers, and significant visitors to the school, including parents. Apart from interaction with people, pupil culture arises out of the pupils' relationship with, and attitude towards, school work and the events that constitute pupil activity in the school. Pupil culture is thus not some kind of an entity in itself but exists only in relation to the many components of school life: in fact it is an ensemble of relationships.

Beginning with the pupil's 'career', which may be viewed as occurring in 'a series of steps or stages' from the age of six plus to 18 years, pupils move through different classes and environs to the final examination and departure. Woods suggests that this 'progression is through a number of status changes occurring at significant points . . .' (1980a: 17). However, while pupil culture does not necessarily change over time, the pupils' experience of it would nonetheless alter as they move through the different stages.[1]

The pupil's career begins with the individual's entry into the school. Pupils come to the school from varied environments and backgrounds with the values and norms of their upbringing already ingrained in them during 'primary socialization'.[2] These values influence the pupil culture as they encompass and are reflected in pupils' views on different aspects of school life, most notably, on school work and the ideology. Once the pupil is in the school, he is in a different environment from that at home, interacting with divers people, events and situations and the process of 'secondary socialization' begins. Secondary socialization may be viewed as the 'internalization of institutional or institution-based "sub-worlds" .... characterized by normative and affective as well as cognitive components'. It also implies 'the acquisition of role-specific knowledge ... role-specific vocabularies ... and "tacit understanding" ' (Berger and Luckmann, 1967: 158). An important aspect of this socialization is school expectations of the pupil role. These differ to the extent that ideological definitions of the role vary from the actual demands made on the pupil by school processes such as the rigorous academic programme in the senior classes. This discrepancy in expectations results in conflicting pupil attitudes towards performance and the ideology.

Pupils are largely committed to school work and conform to what is expected of them in this sphere. They are however ambivalent about the ideology: some of them reject it totally; some others relate to it intellectually but are overwhelmed by other pressures, and a few emphasize the positive change it has brought about in themselves and their lives.

Apart from their exposure to the ideology, the pupils here, as elsewhere, 'are exposed to a number of new experiences and phenomena, such as individual teachers, aspects of school organization, problems of work and knowledge, class cultures, teacher and pupil cultures, peer groups, towards which they are required to make a response. Through this maze of activity and encounters the pupil negotiates his way, making the most of his power and abilities in furthering his interests, often in company with his fellows, discovering and inventing strategies of infinite number and complexity' (Woods, 1980a: 23).

Pupil culture may thus be seen as characterized by strategical action in order to adapt to the complex nature of the many situations confronted by the pupils as well as to fulfil their private goals. At RVS, conformity is the most common behavioural pattern used by the pupils primarily to furher their own interests. According to Woods conformity is a form of negotiation as there is generally 'no bland internalization of institutional goals' (1980a: 15). However, in the case of some pupils, conformity is a result of an internalization of the school's local order and the official and institutional goals accruing from it; it arises from conviction and the affirmation of an ideal: that of the educated, well-trained and successful pupil. This does not however suggest that there is a pro-school pupil culture at RVS. The pupil culture consists of the many strands of pupil experience both positive and negative in attitudes towards the school.

Pupil entry into school

Pupils' entry into RVS is governed by a number of factors. These include both formal and informal considerations. The most important formal criterion is the Management's expectations of the kind of pupil they would prefer to have. Keeping in mind the constraints under which it functions and the goals it has to meet, the school has evolved a policy for admissions.

The entry points for pupils are usually Standard Four (age: eight plus) and Standard Seven (age: 11 plus). A few pupils are also admitted into the Prep. Section (age: seven plus). Pupils are sometimes considered for entry into other classes if there are any vacancies. A brochure containing information on the school is sent to parents who are asked to fill out a questionnaire which includes questions on the pupil's earlier education, academic record, hobbies and interests, and, in particular, his home and social background. A selection committee then selects pupils who are eligible for registration. Finally, the registered pupils are called for an interview and test after which selected candidates are admitted.

The effort to keep the school 'non-sectarian', 'national' and 'international' finds expression in the criteria of 'regional representation' and 'various religious backgrounds'. Children of parents working abroad are also considered so as to have a good mix of pupils in the school. Keeping in mind the school's ideology, pupils who are recommended by Foundation Members as being children of 'parents who are cultured and interested in Krishnamurti's teachings' are given preference as are those who are considered 'sensitive' and are 'vegetarian' in their food habits.

'Sensitivity' is considered a difficult quality to assess but the child spends about 40 minutes with the Committee who watch his behaviour. It is believed by the Management that academic ability could lead to sensitivity thus implying that pupils who are considered bright would be given preference over the others. The pupil's academic performance in the test is thus an important criterion for selection and he is expected to be 'well above average'. Clearly, this indicates a preference for pupils from a certain privileged background, a factor strengthened by the high fee charged. As the school does not accept any government grants or loans, it is totally dependent on fees and donations.[3]

It is not possible, however, for the Management to always follow the admission policy as there are various external pressures, such as the influence exerted by politicians, local bureaucrats, and patrons of the school. Apart from the need to maintain financial viability, there may be certain negative consequences if a pupil with such connections is refused admission. Sometimes admissions continue throughout the year as the Management tries to fill as many vacancies as possible, making compromises along the way. As the school has to maintain the pupil population at a certain level—330–40 pupils—to prevent the loss in income, it becomes necessary to fill in vacancies.

It is apparent that the kind of pupil who comes to RVS does not necessarily meet school expectations. The Principal grants that he is satisfied with half the pupil population while he considers the rest 'passable but lacking in the kind of sensitivity we are looking for'. He feels that such pupils might benefit from being in the school but they might also block school goals by their 'cynical' attitude and influence on their peers.

This dissatisfaction leads to an emphasis on selecting pupils from a 'cultured background with certain sensibilities', once again suggesting a preference for a particular background. Emphasis is laid on the pupil's background for two main reasons: it is assumed that educated and professionally employed parents would understand school goals better and co-operate with the teachers in implementing them; the pupil himself would have a more positive attitude towards both his own goals as he perceives them at this stage and to school processes in general. For example, in some cases, the pupils' background is viewed as being responsible for their lackadaisical attitude towards school work. Such pupils usually belong to the 'business class' and are aware that they would not face any problems regarding an occupation in the future.

The pupils' background in the form of parental aspirations also influences their attitudes, goals and behaviour. Pupils perceive parental aspirations, in their choice of RVS as a suitable school, largely in terms of its reputation as a 'good' school with high academic standards and facilities for co-curricular activities and sport. Parental interest in the ideology appears to be a low motivating factor for sending their children to RVS.

The Principal suggests that only about 20 per cent of the parents are interested in the ideology and the 'total development of the child'. He does however see a large number of parents as being sympathetic to school goals though they may not understand the ideology. Generally, most parents appear to want a 'good career' for their children which is dependent on their academic performance and the Principal feels that RVS fulfils their expectations. Insofar as parental aspirations inevitably affect pupil goals, the pupil may generally be expected to be more oriented towards achieving success in his academic life in preparation for the long-term goal of his chosen career rather than towards fulfilling the school's ideological goals.

It is obvious that a variety of considerations influence a pupil's seeking admission to RVS and his being admitted to it. Here both ideological principles and practical advantage are important.

The ideology suggests that a smaller number of pupils in the school helps establish close relationships between teachers and pupils and facilitates learning and the overall development of the pupil. The Management therefore do not allow the pupil population to rise above 330. The total number of pupils in RVS in 1981 was 327 of which two-thirds were boys. The higher percentage of boys is reflected in each class. Thus, of the 88 pupils who responded to my questionnaire, 69 per cent were boys. The pupils' views on various matters are, therefore, dominated by the boys. The age range of the respondents is 14 to 18 years.

Two factors that perhaps affect pupil views are the number of years one has spent in the school and previous schooling. As most pupils have spent between five to seven years at RVS, it may be assumed that their views, particularly on school processes and goals, have evolved out of a reasonably long exposure to the school. Secondly, for a large number of pupils, RVS is their first experience of a boarding school. This would necessarily affect their views on certain aspects of school life which they may never have encountered before. For example, some pupils find living according to a strictly structured routine tiring while others appreciate the opportunity of living closely with other pupils. The type of school the pupil had earlier been in is of some importance to ascertain his background. Thus, few pupils (18 per cent) had been to government schools, with the majority having earlier gone to 'private' schools.

Although there is a wide regional representation of pupils, the majority belongs to the southern states of Andhra Pradesh and Tamilnadu. Pupils from Gujarat form the third largest group. The Management are aware of the south Indian character of RVS and have therefore, made it a part of their admission policy to select pupils from other areas. This concern is also reflected in the school goal for acquiring a national and international character which would help in developing a 'global outlook' among the pupils. The school's claim to be non-sectarian is confirmed by pupil representation from three different religions although the majority are Hindus.

The most important indicator of the pupils' socio-economic background is parental occupation. About half of the fathers belong to the occupational category of the professions (such as doctors, engineers, scientists, lawyers and teachers at all levels), followed by businessmen, civil servants and similar salaried persons. Of the mothers, very few are indicated as having a gainful occupation. Of these, more than half belong to the teaching profession. It would appear that the majority of the pupils have an upper middle class background. This is in consonance with De Souza's finding in his study of Indian public schools that they 'are patronised by professionals and the business, civil and military elites'. He suggests that one factor influencing this trend is 'the structure of the fees with its built-in tendency to favour the upper social strata' (1974: 238–40). The RVS pupil thus belongs to the upper strata of urban Indian society. It would seem that this is in consonance with the school's local order which, through the admission policy at least, seeks pupils from such a background. The influence of this background on their views and behaviour is evident in my analysis of the various aspects of pupil culture.

Pupil perspectives on school work

The pupil's life at RVS is a mixture of work, sport and leisure. Work, however, is the dominant activity. The extent and content of work is determined by the school in its structured programme for the pupil in the school 'timetable' which is made up primarily of lesson periods. School work also includes the evening preparation (prep.) hour when the pupil is expected to complete his assignments in the classroom. Since the pupil's day is largely devoted to school work, pupil perspectives on it constitute an important part of pupil culture.

To begin with subject choice, the pupils are expected to exercise this in Standards 10 and 11. According to the Standard 10 syllabus, laid down by the Council, the pupils have to study five compulsory subjects and have the choice of qualifying in one or more optional subjects. In Standard 11, the pupils select a group of subjects out of those offered by the school, in addition to one compulsory subject, to qualify for the ISC examination (at the end of the year of Standard 12). The respondents are divided into those from Standard 10 (41 pupils), who take the ICSE examination at the end of the year, and those from Standards 11 and 12 (47 pupils), who take the ISC examination at the end of the year in Standard 12.

For pupils in Standard 10, the school offers Economics, Music and Art as optional subjects. My data indicate that 38 out of 41 pupils have opted for Economics, while the remaining two subjects appear to be favoured by girls two of whom have chosen them. The reasons for subject choice suggest that most pupils view their choice as being, in fact, no choice at all due to the school's inadequate provision of optional subjects. Another influencing factor is the 'utilitarian' consideration of its future value in terms of a job or career, and this applies to pupils who have selected Music and Art as well. It might also be that the pupils' selection of a particular subject, e.g. Economics, may also have been a mechanical process influenced by 'group perspectives'.[4] However, disinterest in their work cannot be posited as most of them have opted for Economics which is a demanding subject. On the whole, the lack of alternative subjects appears to be the decisive factor in this regard.

The pupil's choice of subjects in Standard 11 is also dependent on RVS's organization of the academic programme, which offers three groups of subjects with History and English Literature in 'special' cases. The school, in encouraging the pupils to select one of the three major subject streams, brings their future into the classroom. Subject grouping I (Physics, Chemistry, Mathematics) is considered as preparation for a career primarily in Engineering; II (Economics, Accounts, Commerce) in Banking, Chartered Accountancy and Commerce; and III (Physics, Biology, Chemistry) in Medicine and

Agriculture. Apart from these three streams, the school offers a fourth elective—Economics or Mathematics—as it is thought that most institutions of higher learning particularly medical and engineering colleges, prefer to take pupils who have qualified in four instead of the usual three subjects.

Special English Literature and History are made available occasionally. RVS does not have the staff or facilities to incorporate these subjects completely into the curriculum as the maximum provision, in Standard 12, is for 28–30 pupils. Moreover, the pupils themselves (31 out of 47) prefer Science subjects to the Arts, (only 4 pupils), as they are considered 'job-oriented'; the rest opted for subject grouping II. The Management believes that the pupils are influenced in their choice by their parents rather than the school.

Most pupils however state an 'interest' in and a 'liking' for a subject as the decisive factor, while some others state future occupations and careers as reasons for their choice.[5] The pupils' ability, or lack of it, in particular subjects, is another factor determining choice. Some pupils also express an interest in subjects in terms of a broad interest, such as, 'the study of the human mind', and so on. The factors influencing pupil choice thus appear to be both the 'affective' consideration of interest and the liking for particular subjects over others as well as the 'utilitarian' one of keeping career requirements and ability in mind. A sharp distinction between these two kinds of considerations—as if they were mutually exclusive—is not however implied here.[6]

Pupils' views also reveal that their decisions relating to subject choice, as indeed regarding other matters, are not casually made. The pupil examines all the implications such a decision might entail and discusses them with parents, teachers and friends before coming to a conclusion. For such pupils who have an instrumental view of education, Woods suggests that 'society is a contest system and they are in the contest with a chance. Comparative.success in assessment and selection mechanisms reinforced by social factors (like within-group pressure and parental encouragement), will have cued them into this. This means they do see the future in progressively structured terms, and they do believe their choices have relevance to their future careers. Thus they are much more likely to think in terms of career, ability, examination success, and other factors that promote it' (1976: 36).

While the instrumental rewards of school work are clearly

important to pupils, their views are also influenced by institutional factors such as tightly structured subject streams available to pupils in Standard 11. Most pupils are therefore canalized by the institution into one of the three main streams and further into specific areas of future activity or interest.

The pupils' preference for Science or the 'hard' subjects to the 'softer' options, apparently acts as a pressure and leads to the emphasis on Science.[7] There is also an awareness among members of the Management that RVS is catering to the elite who would not settle for anything less than the best and most prestigious subjects. In thus canalizing the pupils into their occupational careers, the school is, however, diverging from the ideology which emphasizes a broader approach to education. The division between the local and the transcendental orders is evident. Pupils' subject choice and the goals of the local order indicate that the latter appears to operate quite independently of the transcendental order. There is a concern for the bright pupil from an upper class urban background and thereby for reproducing the values and goals of that background. This is quite opposed to the discourse of the transcendental order which in fact seeks to alter or transform the existing state of affairs in society. RVS is nonetheless constrained in widening the pupils' subject choice by its administrative organization which does not allow for an expansion of staff or facilities. It would thus appear that ideological goals, in the ultimate analysis, are constrained by the institutional medium through which they are sought to be realized.

Pupil perspectives on school work are also reflected in their preference for particular subjects and dislike for others, reasons why they find lessons interesting or boring, and opinions on how learning can be made more interesting. Besides the 'practical' content of school work, three important factors that influence pupils' views in these areas are the teacher, in terms of both her calibre and her relations with the pupils, the pupil's self-image, and examinations.

Although very few pupils mentioned the quality of teaching as a reason for their dislike of a particular subject, its importance lies in the implication that pupil interest in work is affected by the performance of the teacher in the classroom. For example, a pupil dislikes Mathematics because his first teacher (in the senior school) 'was so dull that Mathematics itself seemed dull and boring'; another pupil does not like English because 'the teacher doesn't explain everything properly'. Here, the pupils are not so interested in their personal relationship with the teacher but in the latter's professional worth as they see it, i.e., in terms of her contribution to their acquisition of educational knowledge. Pupil views suggest that the poor quality of teaching results from a teacher being 'tired' and 'uninteresting', or when she 'tends to go off at a tangent', and is unable to 'infuse emotion' in the lesson. A teacher's inability to express herself clearly, or a tendency to merely 'rattle off' the topic, is not appreciated. Good teaching, on the contrary, contributes to making a lesson interesting. Teachers who 'enjoy' teaching and are in a 'good mood' tend to make the lesson enjoyable for the pupils. This is also dependent on the teacher being experienced and competent.

Pupil views on how learning can be made more interesting, once again, emphasize the importance of 'practical' work and the 'quality' of the teacher in the classroom. The pupils stress the importance of demonstration through experiments, the use of audio-visual methods, educational tours and debates, dialogue and discussion. They also suggest that teachers need to go beyond 'subject teaching' to explore what is happening in the world outside, for example in 'world technology', and to show them the subject's 'relevance to life'.

Pupils expect the teacher to play an active role in the classroom by questioning them, writing on the blackboard, and making the lesson 'lively' with 'jokes and fun'. Clearly, the teacher as a professional is also important: she should be 'qualified and trained', 'good and experienced', and should have a 'clear idea' of what she is teaching. Relating to the teacher also acquires significance: the teacher is expected to be even-tempered, patient and impartial in her interaction with pupils and it is felt that 'better mutual understanding' between the teachers and pupils would contribute towards creating more interest in the lesson. In the pupils' view, 'by using the right tact and methods, the teacher can turn the students into liking his subjects'.

Turning to the pupils' self-images and self-assessment, poor ability in particular subjects is the main reason for their dislike of them. Their inability to understand the subject or cope with it results in low grades. As the prime pupil goal, in relation to work, appears to be achievement, pupils tend to dislike particular subjects. They are 'bored' with subjects that are 'vague or impractical' and in which they cannot obtain good grades or from which they cannot 'gain anything'. For example, History is considered 'useless for today's advancing world'. Clearly, this is a poor comment on pupils' perceptions of the school's ideology and is primarily a result of the emphasis on Science in RVS. It follows that most pupils have practical considerations in mind in their preference for certain subjects.

Pupils are aware of their role in the pedagogic process. They thus do not view themselves as passive learners and are conscious of the benefits of their participation in the lesson. One pupil's response sums up the different factors that contribute towards creating pupil interest or boredom in the lesson: 'It depends on my mood, the teacher's mood, the time of the day and the subject'.

Pupils are interested in the subjects which they 'like' or 'love', or those which hold a 'unique attraction' for them, arouse their curiosity, and require 'one's brain to really work'. Moreover, they feel that 'paying attention' to a lesson makes it more interesting for them. They express a lack of interest in certain subjects because they are 'too lengthy and void of life', 'monotonous' or 'positively dull'.

In order to achieve the immediate goal of passing the examination, pupils employ the strategy of conformity in the classroom. This does not however imply a lack of pupil participation in the lesson. Pupil talk, directed towards the goal of learning, takes the form of responding to the teacher's questions, questioning her, posing problems, and in general, keenly participating in the lesson. Nonetheless, pupils also seek to alleviate the boredom that is a part of pupil experience in the classroom. This takes the form of laughter and noise, the teacher often being the target of pupil humour. This kind of pupil behaviour is accepted and allowed because of the informality that exists in the teacher–pupil relationship both in the classroom and in other settings.

Pupils' views on their own efforts towards making school work interesting include more participation, paying 'full attention', and 'delving deeper into the topic' by doing extra reading outside the classroom. One pupil emphasizes the importance of 'seeing, hearing and feeling' in the learning process, in an obvious reference to Krishnamurti's definition of learning. Similarly, another pupil writes: 'Learning is a delicate thing. The more sensitive you are, the more you learn. Learning can become more interesting when you become aware of its importance'. Nonetheless, a large number of pupils (57 per cent of the respondents) did not agree that more learning takes place when there are no examinations. The pupil is generally, therefore, oriented towards the school's local order and its goals although he may express an awareness of the ideology which describes learning in essentially different terms. This is further evident from the pupil's view that examinations are necessary to develop the 'competitive spirit', 'to induce learning', to 'urge studying' and to make one 'technically proficient'.

In fact, pupils feel that through examinations, they can estimate their own level or standard in relation to others and can become 'legally qualified'. These responses indicate a highly competitive spirit in the pupil culture as epitomized in the response of one pupil: 'There have to be exams for it gives a person a competitive spirit to do better than his nearest opponent. Having no exams would only make one more wayward and lazy'. This attitude is in clear contrast to the school's ideology, which does not give any place to comparison or competition in the learning process, and is probably a result of parental and social pressures of various kinds.[8]

On the other hand, there are some pupils who feel that they would find learning more enjoyable *without* examinations as there would be less pressure on them, allowing them greater understanding of the subject. They would also not be studying merely 'for the sake of the exams', and could give their total attention to their work. A few pupils also mention the 'fear and tension' created by examinations which tend to inhibit the learning process. On the whole, such pupils would prefer the improved quality of learning that would result by not having to take examinations. As one pupil put it: '[without examinations] you can learn at your own slow pace in a more interesting manner; e.g. in science, you can work like a true scientist if you don't have an exam'.

All the pupils, however, experience the pressure of the examinations, whether they are for or against them. This is also true of some pupils who generally do not give too much importance to their academic life as a result of their interest in the ideology. One such pupil writes: 'In my case I do not consider studying subjects as learning and do not give too much importance to it. . . Learning for me is being more sensitive and aware of one's surroundings. But exams do create a certain pressure on me'.

The examination is, in effect, the culmination of the pupils' academic life in the school each year and the event, and the processes leading to it, acquire a critical significance for him and the teachers. This is however completely at variance with the ideology. By having accepted and evolved a particular kind of academic programme, the Management nonetheless has to see that it works. The pupils have therefore to be prepared in order to ensure their success in the examination. The ideology is in this sense unable to break the competitive spirit engendered by the examination, and the constraints imposed on the school by its external order, and can at best suggest to the pupils the importance of being aware of the consequences of excessive competition.

The picture of the pupil in the classroom that emerges is that of an enthusiastic worker, committed to school work, and conscious of the advantages accruing from success. It is not all hard work, however, as most pupils appear to enjoy their lessons and are interested in their selected subjects thus reinforcing their positive attitude towards school work.

The two most important factors that influence pupil perspectives on work are, as we have seen, the nature of the work and the quality of the teacher within the climate of existing social values, parental aspirations and institutional pressures, which direct pupil work-activity in a particular direction. The preferred nature of the work is dependent primarily on its practical content in terms of how useful and meaningful it is for the pupil. The teacher's contribution in making work meaningful for the pupil lies in her calibre and her relationship with the pupil.

The pupil at RVS is thus by and large committed to the organizational goals of academic achievement and success. These have not however been merely internalized by the pupils who are aware of the long-term advantage in setting similar goals for themselves. In this sense the pupil culture is not articulated independently by its own set of norms or values. It exists in interaction with organizational goals and parental and social expectations, which in fact are influential in shaping pupil culture into a familiar pattern. Educational discourse and the school's local order thus undoubtedly take precedence over ideological discourse in this aspect of pupil culture.

Co-curricular and leisure-time activities

While the school's local order and its heavily pressured academic environment constitutes one strand, there is another aspect of pupil culture which is indicative of more leisurely activity. This includes school organized co-curricular activities in the senior school in such areas as the arts and crafts, music, dance, home science, science, photography, dramatics, current affairs, and the school estate. In the junior school, such activities include project and literary activities, and gardening, apart from the arts and crafts, music and dance. Pupils in the senior school clearly stated that 'interest' is the prime motivating factor in their choice of particular activities. Most pupils choose an activity because they 'enjoy' it, like working with their hands, and are able to give expression to their 'feelings', 'creativity' and 'hidden talents'. Pupils also take an interest in the Literary Club activity: most pupils who are weak in a language (for example, Hindi or Telugu) use the activity to improve their ability in it. The fact that no girls have opted for this activity suggests, perhaps, that they generally select activities out of interest rather than the academic value that may be derived from them. Some pupils are interested in an activity as they think it will help them towards a career (for example, as an artist or a musician) or an alternative occupation. Their interest thus reflects the pupils' largely instrumental view of co-curricular activity which is similar to their attitude towards school work.

Afternoon co-curricular activity is an essential part of the pupil's life in RVS. It has its own ethos as pupils are more informally dressed than during the morning session of lessons. The academic atmosphere of the morning is transformed into one of informal activity conducted in different parts of the school. The tension and anxiety that accompanies school work is absent as the pupils explore their own creativity, or work at a task, or merely 'muck-about', interacting freely with their teachers and peers.[9]

It would appear that leisure-time activities would imply some choice on the part of the pupils but these tend to be planned in residential schools like RVS. Planning for leisure-time activity, however, in terms of providing facilities to the pupils, implies 'an element of control—an invasion of personal freedom to the extent that the pupils' choices are restricted to what is made available by the school' (Hendry, 1978: 107). This is inevitable in a boarding school where the pupils' activities are generally limited not merely physically by the school's boundaries but also by its norms and conventions.

The school routine thus organizes not only the morning academic programme but also 'leisure' for the pupils. Afternoon 'rest' is prescribed for the juniors and the primary expectation during this hour is complete silence in the house. The house-parents persuade, threaten, and bargain with the pupils for this, and the pupils in turn negotiate with the teachers in terms of what they may gain by compliance.[10]

Pupils do not have much free time in the evenings except on the weekends. These are not formally structured except for the organized 'recreation' which includes educational, feature, and other films, 'international' folk dancing, and the drama and musical programmes put up by the pupils and teachers together. Sports events are organized on weekends to fill in time. During the week, such time in the evenings is occupied by house activities in the junior houses and, usually, prep. in the senior houses. The school routine during the week leaves very little free time (four or five hours at the most) for the pupils. They occasionally skip lessons, co-curricular activities, games or *asthāchal* to just sit around in the house or complete their prep. Their absence may be questioned, but, apart from a reprimand from the Headmistress, no stern action is usually taken.

A glance at Table 7.1 tells us that while most pupils spend their free time reading or listening to music, both boys and girls also enjoy going for walks. Pupils who like to observe nature do so when they are out on walks in the valley. Gardening is a compulsory requirement of the prescribed syllabus but some pupils are sufficiently interested to want to continue to work at it during their free time. Pupils' interests are, therefore, to some extent influenced by the surroundings and environment of RVS and are also in consonance with the school's ideology which asks the pupil to observe and experience nature and the physical environment with a receptive mind. Leisure for the pupil in RVS is, therefore, structured by both the school's organization of pupil recreation, and by his own interests and hobbies which may also match ideological interests.

Two thirds of the respondents state that their favourite way of spending their free time is 'reading' and their primary interest is in fiction and detective stories. The boys are also keenly interested in books on science, adventure, and sport, whereas girls prefer books on literature ('the classics'), psychology, and biography. The emphasis on science in the school's academic programme engages pupil interest in the subject outside the classroom as well as inside it. Books by Krishnamurti are read by only a small number of pupils. While this seems indicative of a general lack of interest, it also

TABLE 7.1

Pupils' Leisure-Time Activities

Activities	Responses			
	Number		Percentage	
	Boys	Girls	Total	
Reading	44	16	60	32.26
Listening to music, the radio	12	12	24	12.90
Playing games (indoor and outdoor)	16	1	17	9.14
Going for a walk, trek, hike	9	7	16	8.60
Studying	9	1	10	5.37
Sleeping (daytime naps)	6	3	9	4.84
Thinking, 'day-dreaming', 'stargazing'	7	1	8	4.30
Drawing, painting	2	2	4	2.15
Singing; playing a musical instrument	3	1	4	2.15
Observing nature	3	1	4	2.15
Talking	2	2	4	2.15
Gardening	2	1	3	1.61
Cycling; swimming	2	1	3	1.61
'Cleaning up the place around me'; 'keeping my things in better shape'	1	1	2	1.08
Others	14	2	16	8.60
No response	1	1	2	1.08
Total	133	53	186	100.00

Total number of respondents: 88; Boys: 61; Girls: 27.

suggests that some of them at least are interested in exploring the ideology on their own, besides in set-up situations such as the Krishnamurti talks.

These leisure-time activities do not generally deviate from school norms and conventions. The pupils are aware of these norms but sometimes indulge in other activities in acts of rebellion or resistance to school rules. For example, some pupils visit neighbouring villages for minor purchases (eatables, cigarettes), though such interaction with the villages is prohibited. On one occasion, a pupil ventured as far as a nearby town without this being discovered.

Sometimes pupils inadvertently go against RVS norms by doing something about which the rules are vague or inconsistent. Thus, on the occasion of the festival of *Ganesha Chaturthi* (a Hindu religious festival), the pupils in a junior house performed a *puja* in the evening which was not attended by any teacher nor the housemother. The ceremony was enjoyed by all the pupils who joined in the singing with enthusiasm. The juniors were of the opinion that the teachers did not object to their performing *puja* in the house as the pupils had been doing it at home.

The Management, however, took a different view of the event. The Principal was apparently 'angry' that this had been allowed, as he had made it quite clear that no idol worship was to be permitted in RVS in consonance with the ideology which stresses the importance of exposing the mechanical nature of all ritual and the futility of blindly following tradition. The teachers, some of whom have been exposed to the ideology for several years, however, live their lives in contradiction to its values as they find it difficult to completely give up their traditional upbringing and values.[11]

Teacher attitudes towards pupil activity are also inconsistent, as in this particular case one group of pupils was allowed to perform a *puja* in the house, but in another house the housemother forbade the pupils from any such activity. Moreover, no explanation was given for the teacher's decision as the pupils are considered 'too young' (only the juniors were involved) and the parents are generally held responsible for explaining the school's values to them. The point of the rule is therefore lost in the pupils' lack of understanding of the reasons for its imposition. This can also create a confusion in the pupils' minds who do something at home, with their parents' approval, which is not allowed at school for inexplicable reasons.

Clearly, the school's local and transcendental orders are both important elements contributing to the constitution of pupil culture. Nonetheless, there is an important difference in their contribution: the local order lends a certain clarity and organization to some important activities that are a part of pupil culture whereas the discourse of the transcendental order does not lend itself to easy practical translation and action. The result is some confusion which, in the formation of certain 'guides' to action, as it were, creates inconsistencies and aberrations in both attitudes and behaviour.

An important aspect of leisure-time activity is the pupils' writing which may either be displayed on the Democracy Board or published in the school magazine. The Democracy Board is located in the senior school building and, apart from the pupils' writings, poems and articles by teachers and interesting news items are also displayed. Pupils are permitted to write on anything they want to as long as they reveal their identity and thus assume responsibility for whatever they write. Pupils' writings on the Democracy Board are mainly a comment on school processes usually in the form of complaints about various aspects of school organization. Pupils also make requests to the Management on various issues and senior teachers usually respond to each notice, if a reply is expected, stating their point of view and the decision in each case.

Pupils are particularly critical of teacher behaviour or decisions if they view them as being contradictory to the ideology. Thus, in a piece entitled 'Why such hypocrisy?', the teachers were questioned as to why the pupils have to take 'frequent tests' (in school work) after Krishnamurti has left RVS, while no tests were held during his visit. On another occasion, a senior boy wrote that, after Krishnamurti's recent departure from the school, 'fear' was being used to maintain discipline and that this was not a 'very agreeable' method. This sparked off a discussion involving the Headmistress and an ideologue teacher which, though accusatory in parts, was pertinent to pupil behaviour and the teachers' methods of dealing with indiscipline.

The school magazine, published annually, contains the pupils' writings, mostly in English but also in Hindi and Telugu. It is a compilation of pupil writings in the form of poems, short stories, plays, and essays. The pupils' own perception of the magazine is that it is '. . . a collective awareness. A reflection of what we feel, think and do from dawn to dusk' ('The Editorial', 1981). The pupils' experience of their environment is reflected in their writing. Both junior and senior pupils have written poems specifically on the natural setting of the school. On school life, there are poems on what appears to be the dominant pupil concern in the senior school: tests and examinations. Some attempt to look at the humorous aspects of preparing for tests and writing examinations. Senior pupils also describe their thoughts in the classroom, on what is happening outside, and on their experience of nature from within the classroom. The teacher's teaching technique is viewed as being either exceedingly dull or rejuvenating. Comments are made on the school routine, including humour in the morning awakening for Physical Training (PT), fun at the weekend frivolity in the house, and the dullness of the monotonous schedule, a telling comment on school routine which is generally considered the great organizer of school life. As sport is a major dimension of the boys' life in RVS, cricket and tennis receive special treatment and adventure is also important.

In contrast with their writings on the Democracy Board, which somehow acquires the status of a critical forum, appreciative essays on RVS are written by both junior and senior pupils in the magazine. Their affection for the school, and its special character, emerges as a dominant element especially when they write about their departure which they view with some anxiety. This suggests that they are happy at school, examinations notwithstanding, and in fact are somewhat afraid of confronting life outside. The writings of old students in the magazine also point to the nostalgia with which they remember their experiences at RVS.

The attention paid to Krishnamurti is an editorial policy insofar as the inclusion of his photograph and quotations from his writings are concerned. The pupils also comment on the ideology by either emphasizing the meaning it holds for them or expressing their criticism of some aspect of it or its implementation in RVS. They may summarize Krishnamurti's talks to them, relating these to the present situation in the world, thus suggesting the relevance and importance of the ideology. The pupil culture therefore does not have a coherently articulated stand on it which is primarily a result of the pupils' varied experiences and attitudes towards it.

Pupil perspectives on school work reveal their preoccupation with pragmatic concerns rather than the wider outlook emphasized by the ideology. Similarly, in their attitude to sport, we find that the pupils' views diverge from the ideology. However, as their writings contain, self-consciously or otherwise, several references to the ideology, it is present in a pervasive form in their compositions on diverse subjects and, one presumes, in their thoughts.

I have discussed leisure in terms of what the pupil likes to do in his free time; it implies an absorption with forms of amusement and relaxation and with doing things one would really like to do. The ideology however gives a significantly different meaning to the term insofar as learning is viewed as observation by a mind that is free of occupation which is only possible in leisure. Krishnamurti suggests that the school is a place of leisure where learning can take place: work therefore becomes leisure.

This is difficult to accomplish in RVS as the pupils are under various kinds of pressures, notably examinations. The tension and anxiety that are a result of this pressure inhibit the experience of leisure in work for the pupil who thus generally enjoys all forms of activity that are unconnected with school work. The school's academic programme inhibits the pupils' experience of work-as-leisure and instead they look forward to leisure-time activities. An individual's experience of leisure, according to the ideology, is dependent on an inner perception and understanding rather than an external provision of opportunities. The lack of both however results, it seems, in work and leisure being viewed separately in the pupil culture. Once again, the local order transcends, as it were, the transcendental order.

Sport

Sport is an important aspect of the pupils' lives in school. The RVS pupils exhibit an enthusiastic interest and involvement in games both in the school and in the wider world of sports. This craze for games is a feature of the public school pupil culture in which organized team games are very popular.[12] Contrary to other public schools in India, however, games at RVS are not organized around the competitive spirit in deference to the school's ideology, and their purpose is said to be the effort to keep pupils healthy and physically fit and to let them have some fun.[13]

The pupils are expected to choose from and take part in organized games for 40 minutes every evening on working days. Pupils also have the choice of doing *asanas* (yoga) or swimming. Pupil choice is, however, influenced by the teacher concerned, who watches them at play, and may recommend another game if the pupil is not considered 'good enough' at the chosen one. A Physical Director is in charge with six teachers as instructors in different games; special coaches from outside come to RVS to help the pupils improve their cricket and tennis. Coaching takes place primarily to give extra skills to pupils who are already good at a game, while training is meant for all interested pupils. By the end of January or so, however, all games are stopped as the pupils get increasingly engrossed in preparing for the examinations.

The school has teams in football, hockey, cricket, basketball and tennis and plays only 'friendly' matches with teams from neighbouring towns and districts. Matches with other schools are avoided to keep out the competitive spirit as these schools may not easily enter into the rhetoric of 'friendly' matches. Matches are also played among RVS pupils themselves, for example, between the ISC class and the rest of the school, or between pupils and teachers over weekends. Scores for each match held are maintained and displayed on the notice-board with special mention of the pupils who play particularly well, and these may also be published in the school newsletter. There is an obvious interest in the *results* of the matches played whether or not the competitive spirit is kept at bay.

Pupil enthusiasm is such that they turn out in large numbers to watch matches for hours and to cheer the players. Their behaviour at a basketball match with an outside team is of particular interest. They applauded and cheered highly like any 'home crowd' whenever RVS scored a point. When the opposite team did so, there was only subdued applause, and their failures and faults evoked derisive laughter and snide comments. It is therefore, doubtful that these matches remain 'friendly' either in the eyes of the audience or of the players who set out to win. The teachers often play in the RVS team to help win the game. There is an insistence on winning by the participating teachers and the pupils themselves are motivated in the same direction.[14]

While games are not organized around competition, the matches played induce a spirit of competition into the game. This may be due to the widespread notion that matches in sport may be 'friendly' but are always about winning or losing.[15] The spirit of sportsmanship, which implies playing by rules to win a game, rather than 'fighting' to defeat and humiliate the other side, is, however, also prevalent and influences the participants' attitudes.

The annual Sports Day is another illustration of disharmony between sport in the school and the ideology. Although no prizes or medals are awarded in a significant departure from conventional practice, the pupils compete in several events—primarily, athletics—and are ranked according to their performance. Moreover, as the pupils do not participate in athletics for the rest of the year, the rare event acquires an air of keen competition. The significance of winning an event is symbolized by the 'victory stand' in the centre of the field, even though it is not actually used.

The emphasis on lack of competition in sport in RVS is viewed as lowering its standard by some pupils, who feel that they lack the incentive to play well because of the lack of reward or recognition in the form of cups and prizes. They also suggest that as the competitive spirit is necessary to succeed in the world outside RVS, they would like to prepare themselves to meet this demand.

RVS provides the boys with a larger number of games than the girls. Senior girls thus complain that they are not given sufficient opportunity for participation, and that the school emphasizes the male role on the sportsfield. Moreover, among the teachers who actually participate in games, there is not a single woman teacher. The girls thus do not perhaps have sufficient interest nor the necessary encouragement to participate in the male-dominated games. This difference is accentuated by the fact that girls and boys play separately. They occasionally play hockey and basketball together but here the participants are senior girls and junior boys.

This creates a hierarchy both in sport and among sportsmen/women, which is also evident in the teachers' influence on pupil choice of games as well as the provision of coaching facilities for selected players only and the organization of teams into 'A' and 'B' groups depending on the pupils' ability. Such differentiation between the pupils is not in consonance with the ideology. But, as we have noted in the context of the academic programme, the school is not entirely successful in this for certain distinctions have to be made in the senior school. Moreover, in its attitude towards sportsmen, the school cannot help being influenced by the general sport ideology according to which ability is crucial to determining one's place in the game. The conflict between the ideology and the actual situation appears to be more evident in the sports arena, perhaps because it presents a 'freer' situation, as it were, than the classroom, in terms of the ethos. The extent to which the ideology is absent on the sportsfield is evident from the pupils' enthusiasm for competition in sport. Forty respondents, of whom twenty-nine are boys, are in various school teams; seven boys are in more than one.

There are some pupils, however, who view competition as unnecessary because they feel that their 'interest' in and 'love' for a game are sufficient motivators for proficiency in sport. There is also the factor of the 'fun' derived from a game which is lost in competition. Some pupils are also aware of the 'jealousy' and 'enmity' that arise out of competition leading to an 'unhealthy and undesirable atmosphere' in the school. While the views of these pupils are similar to those expressed in the ideology, it is not clear to what extent they are in fact influenced by the ideology in their attitude. One other factor could be a general lack of interest in sports which would thus lead to their viewing competition unfavourably. However, the competitive spirit in sport prevails in RVS supported by pupil views and endorsed by teacher attitudes on the sportsfield although it may be viewed as 'mild' competition, curtailed as it is by the lack of an explicit reward system.[16]

Pupil–interaction

Pupils interact with one another in different settings predominantly within a sex or age group. The majority of the pupils in fact say that their close friends belong to the same class and house as themselves, thus suggesting that friendships usually remain bounded within certain settings.

Friendships among pupils are central to their life in school. Pupil views indicate that similar interests and attitudes towards life, events and people constitute the most important bases of friendship. These include a shared interest in school work, sport, music, novels, and food (a major interest for pupils in a boarding school). Friendship thus finds expression in talking, doing things and being together.

More boys than girls view their interest in sport and school work as a factor conducive to friendship. Organized games in RVS cater primarily to the boys, thereby explaining their interest in sport. That friendships are based on a mutual interest in school work is typical of RVS pupils whom I have earlier identified in terms of their positive orientation towards school work. Mutual understanding and care are also perceived as a common element in friendship. While these are generally associated with girls, more boys than girls actually make the point.

'Humour' is stated as a basis for friendship by some pupils indicating their association of 'fun' and 'enjoyment' with school life. Thus, they create opportunities for laughter in the classroom and their relations with teachers are characterized by informality, so that the formal learning situation is generally permeated by an atmosphere of cordiality and warmth.

The influence of the ideology on friendships between the pupils is difficult to assess. Some pupils view being on the 'right path' as the basis for their friendships. It is not clear whether they mean their interest in school work and related activities or in the wider aims of RVS. Only one pupil clearly specifies the ideology as 'the main bond' in her friendship with a boy.

It is to be expected, however, that an interest in school-centred activities, such as school work and sport, would form the basis for pupil friendships, as it does, for RVS is a boarding school. In a sense therefore 'pupil friendship . . . rests upon the functions it serves, rather than upon the adult notion of ties formed through love and affection' (Woods, 1983: 97). Insofar as the pupils in RVS are dependent on one another not merely for sharing common interests but also in order to relieve the tedium and tiresome demands of school life, their friendships serve the function of sharing and enduring school life together.

Friendships in RVS are also formed around personality characteristics. In RVS, the pupil culture has a well-defined view of the preferred attributes leading to pupil popularity (see Table 7.2). It is interesting that, in acknowledging popularity, a pupil's attitude towards the teachers or the school is not seriously taken into account. Pupil images of each other appear to be based mainly on their mutual experience of what they *do* rather than on their relations with teachers, the overall structure of the school or its ideology.

Some pupils mention other negative qualities as determinants of popularity: they refer either to a desirable quality that a pupil does not have (for example, the comment, 'being tall also counts a great deal', was made by a short boy), or to qualities which are not particularly admired but are nonetheless viewed as leading to popularity (for example, a girl writes, 'among the boys, I think the people who are easy to bully are popular'). Insofar as the preferred qualities are considered desirable in others, they are also the ones to which the pupils themselves aspire.

Pupil culture has judgements also on what it considers undesirable attributes leading to unpopularity (see Table 7.3). The pupils rank inability to get on with others as the primary indicator of

TABLE 7.2

Preferred Attributes of Pupil Popularity

Classification of Attributes	Ranking of Pupil Preferences					
	1		*2*		*3*	
	No.	%	No.	%	No.	%
1. Good at games	29	32.96	18	20.46	15	17.06
2. Talking against teachers or the school	2	2.27	3	3.41	5	5.68
3. Good at school work	16	18.18	23	26.14	7	7.95
4. Sense of humour	8	9.09	21	23.86	13	14.77
5. Being interested in Krishnamurti's philosophy	–	–	2	2.27	7	7.95
6. Easy to get on with	21	23.86	8	9.09	20	22.73
7. Style of dressing	–	–	2	2.27	3	3.41
8. Being hostile to Krishnamurti's philosophy	1	1.14	1	1.14	2	2.27
9. Others	1	1.14	2	2.27	8	9.09
No response	10	11.36	8	9.09	8	9.09
Total	88	100.00	88	100.00	88	100.00

Total number of respondents: 88

TABLE 7.3

Perceived Attributes of Pupil Unpopularity

Classification of Attributes	Ranking of Pupil Choices					
	1		2		3	
	No.	%	No.	%	No.	%
1. Poor at games	12	13.64	8	9.09	10	11.36
2. Difficult to get on with	45	51.13	8	9.09	14	15.92
3. Being interested in Krishnamurti's philosophy	6	6.82	9	10.23	10	11.36
4. No sense of humour	5	5.68	25	28.41	13	14.77
5. Style of dressing	–	–	3	3.41	6	6.82
6. Talking against the teachers or the school	3	3.41	8	9.09	5	5.68
7. Being hostile to Krishnamurti's philosophy	–	–	1	1.14	2	2.27
8. Poor at school work	8	9.09	11	12.50	5	5.68
9. Others	1	1.14	2	2.27	3	3.41
No response	8	9.09	13	14.77	20	22.73
Total	88	100.00	88	100.00	88	100.00

Total number of respondents: 88

unpopularity. The lack of a 'sense of humour' as a reason for unpopularity comes next. Some respondents also refer to a pupil's poor ability at school work and, significantly, an interest in Krishnamurti. Taking the pupils' first and second choices into account, however, the major determinants of unpopularity are those failings which emerge from and also influence the pupils' relations with one another. That they give these qualities a secondary place in their views on popularity suggests that they may, perhaps, admire those pupils who exhibit ability in games and school work, but they primarily value those personal qualities that enrich their interaction. This is further supported by pupil responses for their third choice: inability to relate to others.

That a pupil's interest in Krishnamurti should be a reason for his unpopularity (second and third choices) obviously suggests that such interest is not particularly valued in the pupil culture. This is evident from the fact that the 'followers' are generally teased and jeered at by other pupils, who refer to them a 'philos', 'junior Jiddus' (the reference being to Krishnamurti's first name), and 'holy men'. One pupil mentioned the extent to which the others would get 'nasty' about his interest in Krishnamurti: for example, when he would borrow books by Krishnamurti from the library, he was told by other pupils that he was just trying to 'impress everybody'. The sceptics' inability to relate to the 'followers' is a result of their negative attitude towards the role of the ideology in school processes.

This lack of interaction between the two kinds of pupils results in the isolation of one lot of pupils, albeit a small proportion of the total, from the rest which is inadvertently supported by the Management and teachers in their attempt to protect 'sensitive' pupils by their segregation into smaller houses. This is not to say that such pupils are totally shunned by their peers but that the extent of interaction is limited. Finally, the unpopularity of such pupils with the others indicates the extent to which the latter are unable to relate to the ideology apart from perhaps an intellectual interest in its content.

While friendship and popularity are aspects of pupil interaction confined largely within age and sex groups, there is one kind of interaction which takes place across these groups. Although interaction between the senior and junior pupils is scarce, relations between the senior girls and the junior pupils are characterized by affection and warmth, the former protecting and 'mothering' the latter.

The relations between the senior and junior boys is somewhat different. The juniors hero-worship some of the seniors depending primarily on their skills exhibited on the sportsfield. The seniors feed the juniors' worshipful attitude by performing for them while they watch with awe and enthusiasm. There is another strand to the relationship, however, namely the bullying (in well-known forms) of the juniors by the senior boys. This often happens in jest but sometimes takes a nasty turn.[17]

The Management have made it clear that they do 'not permit bullying of any nature, with or without the consent of the person who is being bullied', and they take a serious view of any instances of it that are brought to their notice. Their disapproval is vouched for by the expulsion of pupils that have taken place on grounds of bullying. In a letter to the Foundation schools, Krishnamurti himself has warned the pupils about the implications of 'cruelty', for example, in the form of domination by one pupil over another (1981b: 97–8).

The pupils' attitude towards bullying is generally one of disapproval thus suggesting that it is considered a deviant act in the pupil culture. Some pupils have on occasion expressed their desire to leave RVS because of their unpleasant experience. A girl in Standard Nine complained about the extent of bullying in RVS on the Democracy Board: of not only junior pupils by the seniors but also that of classmates and teachers. She commented on how the fear that was being created in the bullied pupils had become a source of 'entertainment' for the seniors. Four boys from Standard 10 replied to this article explaining their action and referred to themselves as 'the bullies'. The Management commented on the two viewpoints, stressing their unconditional disapproval of this kind of behaviour, and asked the pupils to report all instances of bullying to the housemasters or class teachers.

It is evident that pupil behaviour and attitudes may be inconsistent with regard to the same activity. The pupil culture contains both the dominant attitudes, values, behaviour patterns and the others that deviate from these. In this sense, pupil culture is not monolithic: that is, it is not all of one hue and its liveliness is generated by the individual perspectives and activities that consti-tute it.

The nature of interaction that takes place separately among the junior and the senior pupils is obviously different as a result of the difference in age and interests. Junior pupils play a great deal in the house and in their spare time. The senior pupils usually work on their assignments or prepare for tests in the house. Their interaction is thus limited by their preoccupation with school work.

Interaction between boys and girls, except in the very junior classes is either very restricted, with some instances of bullying by the boys in the classroom, or very friendly, leading to 'pair-formations'. The Management would apparently like the pupils to mix across the sexes informally and as naturally as they do within their own sex groups. At the same time, they do not encourage deep friendship between a boy and a girl. Such relationships are 'curbed' lest they should lead to attachments. The Management's attitude towards such interaction is a result of their experience of the unwelcome repercussions of some cases of deep involvement between a boy and a girl.[18] They are also responsible to the parents who generally do not approve of such attachments at school.

The pupils, therefore, sit separately in the dining hall, the auditorium during the morning assemblies, and the classroom except in the very junior classes. The teachers are of the opinion that the pupils themselves do not want to sit together in the dining hall. The senior boys and girls, however, sit together sometimes and enjoy each other's company, talking mainly about school work and particular teachers. Besides the attitude of teachers, peer pressure, in the form of teasing and gossip, also affects the nature of the interaction between them. Thus, one parent mentioned that a very good relationship between her son and a girl (both in Standard 11) had come to an end because of peer pressure and the comments made by some teachers. In senior classrooms, the boys often scoff at the girls, refer to them as 'dames', and make fun of them when they ask questions of, or respond to, the teacher. The girls are therefore usually nervous in the classroom and the teachers, by not correcting the boys' behaviour, inadvertently encourage this kind of interaction between boys and girls.

The western folk dancing that takes place on Sunday evenings is one event when boys and girls interact, though not without strain. Participation in folk dancing is for pupils from Standard Nine upwards but pupil attendance at the dance is low. About 40 pupils in all turn up for the occasion with most of them in the audience. Pupil responses indicate that only 30 per cent of the respondents from Standards 10, 11 and 12 participate in the dancing. The girls appear to be more enthusiastic about the event than the boys many of whom merely watch the dance.

Boys and girls sit on two opposite sides of the auditorium and come together in the centre only while dancing. The teacher who conducts the dances often refuse to begin until more boys and girls dance together. He joins in himself, leading the dances and trying to get the pupils to mix. Very few boys and girls are completely relaxed and they usually dance without looking at each other, often trying not to hold hands. Pupil perspectives are conflicting as about half the respondents are of the opinion that folk dancing enables them to mix better while the other half disagree, thinking of the activity as merely a 'pastime', or emphasize dancing for 'the sake of dancing' rather than mixing.

Peer pressure combined with official disapproval not only inhibits relations across the sexes but also creates a tension between them. According to the teachers, the girls tend to think more about their interaction with the boys who are apparently more involved with their work and games. Thus, the girls are said to pay much attention to their clothes and general appearance.[19] As the girls often question the teachers and the Management about the unstated rules regarding their interaction with the boys, a closer watch is kept on them. The errant pupils are either warned by the houseparent or are summoned to the Headmistress's office and soundly scolded, often threatened with parental intervention or expulsion from the school.

This brings into question the role of the school in controlling pupil behaviour to the extent that interaction across the sexes comes under an unnatural strain. This is not only evident at folk dancing but some teachers encounter the problem in the classroom as well; a visiting drama teacher could barely get the boys and girls to mix at rehearsals, considering it an 'uphill task'. Some of the more liberal parents who select RVS, because among other reasons, it is co-educational, are dissatisfied with the 'unnatural' and 'unhealthy' relationship between boys and girls and blame the Management for 'encouraging' pupils to stay apart.

The tension in the boy–girl relationship does not mean that they do not ever interact in a natural fashion. At a match where the ISC girls played against the rest of the school, their classmates cheered them on, but occasionally also jeered their performance. On St.

Valentine's Day, boys and girls excitedly exchange greeting cards. This is ignored by the teachers, one of whom indulgently commented on seeing their excitement, 'After all, they're 18 years old'! The pupil culture is, however, on the whole, unable to live up to the ideology which emphasizes the need for boys and girls to grow up in a healthy relationship and not in fear of one another.

Pupil perspectives on the school and pupil aspirations

An important component of pupil culture is the pupils' conception of the school—of what it means to them. Pupil views arise from their interaction—direct or indirect—with Krishnamurti, the Management, teachers, and fellow pupils, and their participation in school activities. As stated earlier, I am not seeking to establish a pro-school or an anti-school pupil sub-culture—as has been done by others, notably Hargreaves (1967) and Lacey (1970)—but to identify the different elements in the pupils' conceptions of the school.

Pupil perceptions of the different kinds of school goals and aims is an important aspect of their image of the school. Their views (see Table 7.4) emphasize RVS's ideological or intended goals, as the first three most important aims, rather than its actual or operative goals. School activities which are oriented to the development of 'creative talents' and 'cultural interests', are ranked fourth in order of importance. A significant finding is that, although the pupils are enthusiastic about school work and sport, the school goals which would foster this attitude, are not rated very highly by them. They are perhaps aware that in the official scheme of things, certain aspects of school work and sport are played down in defference to the ideology. Pupil perspectives are therefore concerned with the broader intention rather than actual school processes which may be oriented to the achievement of narrower goals such as pupil success in the examination.

On the other hand, the pupils' rejection of or the low rating accorded to some goals (e.g. goals 1, 11, and 12 in Table 7.4) reveals their understanding of what are clearly not school goals. However, this does not imply that they see them being implemented through school processes in the same order of priority as they perceive them. In fact, pupils comment on the school's inability to 'achieve' its goals, one reason being that today's world 'forces us to give

TABLE 7.4

Pupils' Perception of School Goals

Classification of goals	1		2		3		4		5	
	No.	%	No.	%	No.	%	No.	%	No.	%
1. Train leaders for the future	–	–	–	–	1	1.14	–	–	–	–
2. Give everyone the education best suited to his ability	10	11.36	3	3.41	7	7.95	3	3.41	14	15.90
3. Teach us to respect one another	5	5.68	9	10.23	8	9.09	7	7.95	14	15.90
4. Obtain good results in the examinations	1	1.14	4	4.55	1	1.14	8	9.09	7	7.96
5. To understand ourselves as total human beings	24	27.27	13	14.77	12	13.64	3	3.41	3	3.41
6. Develop our creative talents	5	5.68	11	12.50	13	14.77	24	27.27	11	12.50
7. Prepare us for a suitable job or career	4	4.55	4	4.55	4	4.55	4	4.55	4	4.55

Pupils' Ranked Responses

	N	%	N	%	N	%	N	%	N	%
8. To sharpen our sensibilities to nature and the environment	5	5.68	24	27.27	15	17.05	7	7.95	3	3.41
9. Foster a sense of sportsmanship	–	–	–	–	2	2.27	3	3.41	4	4.55
10. Develop cultural interests	2	2.27	–	–	6	6.82	10	11.36	10	11.36
11. Maintain firm discipline	1	1.14	2	2.27	1	1.14	1	1.14	1	1.14
12. Keep a good reputation outside	–	–	2	2.27	–	–	1	1.14	1	1.14
13. Provide us with an atmosphere in which we can learn to be sensitive to people, nature and things	29	32.96	12	13.64	14	15.90	13	14.78	9	10.23
Others	2	2.27	2	2.27	2	2.27	2	2.27	2	2.27
No response	–	–	2	2.27	2	2.27	2	2.27	4	4.55
Total	88	100.00	88	100.00	88	100.00	88	100.00	88	100.00

Total number of respondents: 88.

importance to jobs and careers'. The school is also viewed as being bound by regulations of the Council, an indication of pupils' recognition of the constraints imposed by external institutions. Some pupils appear to resent RVS's inability to fulfil its ideological intention. They identify 'hypocrisy' and deplore it, among both the teachers and members of the Management, in relation to the ideology and its implementation.

Pupil responses also suggest a lack of sufficient awareness of school goals and consensual aims amongst themselves. On the other hand, some pupils indicate that in terms of the intention, 'the spirit of . . . the desired atmosphere' is present in RVS. One pupil appreciated the role of the school in preserving and strengthening his 'sensitivity', which may have been destroyed in another school, while another suggested that RVS helps the pupil 'to lead a full life'. There is a certain ambiguity in pupil perspectives as there is no dominant viewpoint but rather an intermeshing of various conflicting perspectives that form the pupil culture.

Pupils' own goals, that are revealed in their understanding of why they are being educated are in some crucial ways antithetic to their perception of the school's intended goals. While they consider important such aims as 'sensitivity to people, nature, environment and things', 'understanding themselves as total human beings', understanding 'the problems of society', 'the meaning of life', and learning the 'right way of living', they also exhibit a concern with passing examinations and earning a livelihood. These are viewed as important in making them 'capable' and 'independent' for living in a 'highly competitive world', to help them 'survive' and give them a 'social position' in life. This divergence of pupil goals from the school's ideological goals suggests the influence of parental and social pressures and pupils thus tend to oscillate between the ideology and their perception of social demands in the articulation of their own aims.

That the school's official goals—grounded in the ideology—are realized to some extent appears to be evident in pupil views on the kind of change brought about in themselves as a result of being in RVS (see Table 7.5). The most significant pupil response is the change they perceive in their 'way of thinking', expressed in terms of becoming more 'mature' and 'serious-minded' and a broadening of outlook. For example, one girl writes about the change in her traditional outlook on 'careers and home life', emphasizing that

TABLE 7.5

Pupils' Responses to the Question: 'In what way has being in this school changed you?'

Responses	Number			Percentage
	Boys	*Girls*	*Total*	
1. Change in 'way of think-ing'	15	7	22	15.28
2. More independent	10	9	19	13.20
3. More able to mix with people	6	8	14	9.72
4. Improvement in own be-haviour	9	2	11	7.64
5. Increase in knowledge/ improvement in studies	8	2	10	6.95
6. More sensitive to nature and the environment	5	3	8	5.56
7. Acquired an interest in activities and games	7	1	8	5.56
8. More concern for others	5	3	8	5.56
9. Have become more 'sub-dued', 'calm', 'mild', etc.	3	2	5	3.47
10. Have become more re-sponsible	3	–	3	2.00
11. Recognize the importance of the ideology	2	–	2	1.40
12. Lack knowledge of the out-side world	2	–	2	1.40
13. Developed creative talents and cultural interests	1	1	2	1.40
14. Experienced freedom	1	1	2	1.40
15. Experienced life in a boarding school	1	1	2	1.40
16. Others	15	10	25	17.36
No response	–	1	1	0.70
Total	93	51	144	100.00

Total number of respondents: 88; Boys: 61; Girls: 27.

'having a good job is not everything in life'. A 15-year-old boy observed: 'It has brought the real inner self of me outside. I have realized my real self and also realized the corruption outside the valley. But when here, it seems like a paradise . . .'. Pupils have also learnt 'to look at things more deeply', observing 'properly and carefully', becoming aware of the 'movements of the mind', and taking adverse events and situations in their stride because of a positive change in attitude.

A change is also perceived in themselves in terms of becoming more 'independent', 'self-reliant', 'strong-willed', thinking for themselves, and expressing their opinions freely. Moreover, contrary to the goals they set for themselves as a result of family and social pressures, they say they are 'not afraid of society' or 'the mob'. Pupils also express their consideration and sensitivity to the feelings and opinions of others, to nature and the environment arising from their experience of RVS.

On the other hand, pupils' negative experience of life at RVS indicates their rejection of much that RVS stands for: for example, according to one pupil, the school '. . . has made me a little hypocrite in the hypocritical atmosphere'. More emphatically, a 15-year-old girl writes: 'Before, I liked everything, life at home, my life, my parents, the world. Now, I *hate* life at home, life with my parents, the world'. In this particular case, the pupil's negative experience of school is related to her problems in adjusting to life in a school in India after spending several years in an American school.

In the previous section, it was shown that an interest in the ideology plays no role in pupil popularity. In fact, the pupil culture does not acknowledge its positive influence. Thus for 13 out of 25 pupils leaving school, contact with Krishnamurti and his philosophy has meant 'nothing'. Some of them find it difficult to understand it while others are simply not interested. Their attitude can be summed up in the response of one pupil: 'When he [Krishnamurti] goes, with him goes his philosophy'. Similarly, very few pupils rank contact with Krishnamurti and his philosophy as being the most rewarding aspect of their life in school (see Table 7.6).

The pupils' negative attitude towards the ideology is based on their view of it as 'impractical' inasmuch as it can be practised only by the 'rich and retired' and not by those who have to struggle to earn their living. One reason for this animosity, as noted by an ideologue teacher, is the manner in which Krishnamurti has 'been

TABLE 7.6

Pupils' Ranked Responses to the Question:
'Which of the following aspects of life here have you personally found most rewarding?'

Aspects of life in RVS	Ranking of Pupil Responses					
	1		2		3	
	No.	%	No.	%	No.	%
1. The quality of teaching	20	22.73	12	13.64	7	7.95
2. Opportunities for sport and games	14	15.91	13	14.77	14	15.91
3. Contact with some individual teachers	3	3.41	8	9.09	11	12.50
4. Relationships with a few boys/girls	8	9.09	12	13.64	12	13.64
5. Contact with Krishnamurti and his philosophy	10	11.36	11	12.50	7	7.95
6. Living to a routine	2	2.27	6	6.82	6	6.82
7. Opportunities for the arts, music, drama	14	15.91	18	20.44	11	12.50
8. Living all the time with other pupils	14	15.91	4	4.55	12	13.64
No response	3	3.41	4	4.55	8	9.09
Total	88	100.00	88	100.00	88	100.00

Total number of respondents: 88.

brought' to them. This teacher was referring to an earlier requirement for the pupils to attend Krishnamurti's discussions and taped talks. Pupils also resent the excessive concern with Krishnamurti in the school: for example, a senior boy commented on the caption 'The Man' below Krishnamurti's photographs in the school magazine saying: 'Now "the man" has become more important than the teachings'.

Pupils interested in the ideology, however, view the others' attitude in terms of their inability to comprehend or be 'affected' by it, although they listen to Krishnamurti every year. Visitors to the school observe that mention of Krishnamurti brings about an immediate hostile reaction among *most* pupils. Among my respondents, 17 boys and 11 girls altogether (see Table 7.6) find contact with Krishnamurti and the philosophy a rewarding aspect of school life. For these pupils, listening to Krishnamurti has brought about an awareness in them: for example, of the 'importance of a right livelihood; to be attentive, intense and . . . affectionate with others', and of the 'problems being faced by the world'. They also feel that their values may have remained 'traditional', or been 'imposed by parents', if they had not come into contact with him.

A few pupils frankly state that although they understand him, they are unable to practise his philosophy or totally alter their way of living. They are thus unable 'to get rid of fear', for example: one pupil writes, 'exams still scare me'. Insofar as these pupils accept the ideology and attempt to live by it, as it were, it may be seen as having sufficient influence on their attitudes, values, and, ultimately, their lives, at least while they are in RVS.

This is even more apparent in the case of those pupils who are considered 'sensitive' in terms of having a special inclination towards the ideology. Some of them live in the 'special' houses that have been created for them and are particularly close to the ideologue teachers. They are treated differently from the others to the extent that they may be selected to be later sent to the Krishnamurti school in England or for discussion and closer contact with Krishnamurti. Most of them, however, do not consider themselves any different from the others and are unhappy at being rebuffed by them. By acknowledging the influence of the ideology and exhibiting an interest in it, these pupils have nonetheless alienated themselves considerably from other pupils.

The pupil culture therefore comprises both kinds of pupil

views—those explicitly expressing an interest in the ideology and those that do not. The discrepancy in their views is evident, for example, in pupil perspectives on competition in sport or school work. It is to be expected that, although some pupils may be aware of the ideology's influence on them, they may never acknowledge it explicitly. This would be to protect their self-image, which is dependent on peer approval, and would not be enhanced by such an action.

Pupils' attitudes towards RVS as an institution, and the functionaries and activities in it, reveal their experience of the school and constitute an important element of pupil culture.

Ambivalence in pupil perspectives is even more pronounced in their views on what they 'like' and 'dislike' about RVS, as they express divergent viewpoints on almost every issue. On the one hand, most pupils like the teachers with whom they have a 'free', 'intimate' and 'fantastic' relationship which avoids the 'unnecessary tension' that might result otherwise. The 'understanding' and 'care' the teachers exhibit and their willingness to discuss the pupils' problems with them is appreciated. Similarly, pupils (more boys than girls) find the quality of teaching in the classroom the most rewarding aspect of their life in school. On the other hand, several pupils also dislike the 'hypocrisy' in teachers in terms of their perception of the difference in teacher behaviour and attitudes during Krishnamurti's annual visit and at other times. Some teachers are not appreciated for 'interfering' in boy-girl relations and the 'arrogant' and 'authoritarian' attitudes of the Principal and Headmistress respectively are particularly disliked.

An important aspect of school life that the pupils like is the freedom they experience in terms of lack of punishment and imposed discipline. Some pupils (more boys than girls) however dislike the lack of adequate discipline and competition in school processes which is viewed as being detrimental to their future prospects. While some pupils argue for more discipline, there are others who disapprove of school rules, such as 'being forced' to go for PT, and not being allowed to wear certain kinds of clothes.

It is significant that a large number of respondents like the school's environment which is viewed as being 'beautiful' and conducive to study. The lack of noise and pollution and the vast, open spaces situated away from 'city life' contribute towards the pupils feeling 'calm and peaceful' and 'very happy'. The friendly and relaxed atmosphere in the classroom is valued as it is 'good for learning and becoming aware of oneself'. The environment and the atmosphere create a particular ambience in RVS which the pupils value in terms of not only its practical worth (insofar as it aids learning) but also, the positive effect it has on themselves. Some pupils however do not appreciate the 'isolation from the outside world' that they experience in RVS.

The school's organization of sport and the opportunities for the arts, music and drama are found to be rewarding by many pupils. This is true of the provision for a variety of co-curricular activities and games, special music and chanting assemblies, and weekend programmes. The organization of the small houses and hostels and the School Council are viewed favourably by them. Some pupils (all boys) nonetheless find that there are not enough games, activities or subject choice.

Pupil friendships and relations with peers play a significant role in their lives. Most pupils therefore dislike the bullying, teasing and gossip amongst themselves. Girls appear to be more sensitive on this issue, and are particularly affected by gossip and adverse comments on their clothes and style of dressing. The 'unnatural' and 'hostile' boy-girl relationship is criticized because it is limited or restricted in nature. Pupils not only disapprove of certain aspects of their relations with one another but also of the attitude of some pupils towards school: for example, a lack of 'seriousness' at discussions, the inability to make an attempt to understand the ideology, or feigning an apparent interest in it, and taking undue advantage of the freedom that is granted to them.

To the extent that pupils are dissatisfied with some aspects of school life, let us look at their suggestions for change. These relate to school organization, such as, a wider choice of subjects and activities, a more flexible timetable allowing them more free time, better organization of sport with an emphasis on competition, better houses, more cleanliness and less noise in the dining hall, and the like. As regards school rules, the pupils would prefer less restrictions about school work, sport and, in particular, their attendance at Krishnamurti's annual talks.

There is no consensus however in pupil views on change regarding teacher behaviour and attitudes towards them. They expect a closer relationship with teachers than actually exists: for example, they think that teachers should take more interest in pupils and discuss their problems with them. Teachers are also expected, however, not to interfere and to 'keep off' the pupils.

Apart from attempting to modify teacher behaviour, the pupils are also concerned with their own behaviour. Thus the school is expected to bring about a change in pupil conduct by making them more 'sensitive', developing an 'interest and awareness' in them, and eliminating their 'apathy' during school activities. They would like to have better relations amongst themselves, a closer relationship between boys and girls, and more interaction between pupils who are interested in the ideology and those who are not.

In their suggestions for change, the pupils are thus concerned primarily with the two most important sets of participants with whom they interact, namely, other pupils and teachers, and the physical changes they envisage for RVS. It is significant that some of them resent the requirement to attend Krishnamurti's talks. Any outward or feigned expression of interest in the ideology is also never appreciated by pupils. It however remains a latent and subtle influence in the life of some pupils as is evident from their views and writings.

Apart from their experience of RVS in general, there is also a more personal element of the pupils' lives at RVS. Houseparents are like surrogate or 'second' parents to some pupils who are conscious of receiving 'individual attention' and appreciate the care and concern shown towards them. This concern is, however, viewed as becoming 'too much' sometimes when pupil movement is restricted during the weekend. The positive role of friends is also emphasized as contributing towards the general well-being expressed by the pupil.

There are however a few pupils who feel that they are not really cared for but are expected to take care of themselves. One girl differentiates between being loved and being physically looked after, and feels that while the latter exists, she is not sure whether they are 'genuinely loved'. Such pupils may feel alienated from school processes because they lack close interaction with the teachers or houseparents or feel rejected by their peers.

Pupils also experience different kinds of anxieties and problems in relation to their life in school. School work is the major source of worry for a large number of boys and girls. They are anxious about examinations, and their performance. Similarly, school work becomes a 'personal problem' for those who worry about their lack of initiative to work and the report card sent home to parents, who expect their children to do well. The teachers also press the senior pupils to sustain a high level of performance at the tests. The academic pressures implicit in the organization of the curriculum, the methods of classroom teaching, evaluation and reward are the only cause of pupil anxiety arising directly out of school activities.

On the other hand, a personal problem experienced by most pupils is their relationship with friends of either sex, arising out of misunderstandings, disagreements, teasing, and bullying. The ideology is not completely absent: a particular personal problem is the inability to talk to Krishnamurti out of nervousness and to live by the ideology. It is evident that the pupils' most personal experiences are touched by one aspect of school life or another and by their home life.

In the solution of their problems, pupils tend to trust their classmates more than the teachers, although the houseparents are sometimes consulted. More boys than girls however discuss their problems with their houseparents or teachers. This may be due to the nature of the girls' problems, such as their relations with boys which may inhibit them and restrict their confidences to classmates and friends. When the pupils are seriously disturbed about their work, however, they turn primarily to the teachers and houseparents. Their inability to discuss their 'personal' problems with teachers probably accounts for their desire for a closer relationship with them.

Pupil aspirations for the future are a significant aspect of pupil culture primarily in terms of what they tell us about the impact of the ideology and school processes on them. Most pupils, of course, aspire to earn a livelihood; what is noteworthy is that as many as 94 per cent would like to go to university or to other institutions for higher education or training. These pupils mention as their preferred choices professional institutions, such as institutes of technology, regional engineering and medical colleges, statistical institutes, colleges of architecture, design, home science, arts and music. Degree colleges, preferably in south India, are also mentioned and some pupils would like to go to universities abroad for further education. Only two pupils stated a preference for the

Krishnamurti school in England. The pupils thus have an essential-ly conventional attitude towards their future in terms of aspiring to seek admission into professional educational institutions and this is inevitably reflected in their career choices (see Table 7.7).

TABLE 7.7

Pupils' Career Choices

Careers	Number			Percentage
	Boys	*Girls*	*Total*	
Professions 1:				
Engineer/Technologist/ Architect/ Computer Programmer	21	3	24	19.51
Professions 2:				
Doctor	8	11	19	15.45
Teacher	6	2	8	6.50
Lawyer	1	–	1	0.81
Civil Servant	8	3	11	8.95
Business Executive	9	2	11	8.95
Chartered Accountant	9	2	11	8.95
Artist/Musician/Cine Artiste	5	3	8	6.50
Social Worker	2	5	7	5.69
Scientist	5	1	6	4.88
Army Officer/Pilot	5	–	5	4.07
Creative Writer	1	1	2	1.63
Politician	1	–	1	0.81
Industrialist	1	–	1	0.81
Bank Officer	1	–	1	0.81
Hotel Manager	1	–	1	0.81
Electronics Researcher	1	–	1	0.81
Oceanographer	1	–	1	0.81
Detective	1	–	1	0.81
Interior Decorator and Caterer	–	1	1	0.81
Undecided	2	–	2	1.63
Total	89	34	123	100.00

Total number of respondents: 88; Boys, 61; Girls, 27.

Most pupils, particularly boys, aspire for careers in the category of professions which include engineering, technology, architecture and computer programming. The boys also prefer the civil service, business careers and chartered accountancy, while the girls are clearly interested in the medical profession. The teaching profession attracts very few pupils (more boys than girls). However, 25 per cent of the respondents consider teaching at RVS which suggests that although they are not keen on teaching as a profession, some of them would not mind teaching at their Alma Mater. By and large, pupils appear not to have been influenced by the ideology but by the school's academic programme which trains them for particular careers. We thus find a fewer number of pupils favouring careers which require a commitment and creativity different from that acquired through professional training.

Most pupils acknowledge the influence of their parents in their career aspirations. The influence of the teachers and Management is minimal. It is significant that all the pupils who concede the influence of their housemaster belong to one of the 'special' houses set up for 'sensitive' pupils. One girl mentions Krishnamurti's influence in her aspirations for her career and another refers to 'Rishi Valley (the place)'.

Pupils leave RVS with a sentimental and nostalgic attitude towards the school where they have spent anything from two to eight years. Thus at the staff farewell for the pupils of Standard 10 in 1981, a boy thanked the teachers adding, on behalf of the rest, that their 'experience' in RVS had been 'one of the best' of their lives. Similarly, bidding farewell at the close of a moonlight dinner held for the outgoing pupils, pupils thanked other pupils and teachers saying: 'You are the best juniors, the best people, any school could ever have'. When the senior-most pupils actually leave RVS, the rest turn out in large numbers to see them off, sometimes riding in the buses to the mouth of the valley for the final farewell. Such sentiment and enthusiasm is perhaps evident in every school and is only indicative of the 'we-feeling' the pupils acquire as a result of having spent a few years together.

I have so far attempted to identify the variety of pupil perspectives based as they are on divergent values, backgrounds, and attitudes towards people, situations, activities and forms of discourse. It is apparent that there is no single pupil perspective which might have easily established a common pattern of pupil culture. What emerges really is the conflicting and ambivalent nature of pupil perceptions and feelings towards the ideology, RVS, their teachers, and peers.

Pupils appear to have a very positive attitude towards the school—enthusiastic and committed as they are towards school work, sport, other activities and school life in general.[20] This may lead to the conclusion that their strategical action involves commitment or conformity to school values and processes, since they adhere to them without any particularly significant signs of 'rebellion', 'intransigence' or 'retreatism'.[21] There are muted signs of occasional rebellion, for example, in pupils' writings on the Democracy Board and in pupil talk. The school's policy of sporadically expelling 'difficult' pupils perhaps serves to restrain rebellion among them. An extreme view of pupil conformity to school life however would be a simplistic view of the situation as all pupils do not have a similar outlook.

There is thus an intermeshing of pupil views into an overall perspective which is dominated primarily by two concerns: (1) To attend to school work and participate in all aspects of school life, motivated by their aspirations for a future occupation or career, parental expectations and other social constraints. These pupils are influenced mainly by the school's academic programme. The ideology is in this context largely viewed as being impractical and unrelated to their lives. (2) To study and reflect on the ideology and find some meaning in their lives in terms of it. In this, they are motivated by Krishnamurti's teachings and personality, or presence, as they perceive it. These pupils are also influenced by school organization and parental and social pressures; it is the ideology, however, and Krishnamurti's charismatic presence in the school and interaction with ideologue teachers which emerge as the significant influences.

Insofar as the two sets of concerns are essentially different, the two forms of conformity that arise from them may be viewed as variant forms of 'social strategy' employed by the pupil. In the first case, this may be identified as 'strategic compliance, in which the individual complies with the authority figure's definition of the situation and the constraints of the situation but retains private reservations about them' (Lacey, *MS*: 8). Thus although the pupil may accept the school's official goals and processes for implementation and work within their definitions, he has his reservations about them—as has been amply illustrated by his views and writings. He may also 'work the system' by using official means beyond the point intended by the school. He does this, for example, by observing rules where he stands to gain or by feigning an interest in the ideology at discussions to somehow get through the lesson. Moreover, conformity in this case is to an established, prevailing ideal.

In the second case, the pupils' 'social strategy' may be identified as 'internalised adjustment, in which the individual complies with the constraints and believes that the constraints of the situation are for the best' (Lacey: ibid.). Apart from an internalization of the constraints inherent in the situation, such a pupil internalizes the values and the means used to propagate or implement them. Here, conformity is to an ideal different from that which is generally prevalent.

This however raises the question of the different kinds of goals that are evident in the double-stranded situation in RVS created by the co-existence of the transcendental and local orders in which ideological and educational discourse are respectively located. Pupil conformity to the goals and processes arising from one order, again, does not mean a lack of interest in those of the other. Thus, some pupils conform to the requirements of the local order. They may have an intellectual interest in the ideology which becomes apparent at discussions and in their writings. On the other hand, there are pupils who, while fulfilling school expectations in relation to the local order, are also seriously engaged with the ideological discourse of the transcendental order.

The influence of the two different kinds of teachers in their respective areas of interest, and the particular kind of encouragement they provide, is also obvious. Thus professional teachers encourage hard work leading to pupil competence and an expectedly good performance in the examination. They also make themselves available to the pupils outside school hours for helping them towards this end. The ideologue teacher, on the contrary, encourages discussion on the ideology and helps pupils particularly in the solution of personal problems and acquiring a broader perspective on life in general.

On the part of the teachers, two different kinds of intentionality are involved: while the professional teacher is engaged in the transmission of educational discourse, she is primarily turning out a pupil. The ideologue teacher who may not be more humane or less professional than his colleague, is engaged fundamentally with the transmission of the ideology and is therefore turning out not only a pupil but also trying to turn out a different kind of human being. The result sought in the first case is that of the reproduction not only of knowledge but also of the status quo, as it were, insofar as it implies a perpetuation of the system. In the second case, transformation is sought through the study and understanding of the ideology in relation to the daily life of the pupil.

This underscores the fact that the teacher is a critical element in the making of the pupil and therefore in the pupil culture. Pupil culture is not thus some kind of a static body of information, knowledge, and values which the teachers transmit mechanically to the pupils. It is rather an evolving configuration of several elements which emerges from an active interaction between teachers and pupils in which both kinds of participants are givers as well as takers, and to which they bring different aims and perspectives.

CHAPTER EIGHT

Teacher–Pupil Interaction
Freedom and Constraint

An essential feature of teacher–pupil interaction is that it has a definable form, that some of its constituent relations stay relatively stable over time. It is therefore possible to predict certain modes of behaviour among teachers and pupils in particular contexts. The school's academic programme for the senior classes adheres to the policies and recommendations of the Council, and influences not only the curriculum and related activities but also the goals of the participants. At the same time, RVS is located in a particular institutional and ideological setting which lends it a special character that differentiates it from other public schools.

Coming closer to everyday life, the principal formal settings for interaction are the classroom and other similar locations, such as the staffroom and the auditorium. Less formal settings include the house, the dining hall, the sports field and the 'outdoor'. These physical settings include not only the spatial relationships between the setting and the school but also the 'layout and decor' of each setting itself.[1]

Temporality is an important element as interaction in each setting takes place within a prescribed time limit. Thus teachers and pupils meet in the classroom for a predetermined length of time; interaction in the house is usually limited to outside school hours; and they spend an hour together on the sports field every afternoon. The temporal sequence of events bestows a structure on the activity and contributes to the predictable and orderly manner in which the interaction occurs.[2] The precise content of interaction may vary in different settings but it is the relative persistence or invariability of its forms which lends a sense of structure to social life in the school. Moreover, as the form and content of relations in one setting inevitably affect relations in another, the structure of teacher–pupil relations may be seen as being relatively established in terms of predictability.

Nonetheless, variability in teacher–pupil interaction is also present and arises, for example, from the nature of the situation in different settings. Each situation has a dominant characteristic which appears to be the result of a number of variables. Thus, a situation may be affected by the physical environment, the personality of the teacher, the multiple roles she may be performing, her ideological commitment, her image of the pupils, the nature of the subject being taught in the classroom, a preceding event like a badly done test, a forthcoming event like an examination, and teacher–pupil relations in other settings. Other factors like parental pressure and social expectations also contribute significantly to individual definitions of the situation.

To the extent that the pupils interact with a number of teachers in the course of the day, the nature of interaction inevitably varies from teacher to teacher. It is also dependent on variations among pupils in terms of their age, gender, and their attitudes towards school processes, the ideology and the teachers. Teachers also vary in terms of being professional or ideologue, senior or junior, and members of the Management (such as the Principal and the Headmistress), or those unconnected with it. The kind of image or reputation a particular teacher may have established in the pupil community also affects the nature of interaction. The pupils' image of the teacher may be based on her actual behaviour or a combination of her behaviour and the 'folklore' that exists about her.[3]

The intentions of the participants are to some extent dependent on the purpose of the situation itself: for example, the classroom situation exists for the pedagogic purpose. The participants' perception of this, and the meaning they give to it, defines their intention in a situation. Each setting however has its own rules, procedures and conventions which shape the form of the interaction. In some situations the interaction gives rise to the formulation of certain procedures by the participants. In this aspect of interaction the teachers and pupils make use of strategical action in order to achieve certain goals which may or may not be common to both.[4]

It would appear that negotiation is the key strategy employed by teachers and pupils. It implies the 'search for agreement' inasmuch as 'certain rules of procedure have to be established and maintained' (Woods, 1983: 127) to enable interaction to proceed in a manner agreeable to both sets of participants. In other words, they 'lay the basis for a truce' so as to achieve their goals and maximize their interests (Woods, 1980b: 14).[5] Following Woods, three assumptions may be seen as underlying the concept of negotiation: that of power in the sense that although it is assumed that teachers have more power than pupils, in fact, their use of power is restricted by pupil manoeuvres. Secondly, teacher–pupil relations are variable as they are 'continuously creating relationships, changing them, shifting the bases of them, gaining a point here, conceding one there, devising new forms of them, new ways of getting round them, plugging holes in one's own version, detecting weaknesses in others' (Ibid.). Finally, as both sets of participants generally have varying interests, the use of negotiative strategies is a common feature. My analysis however indicates that in the senior classroom at least teachers and pupils have common goals, though perhaps varying interests, and negotiation is very much in evidence.

The possibilities for negotiation tend to depend on an individual's awareness of his abilities; for example, most children discover that they have important bargaining power in their relations with parents, teachers and peers. If pupils are encouraged to express their opinions freely, as they are in RVS, they become aware of this bargaining power.

On the part of the teacher, the use of this strategy is linked to her need for control over the pupils in one form or another.[6] To the extent that appropriate pupil behaviour can be negotiated by the teachers and pupils, an atmosphere of informality and freedom prevails in the classroom and house. It is only when negotiation fails that teachers resort to the use of punitive measures to establish control. This may also be the teacher's preferred method of teaching. The strategical device of 'domination' which employs verbal aggression as a form of punishment is then used as a measure of control. However, teachers generally refrain from punitive measures in accordance with school regulations.

It has been suggested that the teacher strategically establishes her dominant position in the classroom by imposing her 'definition of the situation' on the pupils by talking, teaching and questioning them (Delamont, 1976: 94–8). It is evident that when their definitions are weak—for example, when they are vague in their use of methodology or unable to define the content of the lesson immediately on entering the classroom—the pupils take advantage of the situation and indulge in disruptive behaviour.

Pupil strategies in the classroom have been succinctly perceived by Delamont: 'The pupil's first strategy is to find out what the teacher wants and give it to her—assuming that they can see a pay-off for themselves, in terms of grades, eventual jobs or peace and quiet. When there is no discernible benefit to be had by giving the teacher what she wants, "disruptive behaviour" is likely to become the major strategy' (1976: 99–100). In my classroom studies, I show that senior pupils who are clear about their goals and the benefits accruing from adhering to the rules generally comply with the teachers' requests. In the junior classroom, the pupils are too young to perceive any benefits, and disorder prevails. The pupils' strategy in the senior classroom is that of conformity to teacher expectations to enable them to meet the proximate goal of passing an examination in an overall positive orientation towards learning. In other settings as well, the use of pupil strategies is apparent as a means to get what they can out of a situation.

The teacher's attempts to introduce humour into the classroom situation is an effort at 'fraternization' with the pupils.[7] This strategy works well with those teachers who already have fairly congenial relations with pupils outside the classroom. If a teacher is aloof and distant from the pupils in general, humour in the classroom does not cut any ice with them. Fraternization is more common outside the classroom, on the sportsfield and on excursions where the expectations for pupil behaviour are somewhat relaxed and where the pupils themselves view their relations with the teachers in a more informal manner. It is obvious that the use of different strategies—notably negotiation and fraternization—allows for greater flexibility in teacher–pupil interaction as it continuously changes and develops in the different settings.

Classroom Study–I

I will now examine teacher–pupil interaction in the 'B' section of Standard 10 where I observed 25 lessons.[8] Pupils in Standard 10 are divided into sections 'A' and 'B', not according to ability but to facilitate learning, with 27 and 21 pupils respectively, whose average age is 15 years.

The 'setting', i.e., the classroom, where the interaction occurs is important insofar as 'those who would use a particular setting as part of their performance cannot begin their act until they have brought themselves to the appropriate place and must terminate their performance when they leave it' (Goffman, 1959: 33). The classroom may also be viewed as a 'situated activity system' to the extent that teachers and pupils are seen as performing 'situated roles' and their performance is dependent on the setting and on one another.[9] This is not to say however that interaction in the classroom is not affected by activities and relations outside it.

The Standard 10 'B' classroom faces a small quadrangle around which all the classrooms in the senior school are located. Inside, 12 boys and 9 girls sit separately divided by a narrow aisle running through the length of the room. This seating arrangement is the pupils' choice who generally refrain from mixing across the sexes in the classroom.

Lessons begin in the senior school at 7.20 a.m. and go on until 1 p.m., with short breaks for breakfast, assembly and fruit juice. After lunch, the pupils may have an activity, laboratory work, or a lesson. They remain in the classroom during the morning spell and the teachers move from class to class taking lessons. A bell announces the beginning and the end of each lesson which lasts for 40 minutes. In 10 'B' teachers and pupils wasted little time on preliminaries or side-talk as the impending examinations seemed to weigh heavily on everybody's mind.[10]

While the pressures of school work may imply a work-oriented teacher–pupil relationship, interaction is generally pervaded by informality and freedom which stem from their cordial relations outside the classroom. The boarding school ethos bestows a greater importance on outside interaction, in less structured settings, than on interaction in the classroom. Moreover, the teachers appear to understand and accept the ideology's insistence on a relationship free of fear in the learning situation. It appears to be a part of the school ethos for them to at least establish informal and friendly relations with the pupils.

The effort to achieve this informality finds expression from the moment of entry.[11] When the teacher walks in, after the bell has rung, the pupils do not rise to wish or greet her which is not viewed as a sign of disrespect. The pupils are also usually preoccupied with the earlier lesson (discussing the subject or rearranging their books) or talking to one another in the brief transition between two lessons. Nonetheless, an important aspect of interaction in the classroom is the teacher's concern with maintaining order so as to facilitate teaching. However, order is not brought about nor control enforced by 'constant teacher directives and autocratic sanctions against deviance'. Instead, the pupil is 'socialized' into a set of rules for 'appropriate' and 'competent' classroom behaviour which he is expected to know and behave accordingly (Hammersley, 1977: 51). These rules may change continuously during the course of a lesson depending on whether the teacher is merely asking the pupils to settle down or is engaged in the 'lesson-proper', that is, 'instruction'. As the rules are 'context-dependent', they vary and the pupils have to adjust to the changing situations. Thus there are rules for late entry into the classroom, for quietening down so that the teacher can begin the lesson, for participating in the lesson, and so on. Rather than a strict imposition of rules, the teachers attempt to induce order by drawing the pupils' attention to the established rules.

The teachers use different strategies in coping with pupil behaviour when they enter the classroom. To quell the initial disorder (pupils banging their desk tops, scraping their chairs, talking to one another, moving around the classroom), some teachers merely reprimand the pupils, but this is usually not very effective. Most teachers gain the pupils' attention by asking them to open their textbooks, or by writing a problem on the blackboard, or by beginning to teach almost as soon as they set foot in the classroom.

It is apparent that the teachers recognize the fact that they need to employ a technique or strategy in order to deal with a situation that may not be conducive to achieving their goals if left unattended. The use of a strategy of this kind is not collectively formulated, not is it a formal teaching technique, but is 'implicit in the hidden curriculum' (Woods in Woods, 1980b). The pupils are also tacit participants in the employment of a strategy. Their compliance is related to the goals of both sets of participants: the teacher, to teach the lesson and complete the course, and the pupil, to learn under pressure of the impending examinations which he must pass in his own interest. The costs of not conforming to the expected behaviour pattern (poor performance or failure) are thus too high to incur.

Once the lesson-proper begins, the teacher encounters another problem of maintaining order. As the pupils are enthusiastic about school work, they actively participate in the lesson: they interrupt the teacher to ask or answer questions, sometimes prompting her in her exposition of the lesson-topic or helping her solve a problem on the blackboard, at times correcting or questioning her conclusions, and so on. The task of controlling extensive pupil participation is therefore a continuous problem for most teachers. However, they do not seek to curb pupil participation completely—in fact they elicit it themselves—but only attempt to control its extent or the disorder that it may give rise to.

Teachers deal with pupil participation in various ways. In Lesson One (a brief summary of which is given below) we have an example of the teacher who allows free pupil participation and his appeals for order are not met. He thus has to cope with the confusion and disorder that results.

Lesson One

The teacher walked into the classroom and quickly read out a problem from the textbook. He then drew a diagram on the blackboard. The pupils began to help him in this by making suggestions, all talking together. He asked them to speak one at a time. A pupil walked up to the blackboard and started changing the diagram, explaining why he was doing so. They discussed the problem and at first the teacher disagreed with the pupil's suggestions, 'So what? Why are you giving all those instructions?' At the same time, he was trying to quieten the rest of the class. He called another pupil to the front who offered another solution. The teacher finally agreed with both pupils' solutions. Pupils: 'It's easier [their way]'. Teacher: 'O.K. For you, it might be easier. But both methods can be used'.

Other pupils continued to talk and interrupt the teacher. After explaining the method, he asked them to work on the problem. He then began to move around the pupils' desks, looking at their work, helping and guiding them individually. After about 10 minutes with the girls, he moved to the boys and asked them for the answer, adding, 'Please don't make noise'. Meanwhile, a girl made a correction in the teacher's method on the blackboard. He gamely accepted it.

A boy was moving around the classroom looking into others' notebooks and discussing the problem with them. The teacher reprimanded him but he did not respond. The teacher then asked the pupils to solve the problem at prep. as he wanted to get on to the next problem and finally told the wandering boy to 'Sit down', and as the pupils were talking together, 'What's going on here?' The noise subsided temporarily.

The teacher wrote the next problem on the blackboard. The pupils were again prompting him. Suddenly, he turned around and addressed a pupil slouching in the front row: 'Sit right. Then you will understand all this'. The pupils asked questions and suggested alternative methods. The teacher accepted some of these, making the necessary changes on the blackboard, explaining why he was doing so.

The teacher was on to a third problem. The pupils began working on it while the teacher erased the writing on the blackboard, looked at his watch and said, 'Oh, we have to discuss so many problems . . .'. Some pupils called him. He asked them to wait and continued talking to another pupil. Soon, all the pupils were discussing the problem amongst themselves. Teacher: 'I won't help you at all. Why are you all talking like that?' They stopped talking but continued after a while.

At the close of the lesson, the teacher gave the class two problems for prep. Just as he was leaving the room, a pupil yelled out the answer to the problem they had been working on. It was wrong. Teacher: 'How will you learn? Think, first of all, think'.

Another teacher uses the method of 'direct selection' to control 'over-participation', naming the pupils from whom he seeks a response, or only using gestures (pointing, nodding, looking), for selection.[12] The difference in the two teachers' methods of attempting to control pupil participation results in two somewhat different situations in the classroom.

Lesson Two

The teacher was revising an earlier lesson, asking particular pupils by name to respond to his questions. Other pupils began to answer and the teacher, very politely, said: 'One at a time. Excuse me, I asked him and you answered. I'm asking him'. He then pointed to a girl in the first row and questioned her. A boy raised his hand, 'Sir?' Teacher: 'Let her answer.' He continued in this manner until he was satisfied that the particular topic had been understood.

Having finished the revision, he began a new topic using the blackboard and drawing the pupils' attention to it, he kept repeating, 'Please look here'. When he finished writing, he asked the pupils to think about the problem and then asked them questions. They raised their hands and he selected particular pupils. As the boys seemed to be doing most of the talking, he turned to the girls, 'From this side, please'. As they took some time, he urged them, 'Quick, quick'. He emphasized throughout that he wanted them to 'visualize' the problem and not merely supply random answers.

The teacher took a long time over the topic asking individual pupils if it was clear to them. Every time a pupil answered in the negative, he would explain a particular point all over again. Meanwhile, other pupils were copying into their notebooks from the blackboard. Turning to the girls' side, the teacher asked, 'Any doubts, this side?', and continued to explain different aspects of the same topic. Finally, he stopped and asked the pupils, 'Is it clear to you? Shall we move on? O.K.?' While most of the pupils replied in the affirmative, the teacher suddenly walked up to a boy in the front row and asked him a question. Surprised, he began to stammer out a jumbled response and other pupils supplied the right answer.

The teacher then started on a new topic, writing it out on the blackboard. As the pupils questioned him or attempted to provide answers to anticipated questions, he controlled them by asking them not to answer, repeating, 'Just a minute, please'. When other pupils interrupted, he quietened them saying, 'Sorry, I didn't ask you'.

While the two methods of control over pupil talk, participation, and behaviour are obviously different, they are not an attempt to publicly denigrate or mock the pupils. Informality is characterized by a relative lack of authoritarian control: the pupils do not formally greet the teacher on her entrance, they are allowed to laugh both with and at her, they call some teachers by their first names, and question the teacher's choice of lesson-topic, and so on. They draw attention to themselves by either raising their hands or calling the teacher: some merely raise their fingers or, in their excitement, snap their fingers at her.

The teachers, too, fraternize with the pupils, bringing elements of humour and fun into the learning situation, but they are careful to see that they do not lose control. One factor that makes their task easier is pupil enthusiasm for school work. For example, when a teacher asks them if she should wind up the lessons before time, they almost always ask for more work in the classroom. And once a problem is set, they work on it to the exclusion of everything else, perhaps a little noisily. Informality in the form of light-hearted banter can however lead to impertinence and disorder primarily due to the inexperience of a particular teacher.

While the school's ideology and ethos facilitate informality and freedom in teacher–pupil interaction, the constraints of the curriculum, embodying the formal school system, give rise to an element of formality that is also present in certain classroom situations. This is another example of the conflicting roles played by the transcendental and the local orders in teacher–pupil interaction. It then becomes apparent that the tension arising from pupil performance in tests, and the teacher's comments on it, are a significant aspect of teacher–pupil interaction. The pupils are obviously affected by their grades and are anxious to improve their performance. There is a difference in the way different teachers may discuss the pupils' performance but the pupils' anxiety is always the same.

Some teachers who have generally cordial relations with the pupils in the classroom are stern and sarcastic in their judgement of pupil performance at tests:

Lesson Three

The teacher began by asking the pupils how they had done in the test. One boy said, 'O.K.' which he clarified on the teacher's inquiry to stand for 'Not good'. The other pupils laughed but were quiet when the teacher repeated his question. Expressing puzzlement at their silence he talked at some length about the necessity of studying in order to pass the examinations. He said that most pupils had not studied for the test which is why they had done badly in it. There was pin-drop silence in the classroom and each pupil's attention was riveted on the teacher. He spoke of the 'ambitions' pupils had of becoming 'engineers' and told them that if they had any such ideas, they would have to work hard. Studying the textbook just a day before the test was no good. Moreover, if they wanted to opt for the Science stream in the next two years, they would have to work very hard. If they did not do so, he sarcastically said that he would be 'very happy'. He also indicated that the Management and senior teachers were planning to hold 'selection examinations' to weed out possible failures. He then went over the question paper in detail explaining where the pupils had gone wrong.

Next, the teacher divided the class into different groups for a series of experiments and started explaining them but was very curt with pupils for the remainder of the lesson. With his back to the pupils, continuing teaching using the blackboard, he asked questions, and when the replies were incorrect, he sarcastically commented, 'Very good, very nice'. Writing the correct answers on the blackboard, he asked them, 'Is this what you have learnt up to now?' He told them there was obviously no point in their remembering what they had been taught in Standards 8 and 9. He then explained the experiment on the blackboard, meticulously drawing diagrams and writing in detail.

This teacher was particularly popular on the sportsfield and otherwise. The significance of school work, and the external world, lies precisely in the fact that it was able to transform an otherwise cordial relationship into one of domination based on the strategy of sarcasm on the part of the teacher and compliance out of fear of impending examinations, on the part of the pupil. Other teachers are less harsh and more restrained in their criticism.

Lesson Four

In contrast to the earlier lesson, this teacher entered the classroom, distributed the answer-books and went out for a short while. On his return, he asked the pupils if they had gone through their papers and then discussed the question paper with them. He emphasized that it did not matter if their answers were wrong but that they should look at the question paper carefully. For each question that the teacher discussed, he stated the number of marks given and told the pupils how much they had obtained on an average in each answer.

He continued to talk about the pupils' expected performance at the forthcoming examinations and quietly repeated, 'I'm very unhappy; very, very unhappy. . .' (about their performance in the test). When he finished, the pupils called him to their desks for individual discussion. At the back of the room, some boys discussed their grades, comparing their performance with one another.

Some other teachers devote only a part of the lesson to such discussions. To illustrate: one teacher discussed the question paper briefly with the pupils but distributed the answer-sheets only at the end of the lesson. She merely made the point about the different ways in which a question paper might be set and suggested that the pupils use their intelligence in answering questions. Another teacher chose to only distribute the answer-sheets to pupils at the end of the lesson without discussion. This however appeared to create great nervousness among the pupils who grabbed their papers from the teacher and were anxious to see that their grades remained hidden from one another.

Such variations between teachers result in contributing towards either increasing or reducing the tension already evident in the pupils. Pupil anxiety about their performance in class tests is obviously related to anxiety about performance in the Board examinations and is not a reaction to the teacher herself. It is obvious then that the informal relationship between teachers and pupils in the classroom is always bounded by the dormant fear of examinations.

A third and final factor influencing teacher–pupil interaction, apart from the school's ideology or its ethos and the formal system, is the personality of the teacher and the use that is made of this by teachers to ensure pupil compliance to appropriate behaviour patterns. A lesson conducted by a senior teacher, who is considered an authoritarian figure outside the classroom as well, was thus loaded with sarcastic comments directed at the pupils, and she kept them alert by asking questions incessantly.

Lesson Five

The teacher began by observing that some pupils were not present and asked the others where they were. The pupils did not respond. Teacher: 'Are they sleeping?' (This was an afternoon lesson). Pupils: 'Yes'. Teacher: 'I hope they continue to sleep until eternity'. The absentees walked in. Teacher: 'Have you woken up? You come late because *akka*[13] [the other teacher] allows you to. If once you are sent back, you will come on time.'

She started teaching, stopping suddenly to tell a girl in the back row, 'Sit up, my girl.' Meanwhile, some pupils continued to walk in late, each one saying, 'Excuse me, *akka*.' Teacher: 'What shall I excuse you from? From the class? Stand guard outside.' Pupil: 'My leg has a pull, really.' Teacher, 'Come in', and to the other pupil, 'What about you? Have you got the push?'

The teacher then asked the pupils, particularly 'those who have been sleeping', questions on the previous lesson. When they gave wrong answers, she said 'Oh!' very caustically. She addressed a question to a girl who merely smiled at first. Teacher: 'I don't want sweet smiles. I want answers'. The pupil said she did not know the answer as she had not read the book. The teacher reprimanded her for not having attended the previous lesson nor bothering to read the book.

The teacher goaded the pupils, questioning them, adding 'Come on, come on'. The pupils were very attentive throughout but hesitant in responding to her. Whenever a pupil provided a correct answer, she said 'Good' which however was a rare comment. When all the pupils were unable to provide an answer, she refused to provide it and asked them to 'find out'.

On the whole, she was difficult with pupils throughout the lesson. She made fun of pupils who answered questions wrongly and other pupils giggled softly. When they responded hesitantly, she commented, 'I must say your memory is very slow and you are supposed to be revising [the lesson]'. She was particularly impatient with pupils who were slow on the uptake, muttering, 'My God!' when they gave an incorrect answer. In complete exasperation, at the end of the lesson, she told the class, 'Oh, my God! You are such ignoramuses. Am I saying something new? I don't know'.

Questioning a pupil incessantly is a strategy to pre-empt control over the lesson and, using the method of direct selection, over the pupil as well. This teacher is therefore in full control of the lesson employing the strategy of domination which serves to ensure pupil compliance. However, as a result of the fear evoked by her domineering personality, she was unable to elicit sufficient pupil participation in the lesson. Her very presence, associated with her style of teaching, laced as it was with sarcasm and censure, inhibited their performance. Although she did not use explicit punitive measures, her verbal aggression indicates an 'unofficial' or 'informal' punishment of a kind directed at 'showing up' the pupils in the classroom.[14] Such a method appears to be contrary to the school's ideology which emphasizes a relationship free of any form of authority or domination and fear. It is obvious that some teachers in the school continue to use a teaching style best suited to their temperaments or one that they have merely adopted over a long career.

This teaching technique is adopted by other junior teachers who seek to establish their position in the classroom which might be otherwise undermined by their informal relations with pupils. Such a teacher, employing a strategic form of action, intentionally presents a 'front', with 'borrowed plumes', as it were, to the pupils so that they can perceive and define their relationship to the teacher accordingly. This was the case with a newly recruited teacher who worked closely with a senior teacher and intentionally simulated her teaching style. The junior teacher felt that it is necessary for a new teacher to establish her position in the classroom lest the pupils take advantage by making noise and disrupting the lesson.

This teacher used a harsh, sarcastic tone in the classroom although she was unable to maintain a stern manner with the pupils outside. Her intentionally developed front would slip at times in the classroom, allowing pupils to have a glimpse of the more informal and relaxed aspect of her personality. She was however quick to move back into her chosen style fearing that the pupils might take advantage of the situation. The pupils on the whole did not show any fear or restraint during her lessons, perhaps because they recognized her front for what it was and related to her differently outside the classroom. Thus her attempt to emulate the senior teacher was not always successful.

Lacey has suggested that the young teacher copes with problems, such as controlling pupil behaviour, by developing a 'teacher persona', which includes establishing 'role distance' with the pupils, a 'formal atmosphere' and 'a presence' which the pupils associate with a set of appropriate behaviour patterns (1970: 174). The use of the teacher persona, however, would be effective only if the teacher maintains a similar distance from the pupils outside the classroom. The case of the junior teacher above indicates that her attempt to present the front of the 'competent' teacher, with its accompanying characteristics of aloofness and distance, did not quite convince the pupils who had a different relationship with her in other settings. Similarly the teacher in Lesson Five was successful as she has a reputation for being a disciplinarian and the pupils generally avoid talking to her, inhibited further by her teaching style. It is clear that an asymmetrical relationship between teachers and pupils arises from the pressure of examinations (as we have seen in Lesson Three above) and from particular teaching styles (Lesson Five).

Classroom Study–II

In the Preparatory (Prep.) Section in the junior school, I observed 42 lessons.[15] This is the junior-most class in the school (age range of pupils: six to nine years), located in a spacious room. Eighteen pupils (nine girls and nine boys) remove their footwear near the door and sit and walk barefoot in the classroom. They do not all face the teacher whose place is at one end of the classroom in front of the blackboard. Most pupils face each other with girls and boys sitting together at the same desk, some with their backs to the teachers.

Three teachers take all the lessons except for the Arts and Crafts activity, and occasional afternoon lessons, which are sometimes taken by other teachers from the junior school. Of these three teachers, one is an elderly lady who has spent 13 years in RVS and had been in charge of this class until recently. The new junior school Head, however, appointed a younger teacher as class teacher as he was proposing a new curriculum for the Prep. Section which he thought might be better understood and implemented by her. Both these teachers were assisted by a third very young teacher (a non-Indian) who was on her first teaching assignment.

The new curriculum had been evolved in an attempt to do away with 'work-book oriented' learning, particularly in Mathematics and English and out of an understanding of 'child psychology'. Certain blocks or areas were seen as being necessary for pupils of this age: (i) a 'physical' block for the canalization of the pupils' energy. This meant physical activity of some kind inside the classroom, either in the form of drama, dance or movement, depending on the teacher's choice. (ii) An 'emotional' period for the canalization of the pupils' feelings. In this block, the teacher usually told the pupils a story attempting to make them experience it as such, thereby evoking the story's emotional content in them. (iii) A 'social' period for encouraging 'verbal expression'. This lesson consisted mainly of conversation on different topics arising out of either the events occurring in the classroom or a subject predetermined by the teacher. (iv) A 'creative period' to develop 'aesthetic appreciation'. The pupils were asked to draw or paint and to compose and recite poetry, songs or stories. (v) An 'intellectual block', which was viewed as being 'necessary' for the pupils' learning, included lessons on reading, writing and arithmetic.

This curriculum was viewed by the class teacher as an 'experiment' which would be adopted in other classes if found successful. The primary aim was 'to work towards Krishnamurti's teachings' through the timetable, thereby giving the ideology an important place in the junior school's academic programme.[16]

Teacher–pupil interaction in this class is thus influenced by such factors as the curriculum and the content of a particular lesson. The pupils' age composition, their relations with teachers in other settings, and the particular teacher conducting the lesson, are other important factors. Finally, it is necessary to consider the influence of the physical organization of the classroom and the junior school ethos which permeates every classroom at this level. As tests and examinations are never held, and homework rarely assigned, learning appears to be free of the tensions that result from such pressures. The excessive noise and chatter in the junior school is in definite contrast to the relative quiet of the senior school. There are, however, other sources of tension or fear.

The curriculum creates a particular kind of atmosphere in the classroom inasmuch as pupils are allowed opportunities for activities that lead to a sense of freedom, at times even disorder. This disorder is primarily a result of excessive pupil talk and movement. The teacher thus spends a great deal of time reprimanding the pupils, often sending individual pupils out of the classroom thereby using punitive measures of a kind. For example, 'conversation' lessons tended naturally to be quite disorderly. This disorder is a result of the young age of the pupils who get excited very quickly and, in the prevalent atmosphere of freedom, find it very difficult to appreciate the notions of order and quietude. Disorder is accentuated in the 'physical' lesson where the pupils are asked to do some form of bodily exercise. This exercise is usually directed and controlled by the teacher but such lessons generally end in confusion.

Disorder in the classroom is also the result of a lack of physical organization such as the disorderly arrangement of desks and the classroom design in general. It is apparently difficult for the teacher to control pupil talk and behaviour as the pupils are spread across the room with many of them seated with their backs to her. In the senior classroom, it was easier for the teacher to control pupil talk and behaviour as they were all seated facing her. The classroom design and seating arrangement also restricted pupil movement and added to the general orderliness.

There also appears to be no predetermined format regarding the content of the lessons and the teacher often uses her own discretion. Moreover, the prescribed timetable is not strictly followed by the teachers who may choose to use the 'physical' or 'emotional' block for written work. Insofar as such factors tend to create some amount of uncertainty in the teacher's approach to the lesson, they accentuate the disorder in the classroom.

The three teachers used different strategies to deal with this disorder. The young class teacher was particularly affected by disorderly pupil behaviour as given the pupils' young age, she found it difficult to sustain their interest in one subject or activity for long. She thus divided most of her lessons into two, doing different things with the pupils in each half, thereby holding their attention continuously. She also tended to use punitive measures such as sending pupils out of the classroom and was somewhat harsh in her reprimands to them.

This teacher generally sought to establish control in the classroom through the use of authoritative injunctions to the pupils such as not allowing them to touch the charts on the wall or telling them several times to keep their 'mouths closed' and their eyes and ears open. When they became extremely noisy, she would sternly ask them, 'Shall the tape-recorder start? Be quiet', thus reminding the pupils of the rules they were expected to follow. (The reference to a tape-recorder was an allusion to her continuous pleading with pupils for less noise.) The use of a code to draw the pupils' attention to an appropriate behaviour pattern is more acceptable than punishment which goes against the school's transcendental order. The use of punitive measures is however a common occurrence in the class teacher's lessons as she believes in putting the errant pupil 'away from the rest' to meet the immediate need for restoring order in the classroom.

The influence of teacher–pupil relations in other settings is evident in the lessons of the older teacher who is also the pupils' housemother. Thus, house matters, particularly problems of discipline, would often enter classroom discussion. Secondly, this teacher's method of conducting lessons was different from the other two as she did not really accept the new curriculum. As a result of her long association with this class and RVS, she felt that she had been doing the right thing all along and was thus inflexible to change. Her lessons were different from those of the other teachers to the extent that they essentially comprised the 'intellectual' block of learning. While this brought a sense of seriousness into the classroom, it did not in any way alter the pupils' tendency to talk. This teacher too, like her colleagues, spent a great deal of time controlling and directing pupil talk and behaviour.

There is an obvious difference in the techniques of the two teachers in coping with the problem of disorder. While the class teacher tended to punish pupils, the older teacher refrained from using any punitive measures. She also often made personal appeals to the pupils (inasmuch as she was an elderly teacher and also their housemother) by threatening to leave the classroom or standing outside until they had quietened down. All the teachers used a code which was quickly translated by the pupils into an appeal for silence. Their first teacher talked about switching on the tape-recorder, the older teacher merely said, 'One, Two, Three' and the pupils were expected to be silent at 'Three'. The youngest teacher's code-word with the pupils was 'Statues' that would immediately silence the pupils. The three teachers thus used different strategies for attaining the same goal of establishing order in the classroom. The pupils' latent participation in the use of these strategies was evident in their compliance with the teacher, although their docile behaviour did not last very long thereby inviting the teacher's disapproval again.

In the senior class examined earlier, the pupils' compliance was linked to their goal of seriously working towards the examinations. In this class, the pupils were not under any such pressure and complied with the teacher's injunctions or appeals for order out of a sense of fear of either being punished, rebuked, or annoying the teacher, depending on the teacher concerned. Thus, although tension resulting from academic pressures was not present, it took another form in terms of fear of teacher reprisal.

In the Prep. Section the informality that is a part of teacher–pupil interaction in Standard 10 'B' is transformed into disorder or commotion as a result of several factors that emerge from the situation. I have identified these as the innovative curriculum itself, the lack of physical organization in the classroom, the obvious lack of any real commitment to the new curriculum on the part of two out of the total of three teachers, and the lack of clearly articulated pupil goals at this stage. The nature of disorder in the two classrooms is significantly different. In the senior classroom, it primarily takes the form of excessive pupil participation in the teaching activity itself, arising from the pupils' attitudes towards the lesson which is related to their learning goals. In the junior classroom, disorder is characterized by noise arising out of excessive pupil talk that may or may not be related to the lesson. Teacher–pupil interaction in the senior classroom is continually evident in the course of the lesson while pupil interaction occurs to a greater extent in the junior classroom. This contrast in the two classrooms is a result, mainly, of the difference in the pupils' ages and hence in their learning goals.

Teachers view the problems they generally encounter in the classroom primarily in terms of the pupils' restlessness, inattentiveness, disorderly behaviour, and indifference or apathy in relation to school work. Their views on how they deal with these problems diverge on two accounts: in terms of their expectations for change in pupil behaviour and of what they expect of themselves to change the situation. They have thus devised various strategies in an attempt to change pupil conduct: they talk to the pupils either individually or in groups and try to explain the situation through discussion, pointing out the repercussions of their indifference and disorderly behaviour on their work. An ideologue teacher who faced a particularly noisy class called five pupils in turn for discussion and after some time, found that he had succeeded in reducing the level of noise in the classroom. 'Talk' may not be always successful and some teachers therefore advocate a 'firm' attitude towards pupils.

In the very junior classes, the teachers emphasize group activity as a method for holding pupil attention, even if the pupils are vertically grouped as in the Prep. Section. On the other hand, some teachers suggest individual attention towards pupils as one way of solving some of the problems in the classroom. The teachers' concern with their own role in the classroom is evident in their recommendations for making learning more interesting for pupils by improvization and the use of new techniques, and by involving them more in the lesson.

One reason for the disorder that prevails in the classroom situation in general could be the teacher's personal relations with the pupils in other settings which may affect relations in the classroom, thereby disrupting what is conventionally considered a more formal situation. Teacher views on this aspect of teacher–pupil interaction are however ambivalent: while most teachers (23 out of 36) did indicate that personal relations do not interfere with interaction in the classroom, the others were not so sure. Thus one teacher felt that it was her young age and close relations with many junior pupils that did not generate any respect towards her from them in the classroom. Another teacher perceived a change in his relationship with pupils from being very friendly to maintaining a distance so that he could induce more order in the classroom. Yet another junior teacher, who was popular with the pupils, found it difficult to establish control in the classroom. She therefore felt that she could resolve the situation by either restricting her interaction with the pupils outside or becoming more authoritarian inside the classroom.

Thus some teachers do experience the dilemma of maintaining friendly relations with the pupils at the cost of order in the classroom. This difficulty is aggravated by the attitude of members of the Management who emphasize the need for order and issue 'warnings' to those teachers who are unable to maintain it. Order in the classroom is thus a pressing preoccupation with both teachers and the Management as a precondition for effective teaching and learning and the emergence of a deeper structure of relations. However, although the ideology emphasizes a close and meaningful relationship between teachers and pupils, they are unable to find an appropriate level between freedom and disorder.

Interaction in the two classrooms also illustrates two different teaching techniques which are a result of the varying curricula. In the senior classroom, the curriculum has been designed to meet the requirements of the Council and the teaching task is aimed towards completing the required syllabi and preparing the pupils' competence for the examination. To achieve this end, physical order in the classroom is necessary and distractions from the lesson such as excessive pupil participation or noise are controlled by the teacher whose demands and appeals for order are usually met. The teacher exercises control by talking most of the time on the subject and by directing or selecting pupil participation. This kind of teaching is referred to as 'discipline-based teaching' by Hammersley inasmuch as 'a definite curriculum is involved, knowledge is objective and universally valid, is hierarchically structured and is contained by distinct disciplines' (1977: 38). Further, 'preferred and predominant techniques are formal organization of the classroom, constant supervision and frequent intervention, the use of imperatives and positional appeals, class tests and grouping by age and ability' (Ibid.). This kind of teaching style creates its own atmosphere in the classroom where order must prevail to accomplish the goals desired by both sets of participants.

In the junior classroom, the curriculum is designed according to a perceived understanding of the requirements for pupils of a particular age and general mental ability. There are however no formal specifications as to the nature of the subjects to be taught although there is a general syllabus for English, Mathematics and General Studies as the pupils are expected to be proficient at a certain level before they can move up to the next class. Classroom organization is informal and teaching takes a different form from that in the senior classroom and, as there are no immediate academic goals or pressures, can be haphazard and undirected at times. Pupil behaviour is often disruptive and the teachers are constantly appealing to them for order.

This kind of teaching may be characterized as 'progressive teaching' inasmuch as the techniques employed are usually 'an informal organization, limited intervention, personal appeal, assessment in relation to past efforts and no formal grouping' (Hammersley, 1977: 39–40). As we have seen, however, the use of positional appeals and authoritative measures to deal with errant pupil behaviour is not completely absent from the classroom.

While the nature of teacher–pupil interaction as it occurs in these two classrooms cannot be viewed as being typical of that which occurs in all classrooms in the school, it illustrates the differences in the relations between teachers and pupils of different ages in the two settings.

Culture Lessons and Discussion and Other Meetings

There is also other teacher–pupil interaction that may occur in the classroom, e.g. during the Culture lessons, or in the staffroom, e.g. during the Discussion and School Council meetings, and other more informal meetings. I will focus primarily on Culture lessons and Discussion meetings as these are prescribed in the curriculum and attendance at them is compulsory for the pupils.

Culture lessons are held weekly in all the classes in the senior school and are conducted usually by the Principal or sometimes by the class teacher (as in Standards Eight and Nine). The purpose of these lessons is to widen the pupils' learning on topics such as religion, philosophy, world events, current affairs, and so on.

Discussions are held weekly in the staffroom between the pupils of Standards 11 and 12 and the Principal, Headmistress, junior school Head and other senior teachers. The content of these Discussion meetings is more or less similar to that of the Culture lessons but the scope for pupil-participation is different. The Culture lesson generally remains another lesson as it occurs in the classroom and teacher–pupil interaction is constricted by the fact that the pupils are interacting with a single teacher. Like any other lesson, the teacher therefore does most of the talking with occasional pupil participation.

At the Discussion meetings, however, the presence of several teachers and the fact that they argue with one another and with the pupils creates a unique situation which is never present in the classroom. Secondly, the staffroom, which is recognized as the teachers' domain, is opened to the pupils and to the extent that this serves to make them feel equal to the teachers, there is intensive and very articulate pupil participation. The Discussion meeting therefore adds a new and important dimension to the pupils' experience of school life.

More informal discussions are occasionally conducted, primarily by the ideologue teachers in an attempt to open communication between the pupils and themselves through the discussion of problems that pupils experience in RVS. These meetings are voluntary but attendance is however low among both teachers and pupils. The professional teachers, who attend these meetings, rarely participate in the discussions which are essentially a dialogue between the ideologue teachers and the pupils.

Teacher–pupil interaction at the Culture lessons varies with the particular teacher who is in the classroom. In the Principal's classes, the pupils tend to participate keenly in the discussion as well as express boredom and apathy. Moreover, the Principal, by virtue of his office is associated with the Management, and thereby, authority, and the pupils apparently like to maintain a distance from authority.

Such lessons, when conducted occasionally by the Headmistress in the Principal's absence from the school, are quite different: she does not brook any nonsense from the pupils who used the lessons I observed for questioning her on the teachers' decisions regarding themselves. She is firm and quick in pointing out the advantages of being in a school like RVS and she also maintains stern order in the classroom. As other teachers rarely adopt this posture with pupils, she immediately has their attention as well as silence in the classroom.

Not all teachers who conduct Culture lessons, however, elicit pupil participation and interest in the subject by resorting to authoritarian action. Thus one teacher had an excellent relationship with the pupils because of his contact with them outside the classroom, primarily on hikes, and the informality between them did not interfere with the lessons conducted by him.

There is a difference in the way an ideologue and a professional teacher may discuss the same issue with the pupils in terms of the ideology which takes a definite stand on particular issues. The ideologue teacher generally handles the discussion keeping in mind the ideology which she tries to convey to the pupils. For example: in one Culture lesson, such a teacher read out a poem on war and a discussion on the causes and consequences of war followed. Concepts such as revolution and violence were avidly discussed. He closed the discussion by pointing out, as Krishnamurti does, that the concept of non-violence is no different from that of violence, perhaps, in another form. The professional teacher on the other hand, may bypass the ideology and not go into any depth in the discussion of the problem. For example, on one occasion a pupil narrated an incident in which Krishnamurti, whilst travelling in a 'posh' car, had observed villagers standing and staring at the car and had commented, 'Why don't they throw stones at us?' The pupil was suggesting that Krishnamurti approved of violent methods to exhibit one's feelings or as a sign of protest. The professional teacher, who appeared not to be particularly attentive, agreed and added that for some people 'violence is the only alternative'.

This contrary approach may create a conflict in the minds of the pupils who would be confused in their understanding of the ideology. I am concerned with the divergent attitudes of teachers insofar as these influence or are influenced by teacher–pupil interaction. Thus, whilst pupil participation and interest varies from teacher to teacher, the purpose of the Culture lessons is gradually eroded by the professional teacher's use of the 'avoidance strategy' out of a lack of interest or a fear of handling the subject inadequately and the Principal's inability to communicate with the pupils, his being an ideologue notwithstanding.

At the Discussion meetings, the content varies from discussion on current affairs, 'right' education, social and psychological problems to the school's ideology. The pupils' knowledge of the ideology is extensive (despite their lack of commitment to it) and they participate keenly in the discussion often quoting Krishnamurti verbatim, for example, in Discussion One below:

Discussion One

The Principal read out an article by a Buddhist monk from a book entitled *The Middle Way* as he had found this particularly interesting and wanted to share it with them. Briefly, the article discussed aspects of Oriental religious thought including Buddhism and their approaches to bringing about a state of 'choiceless awareness'. A pupil pointed out that Krishnamurti also talks about 'choiceless awareness' and that the author of the article, by suggesting 'training' of some sort, makes a contradiction, as there is no 'choice' in 'choiceless awareness'. (Here the pupil was making a direct reference to Krishnamurti's use of the term 'choiceless awareness'.)

Another pupil said that he had taken a course of 'Vipassana' meditation near Bombay (with reference to the training of 'insight') but he 'saw nothing'. The Principal clarified that Vipassana meditation really meant 'insight' and 'understanding' and that there are ways of training which do not necessarily imply choice. He also talked to them about allowing 'space' in their lives, allowing 'choiceless awareness' to embrace everything. A discussion ensued in which the pupils participated with enthusiasm.

At one point when a pupil, in explaining 'choiceless awareness' quoted Krishnamurti almost verbatim, another pupil said, 'That's just quoting

Krishnamurti', and went on to give an alternative explanation which was however similar. Other pupils suggested that the term meant 'the presence of no images', 'being totally alive and alert', 'there being no difference between the observer and the observed', and so on. The discussion ended with the Principal asking the pupils to think about the impact of 'choiceless awareness' on themselves.

At these meetings, the Principal may discuss the pupils' school work, their contributions to the Democracy Board, the pros and cons of going abroad for further study, contributions that they can make to RVS after they leave school, and so on. Such discussions are clearly used by the Management and some teachers as a forum to put across the ideology to the pupils. This may be done in abstract, philosophical terms (as was attempted by the Principal in Discussion One) or by relating it to the pupils' lives.

These meetings also illustrate the openness of communication between teachers and pupils as the pupils are not constrained by the presence either of the Management or their peers. They are also aware that this is perhaps the only opportunity they have of expressing their opinions to the teachers particularly on issues which appear to be of considerable importance to them. One such issue was *their perception* of the general lack of communication between the teachers and themselves on which they incessantly questioned the Principal at one meeting.

Discussion Two

The Principal first told the pupils in no uncertain terms that they could not miss this 'class' because it was like any other class on their timetable unless they had prior permission from him which he may or may not grant. Next, he expressed his appreciation of the photographs and captions on the Democracy Board entitled 'Misery within a Mile' put up by the pupils after a recent visit to Thettu village. One boy, however, doubted whether the photographs had created an 'awareness' among the pupils, saying 'most of us are too concerned with self-centred activity'. The Principal asked them to give their extra shirts to the school which could then be given to the villagers. He also suggested that the school could perhaps help the village. A boy disagreed saying that this was 'charity' and that the problem was one of creating an awareness of the magnitude of the problem which the school was failing to do. The Principal countered this statement by saying that the school could only help the pupils to understand and that the rest was up to them.

The discussion moved on to the possible causes of the lack of 'awareness'. One pupil suggested 'insensitivity' as one reason. Another boy identified 'insensitivity' as implying a lack of 'relationship' between themselves. The Principal questioned this, but the pupil insisted, 'I am telling you, there is no relationship', speaking directly to the Principal. The latter asked the pupils why they felt there was no relationship. He asked whether 'insensitivity' came about because 'we don't respect each other or care for each other'. He further questioned the pupils, 'Do you have a relationship with Krishnaji?' One boy answered, 'Never', while the others were silent. The Principal said that Krishnamurti had something 'vital' to communicate and, although it may not be possible to have a personal relationship with him, because he was a busy person, one has a relationship with him in listening to what he has to say. The pupils remained silent until a boy directly questioned the Principal. 'What are you doing to bring about the awareness?' He replied, 'By talking to you', adding that if the pupil was sensitive, it would come about.

The Principal then told the pupils that Krishnamurti has said that 'nothing' is happening here, asking, 'Where is the new mind?' and his response to Krishnamurti had been, 'I can't do it'. He said, however, that he was doing his best and that Krishnamurti came and spoke to the pupils each year and it was up to them to imbibe what they could or wanted to from the school. Moreover, 'the school can't give you everything. It can only help you'. He compared RVS to other schools saying that here at least there was some form of relationship.

A pupil, however, asserted that there was no point in comparing RVS to other schools. This school, in his opinion, is meant to be different and, recognizing that, was there any relationship at all? The Principal said that he found it 'difficult to swallow' that there was no relationship at all. Although he did not think it was necessary to be related to everyone, he 'promised', on behalf of all the teachers present at the meeting, that they would be open to pupils, welcome confidences, spend time with them and help them. The Principal was pleading with the pupils in utmost despair at the situation as perceived by them. It also seemed as if, in being confronted with the pupils' judgements of his own performance, he was somewhat shaken and anxious to make amends.

The meeting continued into the next lesson and this was the only discussion that lasted for 80 instead of the usual 40 minutes. The Principal also told the pupils that they should see for themselves whether there really was no relationship and not be swayed by 'propagandists' who say several things about RVS. He told them that one of the main criticisms of RVS has been that the 'structure' was all wrong. He was willing to change the structure in whatever way it was possible if that would help. The 'attitude' of pupils, he said, would also have to change.

He had been told by several people, he said, that the school had failed. But he felt that he could not pass judgement on the pupils who had left RVS. They appeared to be doing well professionally but were perhaps 'self-centred'. He could not however judge their lives. He asked the pupils if, after having listened to Krishnamurti for so many years, they could hold the teachings as something 'precious' within themselves and let them grow in future years. He did not receive an answer. He closed the discussion saying 'ultimately we all want freedom but are limiting ourselves. The point is, can we be free?'

This meeting is of particular importance as it brings out Krishnamurti's role in school processes. It took place after his annual visit to RVS when he had instructed the pupils to question the teachers and demand from them what they felt they were not getting from the school, thereby altering the content of interaction at this meeting where the pupils pursued such questions. It is significant that these questions were posed by the pupils at two meetings, both held after Krishnamurti's visit. The extent to which such interaction results in changing the existing situation is difficult to assess but it does serve to act as an initiator for possible change. Moreover such interaction, occurring regularly, appears to be worthwhile to the pupils as it enables them to air their views thereby allowing them a share in school processes other than merely being 'clients' in a system.

A more organized form of pupil participation in discussion of school processes is that which occurs at the School Council meetings. These take place twice or thrice a term and are attended by both teachers and pupils. The teachers represent various areas in the school, such as sport, music, the houses; pupils' representatives from all the classes in the senior school are present, that is, four pupils from Standard 12, three from Standard 11, and two each from the remaining classes. The Headmistress and junior school Head are also present and the meeting is conducted by the Principal. The General Secretary of the Council is a pupil from Standard 12 who presents the agenda (drawn up by the pupils) to the Principal. At such meetings, several aspects of school life are discussed, particularly those areas where the pupils encounter problems on which they would like their opinions to be noted.

The senior pupils, who do most of the talking, appear to be very sensitive and sympathetic to the Management's point of view particularly in matters of pupil indiscipline. They are, however, firm on their stand rejecting the imposition of any form of punishment and refuse to participate in taking any punitive action, for instance, by assuming the role of prefects which they view as unpleasant.

All the meetings discussed here indicate the extent of pupil participation in school processes as well as the teacher's role in seeking and encouraging such participation to a certain extent. The Management appear to reject pupil participation when it goes against the school's image as was the case in Discussion Two. Then, pupil participation seems to acquire a negative content insofar as it is seen as being a threat to, and wrongly exposing, school processes.

Ideologue teachers in RVS organize discussions of a more informal nature which, however, do not occur regularly because of the lack of pupil motivation or sustained interest as they themselves point out. The intention of these meetings was not very clear except to enable the pupils to discuss their problems with teachers. The pupils sometimes take advantage of these meetings to complain against other teachers who they feel are not dealing with their problems in an appropriate manner as in Discussion Three below:

Discussion Three

The meeting started by a teacher asking the pupils what they felt the intention of RVS was apart from teaching and learning. *A boy*: 'Behaviour and the ability to face life'. *A girl*: 'How to live together as boys and girls as this is a co-educational school'. She added that she would like to discuss this aspect of school life with the teachers. All the pupils agreed that there was something wrong in the relationship between boys and girls primarily because the teachers objected to the girls being friendly with the boys. The girl who had brought up the subject gave an example of how she had been talking to one boy for four days and had been observed in conversation with him by a teacher. The same evening, her housemother, 'in front of the whole house', talked to her about it telling her not to do this kind of thing. The boys suggested that the women teachers seemed to raise more objections than the men teachers. The girls agreed and said that while the teachers kept telling them to have a 'healthy' relationship with the boys, and interact more with them, they would also check them or 'lecture' them for doing so. The pupils asserted that amongst teachers themselves a healthy relationship did not exist across the sexes and one of them asked, 'Why do they criticize us when they themselves don't have proper relationships?' A teacher told them that this was done partly out of 'care' because they were the teachers' 'responsibility', and if a relationship between a boy and a girl 'went to an extreme', the teachers would be answerable to the parents. The pupils agreed, and a girl said that their parents would also probably not want them to mix freely with the boys.

Coming to the problem as it existed in relation to one another, one girl said that although she might want to have a relationship with a boy, he would keep rebuffing her. Another girl said that a boy had told her that they like saying 'No' to girls who say 'Yes'.

The teacher told them that this was a form of covering up one's liking for the other and, therefore, boys and girls were avoiding each other. Another teacher intervened saying that it was not a case of specific relationships but that the interaction did not occur in groups either. The first teacher clarified his position saying he was not asking the pupils to 'start holding hands or kissing' but that boys should be with girls as they are with boys and *vice-versa*. The pupils, however, said that they felt more 'free' if they were in the same sex group than when members of the opposite sex were present. When asked why this was so, they blamed the teachers and the teasing and gossip by their peers in the hostels. A girl said that she was afraid of what kind of report her housemother might put on the report-card at the end of the term. Another girl said that she wanted to give a 'good impression' of herself to the teachers.

The teachers asked them to look within, at themselves, to find out the right relationships. The pupils said that they saw that there was nothing wrong in relating to one another but were still limiting themselves. A teacher told them that ultimately, it all boiled down to the essential fact of 'fear', and if they really saw that, they would act from that perception. The pupils agreed but did not quite know how to cope with the 'fear'. The teachers then tried to examine the causes of their fears with them.

At another meeting, pupils of Standard Eight frankly talked about their inability to stop comparing their work with each other and their tendency to cheat at tests in order to score higher grades. Such meetings suggest the nature of the trust the pupils place in the ideologue teachers in discussing their problems with them. This is related to the image such teachers have among pupils of being sincere people who are questioning school processes and attempting to rectify things because of their commitment to the ideology.

These meetings, however, did not take place very often and soon petered out altogether. The difficulties ideologue teachers face in the school are manifold as has been discussed elsewhere (in Chapters Five and Six). It is apparent that they are unable to effectively function unless they have the support of both their colleagues and the Management and the necessary authority that goes with such support. The other teachers' latent condemnation of these meetings was exhibited at one meeting when a teacher barged in and asked for two girls attending the meeting to come out as they had held up the Drama class for half an hour. She told the girls, 'Before you go on to higher things, learn some basic issues like good manners', and led them out of the staffroom. She however later came back and apologized to one of the teachers at the meeting. Her action had its repercussions on the pupils as they received a reprimand from the Headmistress to whom the matter had been reported. The point is that such incidents might have played a role in restricting pupil attendance at these meetings. As long as such meetings lasted, however, the pupils had a forum for discussion on matters which they chose not to discuss with other teachers, for example, at the Culture lessons or in the classroom otherwise.

The House and other Informal Settings

Apart from teacher–pupil interaction in formal settings, there are the more informal settings such as the house, the dining hall and the outdoor. The house in RVS is an effort to re-create a substitute home for the pupil and the teacher is a parent-surrogate which is recognized, for instance, in the use of the term 'houseparent'. The relatively small number of pupils (about 25) in the care of a housemother, or a housemaster, who look after girls and boys respectively, is an effort by the Management to enable more communicative teacher–pupil interaction.

The nature of such interaction in the house is however dependent on three important factors: the sex and age-composition of pupils in each house and the kind of house it is. It is thus apparent that there is a difference in the nature of teacher–pupil interaction as it occurs in the junior and the senior houses. In the very junior houses, the pupils are dependent on the housemother, constantly looking up to her for guidance, support and intervention in their relations with one another. Older pupils have less to do with their houseparent which could be due to the pupils' preoccupation with school work and their desire to be independent of teachers in general.

Teacher–pupil interaction in the house occurs primarily in the course of certain events or situations and in the discussion of particular issues related to the house in general or to particular pupils. The teachers themselves suggest that they spend a lot of time in the house 'nagging' the pupils to perform their 'duties'[17] or maintain order during the afternoon rest-hour. They have thus evolved different strategies for coping with this problem of constantly having to tell the pupils to do one thing or another. That this is a conscious effort is indicated by the remarks made by a housemaster of senior boys: that instead of becoming 'neurotic' as a result of the constant 'nagging' they indulge in, the teachers should 'devise intelligent ways of getting things done'.

In each house, there is thus the system of nominating 'house captains' from among the pupils. The method of appointing house captains varies from house to house depending on the instructions of the houseparent. In the most junior house, the housemother appoints the captains for a period of two or three weeks. That no authority, privilege or status is attached to such positions is in accordance with the ideology and other pupils are free to report an aggressive or domineering captain to the houseparent. The house captains are there mainly to help the teacher in her task of persuading, cajoling and goading the pupils which remains the principal way of getting work done in the house.

Another method used by some teachers is to deny some form of activity to the pupils if they are noisy in the rest-hour. Thus, some houseparents stopped the offending pupils from attending the afternoon lessons until they discovered that the pupils were purposely noisy in order to escape them. In some junior houses, the noisy pupils were segregated in the common room or not given any books to read during the rest-hour. In one junior house, I heard two boys pleading with the housemother not to send them into the common room, begging to be allowed to talk in whispers, and when refused permission, fall silent completely. Thus negotiative activity does not always pay off as the teachers found out when they asked pupils to stay back from afternoon lessons, or when the pupils fail to achieve their goals. It remains, however, a central feature of teacher–pupil interaction in the house inasmuch as relations between the teacher and the pupil are characterized by constant bargaining, on the teacher's part, usually, for order and conformity, and on the pupil's part, for more leeway in yielding to their efforts.

Another form of negotiation is when the pupils themselves impose regulations on their conduct, seeking to fulfil the teacher's goals insofar as these are related to their own objectives. For example, in one house, when the pupils observed that a few girls avoided

morning PT by staying in bed, they formulated a rule that whoever
missed PT would have to miss 'school' as well. As no pupil relishes
the thought of staying in the house during the morning lessons, this
rule ensured full attendance at PT. In this case, the imposition of
rules on their conduct was not out of any sense of moral obligation,
on the part of the pupils, to adhere to the school routine but because
they did not like to see some pupils gain from the lack of formal
rules. Thus, in order to attain their goal of complete pupil
conformity, they aided the teacher in accomplishing her task of
ensuring pupil attendance at PT.

Organized teacher–pupil interaction in the house occurs when the
houseparent meets the whole house to discuss problems such as
whether the house captains are adequately performing their role,
and attending to house problems, or pupils' behaviour and their
sartorial sense in general.

In the senior boys' houses, the nature of the problems discussed
are somewhat different. Oe housemaster specified that at the 'informal' discussions in the house, apart from house problems, teachers
and pupils discuss matters such as 'punctuality, tidiness, manners
and language'. The use of offensive language by the senior boys is a
problem particularly discussed with them by their housemasters who
are of the opinion that 'threatening' and 'shouting' at the boys does
not help in solving the problem. They therefore use the strategy of
'talking' with them, trying to modify their behaviour through
discussion. In 'extreme' cases (specified as being 'continuous
bullying, disobedience or insolence') the pupils are suspended from
attending classes for two or three days. It is maintained, by
the teachers, that there is no compulsion for the pupils to attend
classes. In practice, they are generally expected to do so. An
explicit curtailment of their freedom, therefore, act as a form of
punishment and succeeds in at least temporarily changing their
behaviour.

The methods of dealing with the two most difficult problems
encountered by the senior boys' houses differs from teacher to
teacher. For example, smoking is strictly not allowed in RVS. Some
senior boys, however, do smoke in the house. An ideologue teacher
said that he did not do anything about this unless he found that a
particular pupil was becoming addicted to it. Then, he would talk to
the boy explaining the harmful effects of smoking. These boys are
also dealt with by issuing 'heavy threats' to them, implying either

parental intervention or expulsion from the school. Pupils, however, tend not to take such threats seriously and their behaviour is, therefore, not affected by them. Another senior housemaster preferred to ignore the fact that some boys smoke in the house saying that they only do so in the surrounding countryside.

Another problem encountered by teachers in the senior boys' houses is that of the circulation of pornographic literature. Only one housemaster acknowledged the problem and said that he dealt with it by destroying the literature whenever he came across it. Some other teachers attempted to talk about it at the assembly with the senior pupils but were not encouraged by the Management who felt it was not the right forum for this kind of discussion.

Both these problems were brought to my notice by the pupils themselves some of whom appeared to suggest the teachers' apathy in dealing with them. This is borne out by the fact that the housemasters usually ignored a problem which may have served to accentuate it. The failure to have a policy on how to deal with such issues is perhaps illustrative of the school's inability to accept deviance in any form, thereby either ignoring or suppressing it as and when it occurs.

In the senior girls' houses, the main problem is that of emotional relationships between girls and boys. A girl rarely, however, raises the issue and it is only on the housemother's observation of a particular situation that the problem is discussed individually. The housemother thus 'takes action' when she repeatedly observes a girl becoming 'too friendly' with a particular boy. In these houses, therefore, the housemother has a difficult role to perform which is not always appreciated by the pupils.

One particular problem that pupils appear to discuss with their houseparents, whether they are in the junior or senior houses, is that of their unhappy relations with their parents. They often complain of the lack of care or attention at home, strict parental surveillance, or discord between their parents as being the cause of their own unhappiness. Many pupils also talk to the teachers about their academic problems: for example, their inability to cope with a particular subject or teacher. A third problem, common to all houses, is the bullying or teasing the pupils experience.

Many houseparents feel that the pupils experience a sense of release in merely sharing their problems with another person and soon forget all about them. They also talk to the pupils and help them to view the problem in the right perspective. Thus, going beyond negotiation over appropriate behaviour, teacher–pupil interaction in the house is also characterized by the teacher's sharing some of the pupils' most personal problems and helping in their resolution. This close relationship enters classroom relations between teachers and pupils thus helping them to be based on informality and a certain freedom limited however by the particular context in which it occurs.

Teacher evaluation of pupil behaviour in the house is not based on an arbitrary judgement but has its roots in the situation itself.[18] The attributes that are used to define pupil conduct are qualities that describe interaction and sociability rather than individual ability. These criteria are obviously dependent on the situation of living together in contrast to the classroom where the pedagogic situation dominates teacher evaluation. Stereotypes in terms of which teachers judge pupil behaviour in the house are the extent to which a pupil is 'well-behaved, friendly, cheerful, affectionate, co-operative and gets on well with the others'. Such attributes are considered essential for living together amicably. A pupil who is considered 'short-tempered' is therefore in need of rectifying his attitude in the house. Similarly, a pupil who is 'orderly, neat and tidy, punctual, interested in house activities, responsible and volunteers to do things' is appreciated. On the other hand, teachers are critical of those pupils who lack these qualities. A pupil's 'emotional balance and poise' are criteria that convey the teacher's concern with his emotional adjustment to school life, peers, teachers and the home.

The houseparents' (i.e. 16 out of 36 teachers) views on their relations with the pupils indicate that they have a friendly and cordial relationship, based on affection and understanding, with the pupils in their house. An element of authority however enters their relationship when they are firm in their handling of a particular situation. In defining his relationship with the boys, a senior housemaster (an ideologue) said that the 'function' of a housemaster in RVS is different from that in other schools. It is a 'difficult function' to perform as the housemaster has no formal authority attached to his role. The senior pupils are aware of the situation and the difficulty arises when the housemaster does not want to 'create a strain' in his otherwise good relationship with them. Thus, it is 'difficult to stay with them, and yet stay away from them' as pupils tend to have their own way when they think a teacher is too lenient.

The function of a housemaster is two-fold insofar as his relationship with the pupils is concerned: 'to be firm, mean business and yet, maintain a close relationship'.

Another housemaster identified the dual nature of his task in terms of his perception of the pupils' evaluation of his role. Thus, in his opinion, the pupils attach the two labels of 'strict and authoritarian', and 'kind, affectionate and generous', to him according to their 'mood' and his 'position' in a particular situation. It would then seem that both from the teacher's and the pupil's points of view, the houseparent's role is viewed as one that has elements of both freedom and authoritarianism. Most teachers appear to perform this role without any manifest conflict accepting the dichotomous nature of the role.

Only one teacher (an ideologue) expressed some 'dissatisfaction' with her role performance. She felt that she had succeeded in looking after the pupils physically but she was not so sure about her performance at the 'mental level'. She felt that even if she did not mention Krishnamurti, the pupils were aware she was talking 'philosophy and all that'. They were therefore willing to examine a problem only from an 'external', practical level but refused to look at it 'from within'. Her inability to communicate with the pupils at a 'deeper level' indicated, to her mind, a failure in performance.

It is therefore not surprising that most pupils do not view their relationship with their houseparents as being particularly close. While they have an informal and friendly relationship with the teachers, they feel they are unable to have a more meaningful or intimate association with them. The ideologue teachers are particularly concerned about the need to establish a 'close' relationship with them. Most of the houseparents, however, do not view their relations with pupils at any stage as being closed in terms of communication or lacking in depth. The nature of the personal problems discussed by the pupils with their houseparents also suggests a level of communication that arises out of freedom in relationship unaffected by the teacher's authoritarian role in the house.

The pupils' evaluation of their relationship with teachers is perhaps due to their own preoccupation with school work which inhibits sustained interaction of a more meaningful nature. The significance of the pupils' perception lies in the implications it has for school processes in terms of the ideology. The ideology's expectations of the teacher–pupil relationship suggest deeper relations based on affection and understanding which are seen as aiding not only the learning process but also their mutual understanding of the ideology in relation to their lives in the school. To the extent that such a relationship is not perceived or experienced by the pupils, it suggests the possibility that the ideology has not acquired a significant meaning in their lives insofar as understanding it is partly dependent on their relations with the teachers.

This kind of an ideal relationship, in terms of the ideology, has been established in one of the two newer houses with a view to enabling closer contact between the houseparent and the pupils. In this house, the relationship between the housemaster and the boys in his care may be summed up in the words of one of them as being 'not that of teacher and student'. This housemaster himself defines his relationship with the pupils in terms of 'friendship' and 'respect'. The first implies a 'certain quality of trust and sharing', the second a respect for 'individual dignity'. Moreover, he feels he is able to communicate individually with each pupil aided by his earlier relationship with four (of the seven) pupils who had been in his care at another KFI school for five years.

All the pupils in this house are very close to the teacher and exhibit a complete freedom in discussion and a friendship that extends beyond conventional teacher–pupil relations. They not only discuss their personal problems with him but also talk over more general issues usually related to the ideology and their relationships with one another. At these discussions, which may arise spontaneously, the housemaster helps the pupils to explore the problems from every possible angle continuously pointing out various alternative ways of acting. For example, on one occasion, the teacher said that for himself he required 'space' and that he was put off by the frivolous atmosphere in the house and in the school. He asked the pupils to investigate whether he was a 'crank' in pointing this out to them or whether there was something 'degenerate' about their continuous laughter. One boy agreed with him and another questioned him on the inability of the mind to be attentive. A discussion ensued on the quality of the attentive mind, the difference between 'concentration' and 'attention', and so on. The teacher had thus succeeded in getting the pupils to question their behaviour themselves and, going beyond this, to explore the nature of the mental processes that affect behaviour.

As there is vertical age-grouping of pupils in this house they experienced some problems in relating to one another.[19] They were all of the opinion, however, that the housemaster played a positive role in helping them in this regard by asking them to examine their behaviour, and change it accordingly, without condemning them. The pupils also enjoyed being in a small group as it enabled them to get 'more affection and attention' from the teacher. Moreover, the senior boys in this house felt that it was their relationship with this teacher more than the school or any other factor that had 'made all the difference' and had altered their perception of life.

These pupils were really suggesting that their relationship with their housemaster had facilitated their understanding of the ideology thereby altering their values and attitudes towards their relationships with others, their academic life and the future as they envisaged it. Apart from the changes they perceived in their external life, they had also begun to inquire into their own behaviour, reactions and feelings. They felt that all this had taken place as a result of their continuous contact with their housemaster. This example is important as it illustrates the meaning that such relationships can acquire in the lives of the pupils who explain their experience of school in terms of their interaction with a particular teacher.

Pupils also interact with other teachers (non-houseparents) who visit the houses (particularly the junior houses) twice or thrice a week 'to keep the lines of communication open', as one such teacher put it. These teachers usually talk to the pupils telling them stories or 'incidents' of interest to them, teach music, or watch impromptu performances. One teacher has thus acquired the reputation of holding regular 'gab sessions' (story-telling sessions) with the pupils who eagerly look forward to the fund of 'gabs' that such visits entail. Such meetings are however uncommon in the senior houses as the pupils seem to spend a lot of time in the house over prep. or preparing for examinations.

Moving away from the settings of the house and the dining hall, there is a great deal of informal teacher–pupil interaction that takes place outdoors, that is, on the sportsfield and during hikes. Teachers supervise the pupils at sport every evening for about an hour and their participation in the game is more evident amongst the men teachers who join pupils, the most enthusiastic participation being in soccer.

During the annual Sports Day, the pupils have a special event for the teachers. In 1981, a senior boy sat atop a tree and lowered a pot containing a surprise gift. The teachers were blindfolded and tried, in turn, to break the pot with a pole. The pupils had tremendous fun as they swung the pot and made the teachers run around for several minutes, particularly those teachers who appeared to be unpopular with them. They had obviously decided which teachers were to be allowed to break the pot and many teachers were asked to join in without their having a chance of winning the game. The last event on Sports Day is the game of tug-of-war between teachers and pupils which always arouses much enthusiasm. At the sports events, the teachers interact, in general, with all pupils, but their attention is particularly directed to the ISC class obviously because of the pupils' impending departure from RVS. This is, however, never explicitly expressed· by teachers or pupils.

The freedom in the teacher–pupil relationship exhibited on the sportsfield is even more apparent during hikes and treks: they are friends walking together rather than a teacher escorting pupils on a routine exercise. This is not to say that the teacher is not responsible for the pupils' safety and well-being but the reprimands do not interfere with the general *bonhomie* that prevails. Professional teachers however appear to be more preoccupied with the rules governing an event, sticking close to their teacher role.

Pupil and Teacher Views

In the classroom, teachers and pupils engage in the construction of a special world with the lesson as its axis. Their images of one another emerge through and shape the interaction. Similar images emerge likewise in the house and outdoors in terms of the shared experience of collective living. The house and other settings are therefore as important as the classroom in the construction of the school as a socio-cultural system. Although the activities may be different, the same processes of defining the self and the other in terms of the patterns of interaction are in operation. It is therefore important to consider the participants' views on the form and content of this interaction.

Pupil and teacher views on their interaction tend to be ambivalent. Among the pupils, their views in the senior school vary on account of differences in their perception of their relations with different teachers. There are three broad areas within which pupils are consciously aware of their relations with teachers: in relation to themselves, the classroom and school work, and to the school's ideology, their perceptions emerging, however, from their overall view of teacher–pupil interaction.

They describe their friendly relations with teachers in terms of the kind of relationship that exists between friends and in terms of family relationships. Teacher–pupil interaction is thus likened to other intimate relationships that they experience and can be easily identified by them in terms of affection and informality as well as the element of discipline that is an integral part of parent–child relations. The extent to which the pupils can have a close relationship with teachers is dependent, in their opinion, on the extent to which they feel they can confide in them and receive satisfactory understanding of their problems and guidance. This in turn is dependent on appropriate teacher behaviour that is able to elicit the pupils' confidences. However, while they appreciate teacher concern for their well-being, some pupils resent an excessive involvement in pupil affairs as interference.

Friendly and close teacher–pupil interaction is particularly valued by those pupils who have not experienced such a relationship in previous schools where they were not so 'free' with the teachers as to address them by their first names or communicate so openly with them. However, those pupils who have spent a long time in the school view the interaction in terms of their current experience.

Pupil orientations also consider interaction with teachers in terms of relations with men and with women teachers. Thus some boys find that they are able to relate better to the younger men, although they respect the older teachers. Similarly, some girls feel their relations with women teachers are better than those with men teachers. This inability to interact with teachers of the opposite sex is not experienced by junior pupils. In the senior school, the ethos regarding interaction across the sexes, whether among pupils or between teachers and pupils, is such that it inhibits close interaction.

Pupil experience of the negative aspects of teacher–pupil interaction is primarily in relation to those teachers who keep the pupils at a distance. Such teachers are viewed as being 'aloof and formidable' and 'arrogant' and 'stand-offish' in their attitude towards pupils who are inhibited in sharing confidences with them. Intimate communication with the teachers is thus central to the pupils' experience of what they consider good teacher–pupil interaction.

In relation to themselves, teacher behaviour is also examined by the pupils in terms of the methods of control used by teachers. They are thus put off and 'discouraged' by teachers who 'insult' them publicly, or 'scold' them unnecessarily, especially when the reprimand takes the form of sarcasm. They are also critical of teachers who 'shout' at them. Such teacher behaviour is viewed as a hindrance to close interaction and results in creating 'fear' and a distance between teachers and pupils.

It is significant that while pupil views reject the authoritarian element in the teacher's role in relation to themselves, it is accepted as being integral to interaction in the classroom. Pupils thus point out that while they have friendly relations with the teachers outside, they have a different kind of relationship inside the classroom. It is described as being 'more formal' inasmuch as they 'treat the teacher as a teacher'. An element of deference thus enters the pupils' attitude towards the teacher in the formal setting of the classroom. They tend to approve of the dual nature of their interaction with teachers indicating that the formality evident in the classroom is 'right' and proper. Their approval is apparently based on their perception of the teacher's role in terms of the superior status they attach to the teaching function as such. On the teachers' part, the pupils perceive that they are usually 'serious' in the classroom although they may have an 'intimate' relationship with the pupils outside.

In relation to school work, the pupils expect teachers to 'help' them and value interaction with those who are always willing to do so. On their part, they feel that a more personal or 'intimate' relationship exists if they are 'good' or 'regular' in school work. It is their view that teachers appreciate consistency and seriousness in the pupils' attitude in this regard and hold them in 'high esteem' on account of it. While this is the pupils' construction of the situation, it is also evident in teacher expectations of pupil attitudes to school work.

Teacher behaviour with respect to fairness in terms of treating all pupils alike is also an important factor influencing teacher–pupil interaction. Pupils resent the teachers' 'partiality' towards particular pupils and feel this ought not to exist in a KFI school. Their views also suggest that the teachers tend to have a 'biased outlook' insofar as they form a 'bad impression' of a pupil which persists over a period of time and affects the nature of interaction. Thus some pupils deem it imperative to remain in the 'good books' of the teachers while others suggest that their good relationship is based on the fact that they would never offend the teachers, always behaving in the manner expected of them. Some other pupils however often have 'tiffs' and 'quarrels' with the teachers. They nonetheless seek to maintain the relationship by clearing up the 'misunderstanding' or apologizing to the teachers. Pupils thus adapt to a situation by either conforming to teacher expectations or making up for their own errant behaviour and the interaction rarely leads to a situation of open conflict.

The area where the pupils are most critical of teacher behaviour is in relation to the ideology. Pupils dislike and are 'scared' of teachers who are 'hypocrites' and are, at the same time, running the school. This hypocrisy is defined primarily in relation to either Krishnamurti or the ideology. Thus, teachers who 'preach something, listen to Krishnamurti and behave in another fashion which is the complete opposite' are disliked as are teachers who simulate an interest in Krishnamurti.[20] The pupils' perception of a lack of genuine interest or commitment to the ideology in the teachers who feign an apparent interest, and their negative attitude towards such teachers indicates their expectation that the ideology should be related to the actual behaviour of the teachers and their ability to discriminate between teachers on that ground. The pupils also disapprove of teachers who talk in derogatory terms about other teachers or members of the Management with the pupils.

Pupil criticism of teacher behaviour highlights the strains and tensions inherent in interaction processes. Nonetheless, pupils also perceive the more positive aspect of their relations with teachers. Pupil orientations also indicate that they expect a more personal and less formal relationship in terms of communication at a personal level. They seek a change in the teachers' methods of establishing control and their attitudes towards pupils although they do not state the preferred qualities. Their comment on teacher behaviour in relation to the ideology indicates their expectations of teacher behaviour in accordance with the school's official value system. Finally, in pointing out the extent to which teacher behaviour does not meet their expectations, the pupils are putting forth *their* view of the constraints on teacher–pupil interaction. This is not to say that appropriate teacher behaviour would lead to improved teacher–pupil interaction, as the pupils view it, for teachers have *their* view of the situation.[21]

If pupil views are ambivalent suggesting both cordiality and hostility in teacher–pupil interaction, teacher views express a similar attitude. This ambivalence essentially arises from the conflicting nature of teacher expectations and their actual experience of interaction with pupils. The nature of teacher perspectives are also influenced by the extent to which subjective criteria are present in their evaluation of pupil conduct or performance depending on the situation or setting. It is however important to bear in mind that the teachers may have been more cautious than pupils in expressing their views of the interaction.

Most teachers underscore the 'cordial' and 'friendly' nature of their relations with pupils in terms of the fairly good relations and 'mutual affection' that prevail between them. An ideologue teacher, in particular, considers it a 'pleasure' to work with the pupils: to 'teach' and to 'talk' with them. The authoritarian element in the teacher's role is, however, evident when some teachers say that, although they are friendly with the pupils, they are also firm and take 'no nonsense' from them. This is particularly in relation to the classroom situation where teachers attempt to establish control so as to get on with the task of teaching. This is one reason for the teacher's experience of a 'formal relationship' with the pupils in the classroom as compared to the informality that prevails in relations outside.

The variation in interaction in different settings is particularly evident in the classroom and the house. Thus the housemaster of one of the two 'special' houses in RVS feels that although he has a 'very deep relationship' with the boys in his house, he is unable to establish such a relationship in the classroom. Although the pupils in the classroom may be 'fond' of him, they do not 'care' enough to give up their 'idiotic impulses' such as the desire to talk or act in what he considers a 'silly' manner. On the other hand, a housemother is of the opinion that her outside relationship enters the classroom situation and is, in fact, beneficial in establishing an informal relationship inasmuch as pupils feel 'free' and 'fearless' and yet understand their responsibilities.

In his relations with pupils in the classroom, the housemaster (an ideologue teacher) is therefore seeking a 'deep' relationship of the kind he has with the pupils in his house. His inability to establish it leads to his unsatisfactory view of interaction in the classroom. The housemother (a professional teacher) interacts with the pupils in the house and in the classroom in a similar manner and is therefore satisfied with the nature of interaction. It is possible that teacher expectations differ due to variations in the kind of teachers they are, i.e. whether ideologues or professionals. The ideologue gets to know the pupil as a person in terms of the ideology whereas the professional teacher has her own standards in this regard.

Ambivalence in teacher views is also apparent in their perception of pupil conduct towards them. Thus, an ideologue teacher is unable to 'judge' her interaction with the pupils because of their 'irrational' behaviour towards her. Her firmness elicits an aloofness and distance from them but they are friendly when they require her assistance. The pupils' conflicting attitude therefore confuses her perception and creates an uncertainty in her relations with them.

Interaction between teachers and pupils across the two sections of RVS is limited primarily due to the lack of contact and the tightly structured school routine which does not leave much time for casual interaction. This appears to be particularly common among junior school teachers and senior pupils. A very young teacher in the junior school was thus unable to relate to pupils in the senior school although she had a 'close' relationship with junior pupils.

Teacher assessment of pupil conduct and performance in school work, examinations, and otherwise inevitably affects teacher–pupil interaction. There are two processes through which teachers evaluate pupils that are formulated on the basis of different sets of criteria. The teachers make a standardized formal assessment of senior pupils in terms of their performance at tests and class work in the reports that are sent to parents at the end of each term. Such an evaluation derives from what are considered certain 'objective' criteria of assessment. The teachers also evaluate pupils in other terms such as their behaviour, interest in the ideology, anxieties and problems, and so on. These are more obviously based on the 'subjective' criteria of evaluation. I would however like to argue that both the formal and informal evaluation of pupils take place essentially on a subjective dimension.

The following analysis is based on the reports prepared for 21 pupils in Standard 10 'B' by nine teachers in different subjects.

These reports indicate the formal categorization and evaluation of pupil performance. These stereotypes or typifications then become labels, in a sense, which are attached to particular pupils who are then identified and discussed by the teachers in terms of them. The following teacher typifications indicate the teacher's approval and disapproval of different aspects of pupil performance. Woods, following Hargreaves (1967), suggests that 'teachers rate pupils according to their conformity to their instructional and disciplinary expectations' (1979: 173). Thus, if a pupil fits the teacher's definition of expected pupil behaviour and performance in the classroom, he is viewed as being 'hardworking', 'conscientious' or 'bright', but if he fails to meet teacher expectations, he is seen as being 'lazy and indifferent' or 'not responding adequately' (see Table 8.1). Subjectivity is inherent in the teachers' views inasmuch as an evaluation of pupil performance *in itself* is not taking place but in terms of *an ideal* set up by the teachers.

The basis for the teachers' comments in reports are the grades obtained by pupils in tests which are an objective assessment of their performance. The subjective element is not however totally absent in teacher views in their selection of a specific vocabulary through which they express the objective assessment. Their views on pupil

TABLE 8.1

Report Categories

Positive evaluation	Negative evaluation
Regular	Lacking concentration
Systematic	Lazy and indifferent
Hardworking	Lacking diligence
Conscientious	Frivolous and playful
Industrious	Takes life easy
Steady	Slow in understanding and solving problems
Brilliant	Hasty and confused
Bright	**Weak in the subject**
Intelligent	Not responding adequately
Aptitude for the subject	
Makes a sincere effort	

Source: Reports prepared for 21 pupils in Std. 10 'B' by 9 teachers in different subjects.

performance are, moreover, limited by the classroom situation and a particular teacher's assessment, so that the same pupil may get divergent reports in different subjects. Thus a pupil may be considered 'conscientious' or 'hardworking' in one subject but 'lazy and indifferent' in another. Or, a pupil may be seen as being consistently good or weak in different subjects, and his effort judged in terms of regularity and steadiness or frivolty and a lackadaisical attitude towards learning. To the extent that most pupils get varying reports from different teachers, the method indicates the selective nature of teacher evaluation inasmuch as they emphasize the dominant characteristic of pupil conduct or performance in the classroom to the exclusion of others. The reports therefore capture segments or aspects of a pupil's personality or performance with very few teachers being able to give a rounded picture of the same.

Apart from teacher typifications of pupil performance, they make recommendations regarding pupil progress and improvement in performance, usually encouraging the pupils towards a better performance. They, however, express an excessive concern with the pupils' performance in the public examination, suggesting that particular pupils may 'even fail' in a particular subject. Their advice for pupil progress is by and large related to the manner in which the pupil can adequately prepare himself for the examination, particularly in the case of Standard 10 pupils.

This aspect of teacher views on pupil performance is obviously deviant from the ideology which emphasizes a different kind of 'learning'. The teachers' comparison of pupils in terms of their performance deviates even more sharply from the ideology. Thus a pupil is often judged in terms of 'being better than any in his peer group' and 'one of the best students in the class'. A particular pupil's progress may also be indicated in terms of an expectation to come up to the 'level' of the rest of class. The teachers thus function in a conventional manner by comparing pupil performance (in their expectations for conformity to an ideal norm) and by their recommendations for pupil progress (in their emphasis on an examination orientation).

A more informal evaluation of pupils is in evidence in the teachers' discussions at staff meetings. They talk about pupils primarily in terms of their academic achievement or their 'sensitivity'. Their concern for pupils is evident in their attempt to help those who are poor, and encourage those who are good, at school work.

Teachers also try to cope with examination tension and fear in the minds of the pupils. The Principal often checks on the performance of particular pupils whose parents specially request him to keep them informed of their progress. Here, the teachers are concerned with pupil performance in the classroom and discuss ways and means by which they can help pupils to achieve the goal of examination success with minimum tension and anxiety.

Subjectivity is also present in the teachers' identification of particular pupils as 'sensitive' depending on their apparent interest in the ideology. It is possible that the pupils' interest may be feigned: a professional teacher suggests that those pupils who show an excessive interest in the ideology are in fact the 'biggest rogues'. He does not therefore favour this mode of categorization of pupils. An ideologue teacher, on the other hand, argues that such pupils ought to be nurtured as a deeper interest may emerge from their pretence. This ambivalence in teacher views is characteristic of the situation inasmuch as differences in commitment to the local order and to the transcendental order as such lead to differing viewpoints.

Such a discrimination between pupils in terms of the teachers' subjective opinions affects the nature of their interaction with them. Some ideologue teachers thus pay more attention to a few select pupils which brings in an element of favouritism in their relations with them. Some professional teachers favour other kinds of pupils: for example, a teacher who was privately antagonistic to the ideology had a coterie of pupils in the house who, encouraged by him, supported his opinions. Similarly, another professional teacher interacted closely with those pupils she considered good at school work, polite, well-behaved and with a good reputation amongst the teachers. These are generally regarded as the criteria for identifying the ideal pupil.

Such teacher–pupil interaction is not appreciated by the rest of the pupil community who tend to label the ideologue teachers' favourites as 'philos', 'junior Jiddus', and those of the professional teachers as '*chamchas*' (stooges). Insofar as such interaction is based on the teachers' views of pupils, it is evident that there is a difference between the two categories of teachers (the professionals and the ideologues) in their views. Whilst one category tends to interact closely with the 'ideal' pupil, based on a subjective categorization in terms of the ideology, the other category either does not discriminate among pupils or interacts closely with some pupils according to *their* characterization of the 'ideal' pupil. This differentiation in the nature of teacher–pupil interaction is, however, not evident in the formal setting of the classroom but takes place primarily in informal settings or in casual interaction. Such interaction also raises the question of the role of the ideology in creating cleavages in teacher–pupil interaction by advocating special care of particular pupils. This by no means implies that professional teachers are free from making subjective categorizations about pupils as we have seen above.

Ambivalence, whether or not acknowledged by the teachers, is central to teacher views which do not precisely define the nature of teacher–pupil interaction. This ambivalence emphasizes the complexity in teacher–pupil relations. Thus, although the teachers are aware of their responsibility and affection towards the pupils, and the informality between them, they are also exasperated by pupil behaviour particularly in the classroom and the house. Ambivalence is also present in individual relations between particular teachers and pupils so that a teacher is uncertain about her relationship with some pupils. Finally, ambivalence is present in teacher evaluation of pupil performance and conduct as a result of the lack of consensus arising from the situation itself.

My analysis of teacher–pupil interaction at RVS suggests that the dominant characteristic of such interaction is informality always bounded, however, by the rules of the different settings. I have also suggested that this informality is present in the school ethos that encourages informal and fearless relations between teachers and pupils.

Such a view of teacher–pupil interaction contradicts the conventional viewpoint which stresses that the relationship is one of 'institutionalised dominance and subordination' (Waller 1965: 195).[22] I have acknowledged the asymmetrical nature of the teacher–pupil relationship both in the learning situation and in the more informal settings of the house and the outdoor. This asymmetry derives from certain aspects of the teacher's role insofar as it contains authoritarian elements which are exercised in every situation depending upon the rules, procedures and conventions of the setting. This does not however suggest undue conflict in the interaction. The pupils' tensions, anxieties and fears were noted in relation to the pressures of tests and examinations and the personalities of particular teachers. No situation ever developed into one of open, uncontrollable conflict to the extent that pupils themselves sought to rectify their 'quarrels' with teachers. I have also discussed the interaction in terms of the various strategies devised and used by teachers and pupils to relate without conflict and to achieve their goals. The use of strategies allows for greater flexibility in the relationship and lends a dynamism to it as it continually changes and develops in different settings. If the discussion of strategies appears to be heavily loaded with teacher initiatives, that only serves to bring out the major characteristic of the situation which is essentially asymmetrical in nature. While teachers negotiate, fraternize and dominate in their relations with the pupils, the dominant pupil strategy is that of conformity as a result of their goal perception in the senior school and their relatively younger age in the junior school.

The lack of an essentially authoritarian teacher role *vis-à-vis* the pupils places RVS somewhat apart from other public schools in the Indian setting. De Souza's study of Indian public schools points to the authoritarian structure evident in these schools. Thus 'the headmaster, the housemasters and the prefects occupy strategic positions [in the authority structure] for the surveillance of group behaviour and for the control and co-ordination of the multifarious activities of the organisation' (1974: 84). That such a structured situation, established for the precise purpose of controlling and directing pupil behaviour, does not exist in RVS highlights the lack of a formal authority structure. This enables freer and more informal interaction between teachers and pupils than might have otherwise been the case.

CHAPTER NINE

Concluding Comments

This work set out to examine the relationship between ideology, school and society. The educational processes in RVS are based on a well-articulated ideology which repudiates conventional methods of education and yet, paradoxically, participates in a formal school system. The school's social and cultural setting (namely, the formal system of schooling in which it participates and the particular ideology which constitutes its explicit value base) and the implications all these have for teachers and pupils were the focus of study. The nature and content of interaction between and among the participants in the school were also a major concern.

To begin with, I examined Krishnamurti's world-view and educational thought as a form of ideological discourse. The school however has an objective reality organized around ideological and institutional principles based on both its transcendental and local orders. It may or may not therefore provide the necessary conditions for the implementation of the ideology.

In order to explicate the school's cultural setting, the rituals and ceremonies associated with the daily round of activities and dramatizations of the same were examined. These were seen as representative of the mutually antithetical ideological and educational forms of discourse, thus creating a particular kind of ethos specific to RVS and illustrative of the school's relations to both the ideology and the formal schooling system.

The teacher culture revealed the existence of two kinds of teachers, depending on their mode of recruitment and varying commitment to the ideology in particular and education in general. This was seen as having important ramifications for school processes and for the teachers' relations with the pupils and amongst themselves. Inter-teacher interaction was examined in terms of both its formal and informal aspects and was viewed as influenced by other factors, such as, the institutional status or position of a teacher, the cultural ethos of the school, and personal differences.

Pupil culture encompassed the gamut of activities in which the pupils participate and their differing perspectives on school life. It was apparent that there are two streams in pupil attitudes to the ideology and aspects of school life influenced by pupils' perceptions of social expectations and by teacher perspectives. Pupil culture is therefore not autonomous but articulated in interaction with external influences predominant among which are the home and the teachers.

Teacher–pupil interaction is in fact the central process in the school. It was suggested that informality is the defining characteristic of teacher–pupil interaction at RVS bounded however by the goals of the participants and the rules of the different settings. The relative lack of the authoritarian element in teacher–pupil relations was pointed out as were the difficulties the teachers experience in this regard. Pupil and teacher perspectives were also indicative of the ambivalence in their attitudes towards, and expectations of, one another which are the result of contradictory elements and added to the complexity in teacher–pupil relations.

This work has therefore showed the linkages between the ideology, school processes, the participants' views and external influences in their interrelatedness through an analysis of the different aspects of school life. Thus, a pupil or a teacher is guided, in her participation in school activities, by her perception of the ideology and other school goals, of social expectations and pressures and her own orientations towards school life. Similarly, the implementation of the ideology is not an autonomous process but takes place in relation to other supportive or counteracting forces which are both internal and external to the school. School processes themselves—for example, the functioning of the academic system and the pedagogic process itself—are guided not only by school goals but also by parental expectations, the regulations and recommendations of the Council and pupil interest. All these aspects of school life, seen in their relations to one another, provided significant insights into uderstanding both the crucial and the commonplace features of school life.

Several important conclusions emerge from the construction of RVS as a socio-cultural reality. The most important points to the clash of ideologies in school processes. At one level, there are the contradictions, cleavages and dilemmas created by the confrontation between the ideological and the educational discourses arising from two very different orders. This is apparent in all areas of school life and gives rise, for example, to the division between teachers in their perceived task *vis-à-vis* the pupils. It also creates a conflict between the efforts at understanding or implementing the ideology by some participants and the pursuit of other interests by other participants; the latter may diverge from ideological goals but are nonetheless a part of school processes.

At another level, there is a clash between the ideology of a particular class of Indian society who patronize RVS and the overall world-view of the school. Thus, while the pupils' background and upbringing ingrain in them the competitive spirit and an achievement orientation towards possible careers and occupations, the ideology of the school emphasizes a different kind of learning, pointing to an alternative world-view. This conflict is reflected in other areas of school life and in pupil views on school processes. It is also indicative of the fact that RVS does not exist in a vacuum but functions in interaction with the external environment which is not entirely in consonance with its values and may accordingly exert contrary pressures on school processes. Inasmuch as RVS is dependent on the affluent middle and upper classes for its maintenance, it has to accommodate and incorporate the values and norms of these classes in its functioning.

The clash between the different kinds of discourse and ideology is a result primarily of the character of the institutional structure through which Krishnamurti has chosen to operationalize his educational thought. Thus the organization of the school on the conventional pattern of an academic system geared to meet the demands of society appears to be entirely at odds with the wider goals of the ideology. Other activities organized around the core activity pattern would consequently encounter similar problems of divergence from the ideology. This inevitably creates conflicting situations for the participants who then have to make choices in terms of their commitment to the ideology or to the goals of the institutional setting. Some however attempt to make compromises between the two so as to reduce the inherent conflict.

It would appear that as RVS ˙(in its official goal-orientation) is concerned with ideology through a direct and explicit formulation of the problem, it encounters resistances within its own structure and from external sources. Other public schools, all of which have implicit ideologies of one kind or another, do not perhaps experience similar problems because their ideology is present at a tacit level and therefore does not interfere with the institutional structure or school processes. Alternatively, their ideology may *fit* the structure and functioning of such schools.

To the extent that RVS has an ideology which is explicitly stated and formulated, it emerges as a very prominent feature of school life. Its presence is felt in every area of the school's functioning as it contains the guiding principles against which each activity is compared or evaluated. Although this may result in creating conflict—as it does in several situations—it serves to provide the participants with a yardstick to assess the immediate means used in the achievement of more long-term goals. More positively, it permeates school processes to the extent that some participants identify and explain their experience of school life in terms of the ideology and the meaning it has acquired in their lives. Some features of school life which may be considered a result of the impact of the ideology such as a relative lack of an authoritarian element in teacher–pupil relations may be otherwise viewed merely as the outcome of a more general progressive ideology. In RVS, however, they acquire a significance as their very specific source is the ideology internal to the school and not an externally formulated progressive ideology.

Within the school itself, I have focused more on relations among people, between people and school life, between ideas and school activity encompassed as they are by the ideology, the structural and cultural setting of the school and, in a broader sense, by society. I have not however gone into the implications and ramifications of such a school, and its processes, for society. That is, I have not directly attended to the question as to whether RVS and its products can transform society as envisaged by the ideology. The impact of social influences on school processes and the constraints these impose on performance have nonetheless been pointed out.

This study does, I trust, help to fill in the lacuna in intensive sociological studies of schools in India. Further studies of RVS itself may extend my own analysis, for example, by focusing more closely on the many dimensions of pupil interaction or through an intensive observation of classroom behaviour using audio-visual techniques. More broadly, the school may also be viewed in terms of the divisions created in it not only by the conflict between ideology and education, as I have pointed out, but between the school's specific value system and conflicting social norms and values. This would lead to an understanding of the division this in turn creates in people in terms of their conflicting value orientations. Related to this, a significant area of further study would be the identification of the nature of the school's specific relations with the wider society and the principles of social control and power that operate in such interaction and influence school processes in a particular direction. Such control exercised by the external environment in interaction with the school might prove to be related to the social stratification prevalent in Indian society and to the perpetuation of such differentiation through school processes.

Moving away from RVS, a comparative study of schools with differing ideologies—whether these are public, private or government schools—would be both interesting and important with a view to examining how different kinds of ideologies operate through school processes.

My own analysis of Krishnamurti's educational thought has been concerned primarily with examining its relationship to a particular institutional setting and the people and activities in it. Krishnamurti's thought can however be related to the Indian or, more broadly, the Western philosophical and educational implications of such forms of discourse for schooling. These perspectives are no doubt present in educational ideologies and influence schooling processes. An assessment could therefore be made of the intimate relationship between ideology and education and the different forms of articulation that such relations take.

Finally, there is the general issue of ideology itself. An important question that arises here is that of the purpose served by ideology in educational processes. That is, whether it is merely rhetoric that is adopted for self-fulfilment or whether it is in fact concerned with improving school processes, albeit for its own ends. Apart from the significant need for an explanation of the uses of ideology, such questions indicate the importance of an analysis of the relations of power that emerge as being constitutive elements of the interaction between ideology and education. Further, the significant question of the extent to which ideology is successful in attaining its goals through education needs to be answered. This cannot however always be measured, for example, in RVS where the change sought lies in the psyche of an individual. An understanding of the measure of success an ideology achieves through educational implementation would nonetheless indicate its efficacy and practical contribution to educational processes.

In the final analysis, discussions of ideologies must go beyond utilitarian or practical concerns and focus on the crucial issue of values. Such an exercise would lead us back from the study of the school as a socially constructed reality to our starting point, namely, Krishnamurti's world-view and educational thought embedded in it for a fuller consideration of the same. Additionally, it would also point to the desirability of a discussion of the value premises of those other educational ideologies with which Krishnamurti's world-view is supposed to contend. The manner in which such ideological conflicts are resolved is by no means one of mutual exclusion, or the absorption of the one into the other. A genuine dialectic of ideologies should produce a synthesis: the first task would be to present this dialectic adequately—but this is a task for future research. I trust I have, among other things, cleared the grounds for such an endeavour in this work.

Postscript

On a brief visit to the school in July 1988 it was quite clear that many radical changes, both quantitative and qualitative, had taken place. There are now more teachers in the school (45, of whom 25 are women) and a larger number of ideologues among them. While this may suggest the increasing importance of the transcendental order *vis-à-vis* the local order, it is in fact the latter that continues to dominate school life. The reason for this is quite obvious: it would appear that there has been a major shift in the goals of the school. There is clearly an explicit emphasis on 'academic excellence', as Krishnamurti puts it.[1] The commitment of teachers now is to the 'intellect', as it were, and to its development in the child. This commitment to the academic order and excellence in that order acquires legitimacy from the ideology itself. There is thus an overt emphasis on good teaching, creative curricula designing, innovative pedagogic methodology, and so on. And the school is gratified by, and receives encouragement from, the increasingly good results obtained by pupils in the Board examinations in recent years.

The reinterpretation of the ideology and its impact on the changing goals of the school have resulted in integration among the teachers in the workplace. There are several reasons for this. The ideologues, many of whom are highly qualified personnel, are now committed to the task of creating and developing academic excellence in RVS. The pedagogues, or professional teachers, who are in any case largely committed to this goal find themselves in perfect agreement with current school goals. The result is a shared commitment and joint endeavour towards a commonly perceived task. The ideologue is also now more acceptable to the professional teacher as she is viewed as also working rather than being engaged merely in the elucidation, clarification and propagation of the ideology.

Certain structural changes have also resulted in greater interaction between ideologues and pedagogues. For example, the post of junior school Head (previously occupied by an ideologue) has been removed and three teachers (one ideologue, and two pedagogues) are together in charge of the junior school. For the first time in the history of RVS, a pedagogue (who was Headmistress in 1981) now occupies the position of Principal in the school. A new post of Director of RVS has also been created, in hierarchy above that of the Principal, whose incumbent is both explicitly committed to the goals of the transcendental order as well as to those of the local order. She appears to have also taken into account the work input of professional teachers which has resulted in their overt inclusion into a common endeavour. Their role in the pedagogic process is viewed as being a significant contribution to the accomplishment of school goals. She thus appears to have gained the co-operation and goodwill of most professional teachers in the accomplishment of school goals.

While interaction between teachers appears to have improved in the workplace largely because of a reinterpretation of the ideology and a modification in the goals of ideologue teachers, this does not appear to be true of informal interaction. Ideologues are still considered exclusive persons, somewhat serious and quiet; the younger professional teachers tend to view these characteristics as signs of dullness and intertia. I might add however that these professional teachers appeared to feel threatened by the presence of ideologues who, because of their commitment to the ideology, are certainly closer to the Management and Foundation Members. The informal aspect of teacher interaction thus appears not to have changed very much since 1981.

Apart from the emphasis on the local order in terms of developing the academic system, there is another, somewhat erroneous, indication of movement away from the transcendental order. There has been an effort, probably after Krishnamurti's death, to remove every physical evidence of his presence in the school. His private rooms on the campus have converted into a library and study centre to which access is open. Similarly, his photographs have been removed from school buildings and public places. Quite clearly, these changes have taken place in order to emphasize *doing* rather than preaching, and living in the present rather than sanctifying and preserving the past. The transcendental order therefore appears not to be 'transcendent' any more in the more obvious physical sense as it most certainly was earlier when Krishnamurti's presence was present *in absentia*, as it were. Of course, this may very well result in an actual forgetting of the original intention of the school, but the Management keeps this alive through discussions on precisely this theme in terms of what is being done in the everyday life of the school. The commitment of the Management now appears to be to the development of the intellect as well as to the daily lives of both teachers and pupils in the school. The concerns and problems of everyday life are therefore as important as the demands and pressures of intellectual development. However, it is possible that the pursuit of academic excellence may mean the neglect of ideological concerns and values. The Management is aware of this possibility and is concerned about its implications but the danger of losing the transcendental order, except as a very personal order, remains.

Apart from the intellect, the Management lays an emphasis on 'values' as an extension of the transcendental order. This implies, for example, a concern with ecology and the environment that has taken explicit shape in afforestation and irrigation in Rishi Valley as well as an interest in rural education. The latter has resulted in the establishment of five satellite and two other rural schools. While the Management is actively engaged with building resource materials and other infrastructure for these schools as well as running them, pupils from RVS are involved in these ventures to some extent in the form of co-curricular activity. Pupils in Std. 11 also have a compulsory lesson on 'Environment' for which they are expected to prepare a Seminar Report. This is commendable to the extent that pupils are now more actively engaged with the environment than they were before. Moreover, the concern with ecology results in creating a certain ethos in the school that is in consonance with its natural surroundings.

It is quite apparent that the earlier conflict between the transcendental and the local orders does not exist to the same extent and this results in greater clarity in school processes. There are certain implications, however, for how the school defines itself. RVS is engaged in a process of transformation through the transcendental order but the result of which could very well be an outward negation of that order in terms of a possible neglect of the 'inwardness' of life, as it were, due to an emphasis on the external life of the individual. There is no doubt of course that the 'inward' life is 'invisible' and therefore immeasurable in the sense that the external life of the individual is. RVS perhaps continues to strive to achieve that perfect balance between both streams of life that Krishnamurti so passionately advocated.

The Theoretical Approach

I will now delineate my theoretical approach and refer to those sociological studies of education and the school that have influenced my work. It is this broad theoretical framework which helped me not only to pose specific questions for inquiry but also guided the actual process of data collection and subsequently of the analysis and interpretation of data.

It is from Durkheim that we get the notion of an externally observable social reality. This provides the basic assumption for my study of a social institution in its wider setting of a particular social milieu. The institution is seen to have an existence independent of individual participants and also serves to outwardly regulate their conduct by a set of explicit rules and implicit norms. The individual's conduct is further moulded by her internalization of the appropriate norms and values. In my case study, constraint operates differently on two groups of teachers in the performance of their roles. For one, it is derived from the enforcement of external official regulations and, for the other, from the internalization of specific values. In both cases, however, it is clear that the group (with its exteriority and constraint) encompasses the individual, and secures her participation in its activities.

There is, however, the fundamental question of conflict: how it arises in an institution, how it is dealt with, and whether it is contained or acts as a disruptive force in the social system. There are the contradictions and cleavages that are inherent in any social system and which are, in the case of RVS, partly a result of the lack of clearly articulated goals. Further, these participants are not passive actors in a system: they have different motivations, goals, values, attitudes and ways of acting that influence their mutual interaction. A consideration of these varied factors arising from differences in the orientations of the participants is therefore necessary for an understanding of the school as a social system.

Weber draws our attention to the necessity of 'verstehen' or 'interpretive understanding' in the attempt to examine the subjective point of view: 'Action is social insofar as, by virtue of the subject meaning attached to it by the acting individual (or individuals), it takes account of the behaviour of others and is thereby oriented in its course' (Weber, 1947: 88). It follows that for an adequate explanation of society 'the object of cognition is the subjective meaning-complex of action' (Ibid: 101).

More specifically, the conception of the social reality of the school adopted by me emphasizes the processes of social interaction. My primary concern is with the 'world of everyday life' which 'presents itself as a reality interpreted by men and subjectively meaningful to them as a coherent world' (Berger and Luckmann, 1967: 33). This world has social meaning and being, insofar as it is not 'my private world but is from the outset an intersubjective one, shared with my fellow men, experienced and interpreted by others' (Schutz, 1970: 163).

Symbolic interactionists conceive of social interaction as 'an essentially interpretive process in which meanings evolve and change over the course of interaction' (Wilson, 1970: 700). Further, central to symbolic interactionism is the view that 'human beings construct their realities in a process of interaction with other human beings' (Meltzer *et al.*, 1975: 54). In the school, social interaction constitutes the ongoing social reality—the world of daily life—that is observable in the different settings and situations and in the variety of encounters between and amongst participants within the overall processes of the reproduction of educational knowledge and the creation of a different kind of human being.

In order to understand 'intersubjectivity' in the processes of social interaction, one has to examine the 'mutually understood, "negotiated", shared definitions' of the participants (King, 1983: 26). This would lead to an exploration of what constitutes the 'ground rules of everyday life' (Robinson, 1981: 16). In my analysis I am therefore not only concerned with the formal expectations of individual behaviour but with individual perceptions, alterations, adaptations or acceptance of the same as these shape the nature of social interaction. The recognition by the participants of the variations in individual definitions of the situation, whether these are shared or not, reflects a mutual awareness of individual orientations. The teachers' understanding of one another's orientations towards the ideology is in fact one factor responsible for the cleavages in their interaction which I discussed in Chapter Six. Moreover, differences in teacher perceptions of the ideology and in their commitment towards implementing it necessarily affects the nature of their interaction with the Foundation Members insofar as the latter tend to include ideologically committed teachers into an inner circle of the 'ideologues' whilst maintaining cordial relations with the rest but excluding them from a shared ideological domain.

Teachers and pupils also behave according to their perceptions of one another in different settings and situations. Their interaction is thus affected by previous experience which results in the formation of 'typifications' or 'constructs' which then serve as a guide to interaction. Interaction may also arise spontaneously but is normally influenced by mutually understood rules. The latter are a result of 'negotiation', for example, between teachers and pupils for order in the classroom or the 'house', between the Management and the teachers for incorporating activities related to ideological implementation into the already crowded daily routine, between different kinds of teachers over the nature of their work in the school, and so on. Negotiation is a central interpretive procedure in the interactional processes in the school. It is also evident in the 'strategies' developed by teachers and pupils—the former more than the latter—to cope with difficulties in the situation or in the processes of interaction.

I am also concerned with the dramaturgical element in social interaction—as developed by Goffman—whch is suggestive of the 'manipulative penchant of humans' (Meltzer *et al.*, 1975: 81). The basic premise of this approach is that 'when human beings interact each desires to "manage" the impressions the others receive of him/her. In effect, each puts on a "show" for the others' (Ibid.: 68). The participants in a social system, singly or in 'teams', therefore 'perform' a 'part' or a 'routine' for other participants ('audience') in a 'setting' with appropriate 'sets' and 'props'. This performance may take place in a 'front region' of the 'scene' or 'backstage' which is hidden from the audience (Goffman, 1959). Further, the performance is a part of 'focused interaction' and the 'unit of social organization' in which this occurs is 'an *encounter*, or a *situated activity system*' (Goffman, 1961: 8).

The teacher in the classroom, the Principal interacting with pupils, senior pupils in front of junior pupils are thus basically 'performing' for an audience; a staff meeting becomes a 'performance' for visiting Foundation Members; occasionally, a teacher puts on a particular 'front' with pupils to elicit appropriate pupil behaviour; the 'front region' of visible individual behaviour may accord with formal expectations but the 'backstage' may indicate the dilemmas and tensions inherent in the situation, for example, in teacher interaction. The dramaturgical element is therefore at work in the processes of interaction at different levels and on different occasions in the setting of the school.

My concern with the social reality of the school in terms of interaction might suggest that I merely consider the episodes, situations and encounters in which this interaction takes place and ignore the substantive content of the interaction itself. I do however take account of the overall structure of the school, its dual function of reproduction (of knowledge) and production (of a new generation of human beings), the implications this has for the people in it in terms of their mutual orientation and interaction, and its relations with wider society. In particular, I am concerned with examining the school's specific ideology and its relations to the processes of schooling and interaction. The ideology, in a sense, lends a specific meaning to the interaction and brings the episodic strands of interaction together insofar as the teachers are engaged in the school's dual task which is perceived as being a holistic form of education.

The school's relations with wider society are evident at all levels of its functioning: in terms of the social background and expectations of the pupils and the teachers; in the pedagogic relationships in the classroom that are shaped by the requirements of the syllabus which is set by the Council; in pupil attitudes towards school work which are dependent on parental expectations and on the requirements for admission into institutions of higher learning, and so on. I therefore attempt to move beyond what might otherwise be viewed as a narrow consideration of the processes of interaction within the school into an analysis which broadly views the relationship of the school to an external social order and the individual to society.

My analysis is also concerned with the place of authority and control in the school—how it arises, what purposes it serves and what forms it takes—and with the resultant relations of power that emerge.[1] My attempt is to examine the extent to which relations of authority and modes of control define and shape interaction as well as orient activity in a particular direction in the school. Thus, for example, while the 'negotiation' of meaning is a central theme in my analysis of interaction, the significance of the extent to which reality is negotiated by some who have 'the differential power . . . to define reality over others' is not lost. It is evident that 'not all parties to interaction have equal power to define the . . . parameters of "acceptable social reality"' (Sharp and Green, 1975: 29). Teachers therefore have more leeway in framing the rules of negotiation *vis-à-vis* pupils, Foundation Members over the school Management and the teachers, the Management over teachers and pupils, and certain ideologue over other professional teachers.

The work is finally an attempt to show the dialectical nature of the individual's relationship with society. Woods, who affirms the interactionist view of the dialectical relationship between the individual and society, suggests that the implications of such a viewpoint are that 'actions are rarely totally original, nor is the individual totally bound by cultural and structural constraints' (1983: 4). It is rather a process of mutual interaction through which the individual both gives rise to society as well as is influenced by social processes and society at large.

Building upon the theoretical approach, I follow along the path in the sociology of education and the school opened by the so-called 'new sociology of education'.[2] This approach, drawing essentially on interactionism and phenomenology, opened up a wide range of research in the sociology of education which now concerned itself mainly with the *content* of education which had hitherto been neglected. Lacey has suggested that previous research methods— what he calls the 'black-box' model of research—assume that 'in order to demonstrate an effect it was necessary only to show correlations between inputs and outputs. The contents of the black-box, the social mechanisms and process, are neglected . . . ' (1976a: 56–7). The new approach—'an emergent "alternative paradigm" '—therefore sought to fill in this lacuna in research in the sociology of education.

Young, one of the initial proponents of this approach, has argued for the need to move 'to explanations of how pupils, teachers and knowledge are organized', and to consider ' "what counts as educational knowledge" as problematic, so that one major focus of the sociology of education becomes an enquiry into the social organization of knowledge in educational institutions' (1971: 2–3).

Bernstein's significant work in this context has drawn attention to the 'distribution of power and principles of social control' that are 'alive in the context, contents and institutional embodiment of education' (1975: 149).

Thus, contrary to earlier approaches which concerned themselves with analysis at the macro-level, within which 'education is discussed as it relates to the economy and the opportunity structure, as well as to the attainment of political ideals, like equality of opportunity' (Robinson, 1981: 22), the new approach emphasizes analysis at the micro-level. The latter focuses on the specific contexts and content of the processes of interaction as they occur in the school.

Woods, who in recent years has argued for an interactionist approach to the study of schools, identifies six main concerns of this approach from the extant literature which have a direct bearing on this work. A school consists of different *'contexts'* and situations which are differently interpreted by the participants. The individual's 'definition of the situation' is therefore of considerable importance in identifying the various situations and their construction by participants. Further, teacher and pupil *'perspectives'*, the 'frameworks' through which they 'construct their realities and define situations', are central components in the construction of the social reality of the school. These perspectives are both 'culturally specific and context-bound' and different situations may lead to the formation of different perspectives.

It is important to note that these perspectives arise out of *'cultures'* which 'develop when people come together for specific purposes, intentionally or unintentionally, willingly or unwillingly' and, further, are not 'formally regulated but heavily implicit'. Thus an understanding of teacher and pupil cultures serves to render clear the background within which perspectives are formed and articulated.

Central to the interactionist approach is the concept of 'strategies' which are viewed as being the link between perspectives and action and the point where 'individual intention and external constraint meet'. In schools, teachers and pupils devise strategies or plans of action to cope with difficult situations to meet their goals.

It is, however, of considerable significance that school life is a 'continuous process of *negotiation*' insofar as 'the persistent properties of the act of identifying, interpreting, reckoning, and choosing, maintain a dynamic which . . . makes the actual interplay between persons the most important element, as each seeks to maximise his own interests'. Negotiation, as a central feature of interactional processes, also raises the question of the relative power of participants. The teacher, for example, tends to benefit more from negotiation than do the pupils.

Woods' final point is that of the 'subjective *career*' of the participants which is a means of 'linking the individual's experience with the institutional provision of formal careers and ultimately society at large'. Two important aspects of careers are commitment and the development of identities, the identification of which primarily serves to highlight the nature of interaction between the individual and the social system of the school as well as wider society.

These aspects of social life in the school, as identified by Woods (1983: 6–16), and also found in other works on the subject, are not examined independently but in their relations with one another in my construction of the social reality of the school. My central concern, quite clearly, arises from an important question: what is life at school all about? I am not only concerned with interaction between participants (which is the central focus of my work) but also with interaction between ideas and institutions (i.e. between the ideology and the school), among institutions themselves (such as the Council and the school), and between the internal and external orders of the school (i.e. between the internal mode of functioning and the external influencing factors).

It should be clear that my analysis is mainly located within an interactionist approach which 'recognises both the autonomy of the moment and the range of choices open to the actor in any situation, *and* the existence and influence of social structures which not only constrain but also make possible particular activities. It is concerned with the analysis of micro situations, . . . and with the macro-societal context in which they occur' (Hammersley and Woods, 1976: 7).

Work on the sociology of the school describes and highlights different aspects of the school. In order to understand the world of the school, it is important to identify, describe and analyse the various elements that contribute to the richness of school life. Thus the '"charting" or "mapping" of areas of social life within the school is a necessary task in its own right' (Woods, 1983: 178). Criticism has been levelled at 'descriptive research which maps the vicissitudes of a problem' but leaves the analyst wanting 'to grasp somehow the underlying principles of the map itself' (Bernstein, 1975: 2). I would however agree with Hammersley and Woods that 'intra-school processes . . . have some *explanatory* significance' (1976: 3) for it is in the 'mapping' of school processes that the underlying principles of the relations between the relations, as it were, of the different aspects of school life come to the surface and provide us with an explanation of the complex social reality of the school.[3]

It is clear that the theoretical framework relies primarily on symbolic interactionism but incorporates other sociological perspectives to enable us to view the school not merely as internally constructed but also as externally given. Symbolic interactionism proved to be helpful in understanding the critical nuances of everyday life through an analysis of the participants' perspectives and the meaning they bring to interaction in the daily round of activities. It helped to gain significant insights into the functioning of the school, not merely in terms of what happens, but also of how the participants both perceive and contribute to what happens in RVS. I was thus able to render the school sociologically intelligible in relation to ideology and society within an overall perspective that includes both objective facticity and the subjective meaning brought to situations and processes by the participants.

It is possible however that one has perhaps to move away from the symbolic interactionist approach if one seriously considers the problems of power and control that operate in school processes. It has been recognized that interactionist research in schools needs to go beyond 'the first rough mappings of the hitherto dark unknown of the "black box" interior' to include 'further mapping of uncharted areas of school life, formal theory and macro links' (Woods, 1983: 180). Marxist criticism of the interactionist approach to the study of schools in particular indicates the neglect of macro-level theory. However, it is also important to consider another viewpoint which suggests that the claim 'that micro phenomena can only be understood correctly in terms of the right macro scheme is to beg the question of how we produce and test the latter; and also to confuse the completeness of an explanation with its validity' (Hammersley, 1980: 199).

In terms of the significance of understanding the underlying principles of the distribution of power and social control in school processes, attention would have to be paid to what have been described as 'structuralist sociologies of the school' (Tyler, 1988: 148 ff.). Bernstein and Foucault, the major proponents of this approach are seen as being 'concerned with the systems of control which produce *discourses*—those fields of practice constituted through the interpretation of knowledge and power' (Ibid.: 164). Such a viewpoint necessarily entails the denial of 'the intentions and meanings of the individual subject . . . since the conditions of experience depend on the possibilities which the individual does not himself control' (Ibid.).[4]

Similarly, Bourdieu examines the role of education, and more specifically, of the school, as the agent for the reproduction of the power structure (Bourdieu and Passeron, 1977). While an understanding of these perspectives no doubt helps in providing us with an alternative and perhaps more realistic view of school processes, it also becomes necessary to examine their view of the human subject. Is the human subject a passive being who merely internalizes the values and norms of the dominant culture or is the human subject an active agent in the construction of socio-cultural reality? Resistance theory in education would have us believe that the human subject, through acts of resistance and rebellion in the school, can in fact alter and sometimes transform 'the educational code'. I am of the view however that such 'resistance' that takes place in school processes can at the most temporarily displace the code rather than change it altogether.[5]

The symbolic–interactionist perspective certainly helps us to gain important insights into life at school. We see the human subject in interaction with people and ideas in everyday life. It does not however provide us with the tools with which we can uncover the underlying principles of the distribution of power and social control in school processes. Without an adequate understanding of the latter, it would appear that our understanding of life at school is incomplete. Surely, however, in order to explain power and control in school processes, we must *first* know what in fact life at school is all about. This work may thus be seen as a contribution to the endeavour of understanding life at school, albeit at a particular kind of a school.

A Note on Fieldwork

Fieldwork for me resulted from an attempt to render an educational institution intelligible in sociological terms. I was interested, specifically, in the implications of a particular ideology for the schooling process; in the nature of interaction between the participants in the school and between school processes and the wider society; and in the various dimensions of school life itself. In more general terms, I was interested in arriving at an understanding of the school through the process of observing and interacting with the ongoing reality and 'lifting the veils that obscure or hide what is going on' (Blumer, 1976: 15).

In this process, the most crucial problems were raised by the seeking of information, both public and private, and the hiding of it by exercising control which created barriers between the ethnographer and the 'field'. The barriers I encountered raised some important questions of censorship and control: Who restricts information and thereby creates barriers? When is it considered appropriate for information to be freely given and when is it concealed? What constitutes free knowledge and restricted knowledge and what are the repercussions of this distinction on the ethnographer and her research? Here, I will present some of the problems generated in the 'field' by the continuous interplay of the ethnographer's search for information and the participants' masking of it and attempt to seek answers to some of the questions raised above.

I selected RVS as my field primarily because of the explicit presence of an underlying ideology. I carried out fieldwork in RVS for a period of nine months during 1981 and stayed on the school premises in accommodation provided by the school. This afforded me the necessary facilities and opportunities for sustained observation of school activities and for building intimate relations with teachers, pupils and other school personnel.

To begin with, I had no clearly formulated 'research design' as the basis for study as I was not testing any hypothesis. A rounded case study was the aim. I was therefore not interested in any specific areas of school life to the exclusion of others and my focus on 'interaction' as the subject of study and as a methodological device emerged during the course of my stay in the school.[1]

The first difficulty I encountered was in gaining 'entry' into the school. The school Management are the 'gatekeepers', as it were, of the institution and wish to protect teachers and pupils as well as themselves from an outsider who seeks to observe school processes. I wrote several letters to the school which remained unanswered. I therefore had to seek the assistance of the Foundation and approached a Foundation Member who readily granted me permission to study the school.[2] Her decision was based on the expectation that my work might serve as a feedback to the Foundation and school Management on the functioning of RVS as seen by an interested but impartial observer. Her faith in my ability to undertake this task was not however shared by some other Foundation Members who were apprehensive as to whether I, a doctoral student, had the 'maturity' and 'right understanding' to view the 'experiment in human education' which was going to be 'exposed' to me. What I did not realize at that time but which became evident later was that as I had come to the school through the Foundation, I was viewed with even more suspicion and distrust than usual as I was at first considered a 'stooge' of the Foundation by some teachers and the Management.

It was with some trepidation combined with scholarly fervour that I arrived at RVS. My first few weeks there were fraught with tension and anxiety for the Management and the teachers regarding the impact of my presence on the school, and this inevitably affected the nature of their relations with me. I briefly spoke to the teachers at a staff meeting about the nature of my work and sought their co-operation and assistance. At another meeting, however, where I was absent, the teachers were told by the Principal to consult the Headmistress before speaking to me so that there would be 'no confusion or contradiction' in their statements to me. In this manner, the Principal sought to control the flow of information by imposing an intermediary between the teachers and myself, who would determine what was appropriate for disclosure (free knowledge) and what was restricted to themselves (secret knowledge).

The teachers were thus very restrained in their relations with me in the beginning.

At this time some teachers did approach me for discussion but they were either those who were to shortly leave the school, and had nothing to lose by talking to me freely, or those who were in general disgruntled with the school's mode of functioning. These teachers mainly complained about what they considered the Management's misdirection, the pupils' preoccupation with themselves and lack of sensitivity to what was happening around them, parental disinterest in school goals, the Foundation's 'interference' in school processes, and so on. Some of these teachers were identified by me as the 'ideologues' who were particularly critical of school processes and also dissatisfied with their own role at RVS. I was perhaps used as a sounding board by them and, while I listened carefully and took down notes later, I was all along aware that I was hearing only one side of the story.

Some other teachers were antipathetic to my presence in the school. Their questions and comments, however, often reflected their own insecurities and fears. Thus a senior teacher who was unsure about how I would portray the school asked, 'Will you be writing what you are *told* to write or whatever you *feel* like writing?' I handled their rather derogatory comments as best as I could under the circumstances but I remember being embarrassed and upset by them.

The pupils were not quite clear about my position in the school. I spoke to them as I met them casually—individually and in groups—and told them about my work and made it clear to them that I was not a teacher in the school. It took me quite a while however to 'make friends' with them and to get them to be relaxed and comfortable in my presence.

It was evident to me from the outset that I had to first immerse myself in school life to the extent I could, and to the extent I would be allowed to, in order to penetrate the closed wall that stood between me and my 'understanding' of the school.[3] Before coming to RVS, I had decided not to participate in any teaching as I felt that this would leave me with very little time for my own work. Nevertheless, had I participated in teaching, I might have gained a quicker understanding of school processes. As it was, I was left with the option of joining in activities—other than that of the classroom and staffroom at first—such as the morning assembly, and accompanying pupils and teachers on hikes into the neighbouring countryside, interacting with them informally in the dining hall, and the houses. I also attended the yoga lessons, watched teachers and pupils at sport and gardening, and took part in the co-curricular activities, such as, music and drama.

During this time, I was engaging in what Berreman, following Goffman, calls 'impression-management' in the field (1972: xvii–lvii). That is, I was trying to present myself in a manner that would be acceptable to teachers and pupils so that they could begin to trust me. I was behaving differently with teachers and with pupils who had differing codes of conduct. Thus I presented an amiable but serious front to teachers and a more informal one to pupils. With teachers, I was genuinely interested in what the ideology was striving to achieve through school processes *as well as* in the problems that ideological expectations might pose for the practical tasks of running a school. This appeared to be the most crucial dilemma for teachers and the Management and by not taking sides for or against the ideology I was able to participate in discussion on related issues. By my participation I wished to make it clear that I was not merely an observer but also sufficiently interested in their problems so as to share and discuss them.

I realized that the only way in which I could interact with pupils was by being where they were, outside the classroom: at hikes, sport, after-dinner activities. Slowly they began to accept my presence amongst them and soon began to invite me to accompany them on hikes or to visit them after dinner. After about three weeks of my stay at RVS, the Principal invited me to attend all the staff meetings as well as his meetings with the senior pupils. I thus began to take part in as much of school life as I could in the staffroom and the classroom—the two main arenas of school activity—and outside. This was done in an attempt to establish rapport with teachers and pupils and to get a picture of the community in the round, as it were.

Intimate and sustained observation helped in understanding the subtle and hidden as well as the manifest aspects of school life. I could thus perceive some of the ' "*imponderabilia of actual life*" which cannot possibly be recorded by questioning or computing documents, but have to be observed in their full actuality' (Malinowski, 1922: 18). While not participating as a teacher, I was very much 'involved' in the everyday life of the school.[4] I was not only attending and taking part in many of the activities but also developing close personal relations with teachers and pupils and my role in the school gradually began to be viewed with less suspicion by everybody.

'Involved observation' was therefore an important research technique I used. I have emphasized the significant role of 'understanding through talk' which is necessary for obtaining the participants' view of themselves, of their relations with one another and of school processes.[5] I thus conducted interviews, discussions and conversations with not only teachers and pupils but also with the founder, Foundation Members, some parents and other visitors to the school. I relied on formally structured interviews, informal discussions and on what Woods calls 'naturalistic or behavioural talk' which is heard and noted by the observer in the 'ordinary course of events' (1979: 263).[6]

I conducted formal interviews with the key personnel in the school such as the Principal, Headmistress, junior school Head, and others in order to obtain answers to specific questions on school processes, namely, the official definition of school aims, the procedures for the recruitment of teachers and the selection of pupils, the structural organization of the school, and so on. I would begin the interview with questions from a prepared list and, apart from asking the interviewee to provide specific information, I also used the method of 'non-directive' questioning. This involves asking questions that are more open-ended than those which are formally phrased and are 'designed as triggers that stimulate the interviewee into talking about a particular broad area' (Hammersley and Atkinson, 1983: 113).

In the course of informal conversations with teachers, I attempted to let them elaborate their formulations, perceptions and meanings of school processes as well as their own roles and lives in the school. Through these interviews and conversations, observation of activities, discussion of topics unrelated to actual school processes, and listening in to casual staffroom talk, I was able to construct the major ideologies of the teacher culture. This resulted in the formulation of a teacher typology based on the mode of recruitment, the teachers' perception of their roles, and the nature of their commitment. I then selected four teachers on grounds of their being either 'professional' teachers who were primarily committed to teaching and a career, or 'ideologue' teachers who were mainly committed to the elucidation, clarification and propagation of the ideology. I interviewed them intensively on the course of their lives, careers, roles and their views on school processes. It is from these teachers that I derived the vital elements of the differing ideologies they subscribed to which proved to be crucial to my understanding of the teacher culture.

It was in my conversations with teachers and the Management that I became aware of the extent to which personal relations can either hinder or facilitate an interview. I rarely obtained any information from the Principal with whom I had a very reserved relationship. I also encountered resistance from some teachers who were clearly disinterested in expressing their views on any aspect of school life. They just did not trust me sufficiently which was evident in their lack of response to my efforts to relate to them ouside my role of ethnographer.

Good personal relations would, on the other hand, lead to an interview being transformed into a more informal encounter and I would often be supplied with rich and valuable information beyond what I had originally sought. Some teachers spent much of their 'free' time speaking to me at length about various aspects of school life. When they realized that they were sometimes saying more than they should, to someone who was really an ethnographer and therefore an 'outsider' in a very elementary sense, they would ask me not to quote them or say that a particular piece of information was 'off the record'. Here the teachers themselves sought to impose controls on the information which they could not however help sharing with me due to the rapport that had developed with time. Although the masks were removed at such moments, the distinction between ethnographer and participant nonetheless remained. This was evident to the extent the teachers were conscious of my role even while sharing confidences *and* I remembered to file away every bit of information I received whether or not I used it later.

With the passage of time, I had established very close relations with some teachers who became my 'key informants'.[7] I did not select them as informants but in the course of time they entered into this role and provided me with not only important information but also with an overall perspective which might have been difficult to obtain otherwise. This was particularly in relation to the ideology and its association with school processes at both the manifest and the latent levels as this was not always easy to ascertain from observation. I was fortunate in finding informants with divergent attitudes and commitments to the ideology and their role in the school so that my understanding was not dependent on only one kind of perspective.

There were however two problems I encountered during the course of attempting to understand through talk. 'Talk' can readily turn into 'gossip' which is important as data but irrelevant beyond a point. It is important inasmuch as it plays a crucial role in the 'folklore' of a community and can lead to meaningful insights into interpersonal behaviour. Interaction in an institution is constituted by both formal and informal relations between participants which are based on status and position, personal friendships, likes and dislikes, and so on. Gossip helps in understanding informal relations in themselves and the manner in which the participants view them and their more formal relationships. I was often compelled to listen to teachers gossiping about other teachers' private lives, pupils' relations across sexes, their relationships with their parents, the financial status of parents, the lives of Foundation Members, and so on. The ethnographer is allowed to peep behind the mask of what is considered 'proper' social behaviour and thus deciphers some of the critical nuances characteristic of complex social interaction. I was however always conscious of the tenuous but important dividing line between fact and fiction in gossip and balanced data from gossip with other sources.

The other problem I encountered in my conversations with teachers and the Management was when my opinion was sought on sensitive issues, such as the implementation of the ideology in the school, or the role performance of certain teachers, members of the Management and Foundation Members. It was even more embarrassing when I was expected to join in the gossip and asked to comment on a particular teacher's behaviour or activities even though this might have been viewed as a sign of inclusion in the community.[8] I had to use some tact, and at times I was circumspect, in my answers as I was always expected to respond and could in no way avoid such questions.

In this situation it is clear that controls on information are lifted by the participants themselves and the ethnographer is invited to participate in 'backstage' activity, as it were. This may be due to the fact that this activity is viewed by the participants as being irrelevant to the ethnographer's research and is therefore considered safe for exposure. The ethnographer however imposes her own controls, as I did at RVS, so as to steer clear of controversy as well as to direct talk into more relevant areas of interest.

Secret or restricted knowledge is shared not only as gossip which is not really private but external, as it were, to the speaker. More personal areas may be revealed depending on the rapport that has developed: one teacher, for example, showed me his diary and allowed me to read it over several days. It mainly contained an account of his experience of the ideology and attempts to implement it in RVS. While one may not use the 'confidential' material one is able to obtain in any direct manner, it cannot be denied that some of it is responsible for the insights one derives about the intricacies of everyday life that cannot be obtained in any concrete form. These insights inevitably find their way into the analysis although one may not refer to them or to the source so as to avoid revealing the personal or secret nature of the information received or the identity of the informant. Thus although mutual trust and rapport leads to the gain of vital information, the ethnographer then faces the ethical question of the *use* of the material obtained. This problem is a dilemma experienced by every ethnographer who has to first worry about breaking the barriers of suspicion and distance and having done this, about how to use the sensitive information without betraying the informants.

While it was relatively easy to gain access to the teacher culture and understand it through talk and observation, it was more difficult to do so with pupils. It is simpler to identify with teachers and to relate to them than it is with pupils. At RVS, the difficulty in getting to know pupils did not lie with those who were younger and junior but with the older, senior pupils. My strategy in attempting to mingle with senior pupils, boys in particular, and thereby establish rapport with them was by gaining entry into a particular house and first forging links with them through informal visits and conversation. Once these pupils came to know me well enough, it was relatively easy to understand their perspectives through discussion. Through them, I came into contact with their friends outside the house and with other senior pupils in the school. My understanding of pupil views on different aspects of school life also developed in the course of my conversations with them in casual encounters and in watching and listening to them all over the school—in their interaction with teachers and amongst themselves.

A few pupils considered 'different' in both positive and negative terms by the teachers became particularly friendly with me. There were some who were viewed as having a special interest in the ideology and were therefore considered 'serious' and 'sensitive' in their attitude to both school work and the ideology. Such pupils, and others who were not very interested in the ideology but serious about school work in any case, provided me with an overall perspective of the dominant pupil culture.

There were some pupils who were disinterested in school work and in school goals in general. One boy who was considered definitely deviant and treated in a casual manner by the teachers due to his total lack of interest in school work used me as a 'relief agency' (Woods, 1979: 261) in telling me at length about his personal problems and apathetic relations with the teachers and other pupils. This pupil became an important informant in providing me with a 'peep-hole' view, as it were, of the 'underworld' of pupil culture (in this case, of senior boys) which appeared to consist largely of bawdy talk about girl pupils, the use of what was considered 'foul' language by the pupils themselves, smoking cigarettes surreptitiously, eating non-vegetarian food (which was not allowed at RVS), and so on. My only problem arose from the nature of information he sometimes supplied me. As he continuously broke school rules and told me about his exploits, I worried whether the teachers' trust in me would be undermined if they discovered that I was aware of his breach of rules but did not inform them. In order not to betray the pupil's trust in me, I censored my discussions with teachers by suppressing the information he made available to me. I was however always aware that I would lose the teachers' trust completely if they knew I was concealing 'deviant' forms of pupil activity from them. It therefore becomes the ethnographer's practical concern to hide some information obtained from one source from other participants in order not to lose credibility among different people. On the other hand, the sharing of some information may lead to the gain of further information. It is a situation of balancing one against the other in a continuous game of hide-and-seek with information.

Among the research methods I used to decipher school processes, classroom observation was particularly useful in understanding interaction in a situated setting. I did not use any of the conventional aids to classroom research such as the tape-recorder, nor a predetermined set of categories into which I sought to 'fit' classroom behaviour. I wanted to remain open to everything that was taking place in the classroom to the extent that it was possible by being an unobstrusive observer sitting at the back of the room. My main task was to listen to and observe classroom talk and activity and take down detailed notes. By not using a recording device, which incidentally may have altered the 'normal' flow of activity, I am however aware I may have missed what was happening in different parts of the room.

I was primarily interested in observing the nature of teacher–pupil interaction in two different classroom settings: in the junior and the senior schools. In the senior school, where I had selected a particular classroom for study, I faced no problems of entry. The teachers' permission was sought by the Headmistress on my behalf at a meeting where I was not present and they agreed to my presence in the classroom. The teachers were, by and large, unconcerned by my presence as were also the pupils who would only sometimes glance at my notebook while passing by to see what I was writing. Some teachers however would later come up to me with explanations as to why they thought a particular lesson had not proceeded well. Only one teacher mentioned my presence as being responsible for the pupils' inattention in the classroom.

Apart from the evidence of the teachers' need to provide explanations to the observer so that their competence was not misjudged, they appeared to behave naturally in the classroom. Over a period of time, I observed almost every lesson taken by different teachers—some several times over—and faced non-cooperation in only one instance. I did not face 'withdrawal' or other tactics employed by teachers in the classroom to minimize observation as Hargreaves did (Hargreaves, 1967: 196). An important reason for the relaxation of such control in my case is that I sought to observe classrooms in my second term at RVS by which time most teachers had accepted me to the extent that they scarcely noted my presence as an observer at meetings and on other occasions.

It was in the classroom that I most directly experienced and shared pupil experience of school processes. For example, the pupils had often told me that they found a particular teacher's lesson 'very boring'. I would invariably find them yawning their way through it, looking out of the window, participating half-heartedly in the discussion and glancing at their watches several times waiting for the lesson to come to an end. Their description of the teacher as a 'bore' and their behaviour in the classroom enabled me to experience the situation as they did and I found this teacher's lessons boring myself.[9] I could also experience the pupils' enthusiasm for discussion when a teacher stimulated them into avid talk as well as their ability to listen in silence to a teacher who could hold their attention.

In the junior classroom, I faced some problems. I had selected the junior-most class where an experiment in learning was conducted by three teachers. The class-teacher was initially very apprehensive about my presence in the room and it was only with the intervention of the junior school Head, and my assurance that I would only quietly observe and not disturb the lesson, that I was allowed to sit in the classroom. I was not however permitted to take notes during the lesson. I had to employ a strategy to circumvent the control that was being imposed: I began to attend every alternate lesson and took down detailed notes during the intervening period. Sometimes, in order to retain the immediacy of the situation, I would casually leave the classroom and quickly take down notes before coming in again. My experience in this classroom was however different from that in the senior classroom, not only because of the younger age of the pupils who were easily distracted by my presence, but more importantly because the class was fraught with many difficulties due to the new curriculum.

The problems resulting from the attempts to implement the new curriculum escalated to such an extent that the junior school Head had to intervene and the structure was reorganized. This was the only instance when I 'interfered' in school processes and the 'interventionist research strategy' unwittingly came into play.[10] My role in the process of change was triggered by a teacher seeking my advice as to what could be done as she was finding it difficult to handle the situation. I asked her to speak to the Head who until then was not aware of the deteriorating situation in the classroom. He first held a meeting with the three teachers concerned and also consulted me about possible changes and then took the necessary step of reorganization. An improvement in the situation however quelled my doubts about what I viewed as my lack of detachment from school processes.

In addition to observation and understanding through talk, I also distributed questionnaires to all the teachers and a section of the pupils in order to ascertain their socio-economic background, role perceptions, views on the ideology, education, and various aspects of school life. The Management sought to control the kind of information I was seeking from teachers by deleting two questions from the questionnaire which had to pass the inspection and approval of the Headmistress before distribution. The two very disparate questions, which I considered crucial to my questionnaire, were aimed at eliciting the teachers' views on the influence of the ideology on their lives and their description of a serious problem they had encountered in the classroom and how they had dealt with it. The reason given for their deletion was that the questions were 'personal' and probing too closely into the teachers' lives. This was the view of the Management—the gatekeepers—who were protecting not only the teachers but also themselves as the teachers' answers to these questions might reveal more than they would perhaps like the ethnographer to know. The teachers in general however remained unperturbed by these questions which I raised in my conversations with them thus evading the imposed control.

I examined school documents to obtain information on specific topics such as rules for teacher conduct, the criteria for pupil admission, reports on pupils, statements on finance and annual reports, and so on. I also studied documents pertaining to the history of the school and to its relationship with the external order such as the Council. Access to these documents was relatively simple: I was shown every document I asked for including those that were considered 'sensitive' as they contained accounts of Executive Committee meetings. I saw some of these papers only in the last few weeks before I left the school. By then I was a completely trusted member of the community which incidentally adds to the dilemma of the *uses* of the information obtained.

The various methods I used for the collection of data generated insights into school processes and thereby contributed to my understanding of the social reality of the school. The combination of different research methods resulted in what, following Lacey (1976), I may call the 'spiral of understanding'.[11] It is important to note that each level of understanding is associated with a particular mode of data collection but each level also contributes to an understanding of the whole. Thus, for example, classroom observation contributed as much to my understanding of the school and to my theoretical explanation of school processes as did understanding through talk. The latter was however my main research tool. It was partly imposed on me by the situation itself which necessitated intensive interaction with different kinds of participants. Initially, talk helped in establishing mutual trust and rapport and later led to the gain not only of detailed information on everyday life but an understanding of the complexities of school processes.

Although this has been discussed by almost every ethnographer, I would like to briefly comment upon the role and importance of 'subjectivity' in fieldwork, besides that of 'objectivity' which is generally acknowledged. For me, fieldwork has been not only an exercise in the collection of data but also a rich human experience to the extent to which I was completely immersed in and personally involved with the many dimensions of school life. I attained the status of a member of the community when my name appeared on the list of teachers put up on the notice board in my second term at the school. This did not raise any objections from either teachers, pupils or the administrative staff as it was assumed that I was one of them although I was clearly not a member of the teaching staff. Similarly, I was expected to participate at staff meetings and was invited to staff dinners and other occasions. I had established close relations with some pupils who would visit my room off and on and share their lives with me. I was also invited to attend their 'house functions' in the evenings and took part in as much of pupil activity as I could.

My involvement in school processes was such that I would be tense in sympathy with the pupils during examinations, fret over the problems being experienced by the teachers *vis-à-vis* the pupils such as indiscipline, experience the humiliation of a pupil when s/he was being ticked off by a teacher or was recounting such episodes to me, worry about the implementation of the ideology and try to examine ways by which it could be accomplished, and also feel perturbed about the professional teachers' role in such a school and the problems they faced apart from the limitations their presence imposed on ideological goals. I used to look forward to special events like 'moonlight dinners' and outings to a neighbouring city as other participants did. A 'tea-party' with teachers or a 'gab session' with pupils became pleasurable occasions as they were for the others.

All this while, I was also conducting fieldwork in what I hoped was an 'objective' manner. I was constantly aware of my role as ethnographer and worried about my involvement in school matters.

It was in the process of taking down detailed notes and maintaining a field diary that I was able to sustain the 'detachment' that appeared to be necessary for 'objectivity'.[12] The significant role of subjectivity was however obvious to me all along in terms of 'trying the intimate experience of "the other" in oneself' (Levi-Strauss, 1973: 9) in order to 'reach down into the "grammar" of the . . . culture, so as to establish a translation, not just of the words but of the poetic meaning' (Leach, 1973: 12).[13]

In conclusion, I would like to draw attention to some of the problems that arose from the use of particular methods of data collection. I would also like to make some observations about the relations of power and control that exist between the ethnographer and the participants in the fieldwork situation and the problems these may pose for them.

In the study of complex organizations, like schools, the ethnographer engages in 'both explicit and implicit forms of sampling', which, following Ball (1984: 75), I use to refer mainly to 'problems of selectivity'. The first and most important point of selection is the choice of the field. Why did I choose RVS as my study school? My selection was influenced by a number of factors including the lacuna in sociological studies of schools in India, my interest in Krishnamurti's work and my own experience as a teacher there several years earlier. Both academic and personal concerns thus motivated my decision. As stated earlier, I was interested in examining the relationship between ideology and education and the repercussions this had for schooling based on the case-study of a particular school. It could be argued that such a school is such a unique educational institution that the sociological findings would be insufficient for comparative purposes and have no bearing on wider social phenomena. It is however possible that while ideological discourse is explicit in one school, it may be hidden or underdeveloped in another. That is, in some schools there may be two forms of discourse: an official discourse, based on an ideology about education, that governs the functioning of the school, and an everyday discourse, as it were, that directs actual school processes and is shaped largely by the pressures and demands of the situation. In other schools, such forms of discourse may be muted in expression or simply do not exist. Such being the case, as well as the fact that private schools (both aided and unaided) constitute about

60 per cent of all schools in India, my understanding of the social reality of RVS is located in the overall context of schooling in India.

Apart from the general considerations regarding the selection of the field, there are the specific problems of sampling in the fieldwork situation. Thus, why does one choose to study two particular classrooms in preference to other classrooms? The reasons for this are related to the kind of information one is seeking. For example, I was interested in examining teacher–pupil interaction in the informal setting of a junior classroom where the pressures of school work and examinations did not exist as well as in the more structured setting of a senior classroom where both teachers and pupils work under the pressure of imminent examinations. Although I made an arbitrary decision regarding exactly which classrooms I would observe, this did not in any way affect the kind of data I was able to obtain. What did happen was that in focusing on teacher–pupil interaction, I neglected a very important dimension of school life, viz., inter-pupil interaction in the classroom. Moreover, in my interaction with senior pupils outside the classroom, I was able to interact more closely with boys (who were more forthcoming) than with girls. I therefore had to supplement the data obtained through talk with other sources such as the questionnaire which was distributed to the three senior-most classes in the school.

Among teachers, the culture of the ideologue teachers emerged more predominantly than that of the professional teachers although the latter outnumbered the former. This is due to the encompassing nature of the ideology in school processes in terms of the superior value attributed to it by a dominant section of the participants although the focus of everyday life is educational transmission.

It is evident that the ethnographer *and* the participants censor and control the flow of information and thereby shape the nature of interaction between them. The ethnographer thus has little power over the participants as 'each works to place it (interaction) in particular social, emotional and political contexts' (Cassel, 1980: 30–31). In this sense, power is distributed between them and interaction often involves negotiation rather than the stringent application of rules of procedure (Barnes, 1979: 24). It is the ethnographer however who seeks to elicit the participants' co-operation and has thus to take the initiative to negotiate, cajole, and use alternative strategies to tease out, as it were, information which is secret and therefore restricted. This may include presenting different fronts to different kinds of participants, as I did, to make oneself acceptable to the entire community and thereby eligible for receiving secret information. Success with participants depends on the ethnographer's ability to handle interaction in a manner that engenders confidence and trust. Some participants may of course decline to enter into interaction and the ethnographer has no power to make them do so. Once the ethnographer has obtained the information from others, who become friends and informants, the balance of power shifts from the participants to the ethnographer inasmuch as the latter may choose to use the information in any desired manner.

It is here that the ethnographer encounters one of the most thorny problems in fieldwork. This is primarily ethical in nature and, following Barnes (1979), may be succinctly phrased in terms of the question: 'Who should know what?' The dilemma of the use of the material obtained first occurs in the field itself. For example, I encountered situations in which I was censoring my conversations with different teachers and pupils to protect other teachers or pupils in the school. The ethnographer thus has to continuously be on guard so as not to betray other participants and lose their goodwill and credibility in the field. Apart from this practical consideration, there is also the moral aspect in terms of the trust and confidence which has been placed in the ethnographer and which, in human terms, is not usually possible to betray.

The ethnographer also experiences the dilemma of the use of the material while providing an analysis of the acquired material. This can be overcome by not revealing the names of the participants who supplied controversial or sensitive information which is sometimes the most useful in revealing the underlying reality of the field. However, an extreme result of such a dilemma occurs when one has to drop the information altogether as any use of it would be completely unethical. This happened, for example, when I chose not to use the material from the teacher's personal diary although it would have helped in providing an interesting dimension to my understanding of the teacher culture from the viewpoint of one kind of teacher.

The crucial point that emerges is that the ethnographer does not really have the kind of power that is generally assumed to exist due to the acquisition of sensitive and important material. The ethnographer's use of the acquired material is generally governed by practical, moral and most important, human considerations and an attempt is made to protect the identity of the participants and the efforts of the particular community to achieve their goals. It is possible however that some ethnographers do misuse the information they acquire to further research in the area which has resulted in the extensive debate on ethics in social science research (see, for example, Barnes, 1979).

Fieldwork thus implies not only the straightforward collection of data but the complex task of uncovering the masks or lifting the veils that lie between the facade and the reality within a framework that is guided by both practical (in terms of the ethnographer's objectives) and ethical considerations. To accomplish this task, the nature of interaction between the ethnographer and the participants is crucial to enable the ethnographer not only to gain information but to 'understand' the social reality of the field.

NOTES

Chapter One: Introduction

1. Foundation Members are members of the Krishnamurti Foundation (India) which runs the Krishnamurti Schools in India. Their role in the school is discussed in Chapter Three.
2. For details of my theoretical approach, see Appendix A.
3. See Appendix B for details on how I conducted fieldwork in the school over a period of one year.
4. See Holroyd (1980) and Jayakar (1987) for a more complete exploration of Krishnamurti's world-view.
5. My specific use of the term 'ideology' is explained in Chapter Two where the relationship between ideas and education is also discussed.
6. This has been taken from Weber (1947: 99).

Chapter Two: Ideology and Education

1. I am using the term 'charisma' as it is defined by Weber: 'a certain quality of an individual personality by virtue of which he is set apart from ordinary men and treated as endowed with supernatural, superhuman, or at least specifically exceptional powers or qualities' (1947: 358).
2. Krishnamurti's charismatic personality plays a significant role in his communication with both a public audience and with the many individuals who are close to him. For accounts of his charismatic impact on different people see, for example, Anon. (1933:116), Huxley (as quoted by Bedford, 1974: 296) and Jayakar (1981) and more recently Jayakar (1987: 2).
3. Krishnamurti's repudiation of authority comes through clearly as he is seen as not offering 'a system of beliefs, a catalogue of dogmas, a set of ready-made notions and ideals . . . not leadership, not meditation, not spiritual direction, not even example. It (the teaching) is not a ritual, not a church, not a code, not uplift or any form of inspirational twaddle' (Huxley, 1954: 14–15).
4. See Krishnamurti (1929: 1–3) for his celebrated and oft-quoted speech dissolving the Order of the Star (an organization of which he was the Head) wherein he stated his position on his role as a 'World Teacher'.
5. Source: Interview with Krishnamurti.
6. Krishnamurti however rejects the view that the Krishnamurti Foundation schools are 'organizations'. His abhorrence of organizations of any kind leads him to define the schools as 'communities of people working together'.
7. For a recent work on Krishnamurti and the educational process, see Khare (1988).
8. One must not forget however that Krishnamurti was a mystic and not a social philosopher. This might help explain his neglect of certain important aspects of social reality.

Chapter Three: School Organization

1. This is not to suggest that such schools are not interesting or that RVS does not face any problems in its paradoxical situation but only to highlight the somewhat 'different' organization of RVS in relation to other public schools in India.
2. For Besant's views on education, see Besant (1938, 1942).
3. For an enunciation of Krishnamurti's association with the Theosophical Society and of the gradual changes occurring in the Theosophical Society as a result of Krishnamurti's evolving world-view, see Lutyens (1975) and Jayakar (1987).
4. The school's association with the Theosophical Society and its initial organization and development has been compiled from *G. V. Subba Rao: His Life: A Dedication to Educational Pioneering*, Madras: The G. V. Subba Rao Trust, 1980.
5. Of the five schools, two are residential at Rajghat, Benares and Rishi Valley, Andhra Pradesh while there are two day schools at Madras and Bangalore. The Foundation also runs an after-school centre 'for the poor' in Bombay called Bal-Anand. Source: Pamphlet on the Krishnamurti Foundation India, Madras: Vasanta Vihar; and interview with a Foundation Member.
6. *Indian Express*, Bangalore, 2 February 1981.
7. Lambert *et al.* suggest that 'expressive goals' in schools 'are concerned with things which are not means but ultimates' (1970: 56). I am using the term in a similar sense.
8. Perrow makes a distinction between 'official' and 'operative' organizational goals (as quoted by Hall, 1973: 83).
9. Pupil views are discussed at length in Chapter Seven.
10. In my discussion of teacher culture at RVS, I develop a typology of teachers where I draw a distinction between the 'professional' and the 'ideologue' teacher based on the mode of recruitment, and the teachers' commitment to the ideology and perception of their roles.
11. I have noted the Principal's defensive stand in discussion with teachers, for example. See Chapter Six.
12. Source: Minutes of the adjourned meeting of the Rishi Valley Executive Committee held on 5 December 1980. Subsequently, in November 1982, an Education Committee (consisting of four key functionaries) was formed to share the Principal's task in the 'communication of the teachings' through the educational process.
13. I discuss these forms of constraint and the sanctions used to regulate behaviour in my discussion of teacher culture and pupil culture.
14. In 1983, a middle school consisting of Standards Seven and Eight with two sections each was established and is viewed, by the junior school Head, as a 'transition period' for pupils between the junior and the senior schools.

Chapter Four: School Culture

1. Bernstein distinguishes between rituals in terms of their being either 'consensual' or 'differentiating' in function (see Bernstein, 1977: 54–66) but, as I point out later in this chapter, 'consensual' rituals themselves contain elements of differentiation within them.

2. In an interesting discussion and application of Mary Douglas' work, Wuthnow *et al.* (1984: 99–102) suggest that 'dawn' and 'dusk' may be treated as margins of social reality wherein a variety of experiences can take place. There may thus be a 'sense of danger, sacredness and ecstasy' and other 'out of the ordinary experiences'. If we view dawn as being postponed for the morning assembly to take place, and since *asthāchal* usually takes place at dusk, the participants' experiences at these times may be viewed as being extraordinary and 'quasi-religious' in a sense that they are not during other times in the day.

3. Teachers, particularly houseparents, admit that they are afraid of 'too much' interaction across the sexes, especially in the senior school, as this often results in 'pair-formations' which can easily 'get out of hand'. They thus tend to watch such interaction very closely which inhibits pupil activity.

4. If one were to follow Tambiah's approach to the study of ritual, *asthāchal* would belong to those 'classic constitutive ritual acts, whose very performance achieves the realization of the *performative* effect' (1981: 128).

5. For a discussion of this aspect of teacher–pupil interaction, see the section on Classroom Study–I in Chapter Eight.

6. Members of the Management often take visitors around the school showing them the various activities and areas of school life. Goffman (1961) uses the term 'institutional display' to describe such invitations to visitors to 'inspect the premises'. They are thus given an ' "appropriate" image of the establishment' mainly in order to allay any doubts they may have about its functioning. Of course, the participants also like to 'show-off' the school, as it were, to visitors.

7. In their response to the questionnaire, both boys and girls mentioned school work as their major source of anxiety. It becomes a 'personal problem' for those who worry about their lack of initiative to work and about the report card that is sent home to parents at the end of each term. The academic pressures implicit in the organization of the curriculum and the methods of transmission and evaluation that are characteristic of the local order in general have been described as amounting to a 'pressured academic environment' (Lacey, 1976: 290). In RVS this would obviously contradict the transcendental order but is nonetheless a part of school processes.

8. In the following chapters I discuss the different forms of resistance to both the transcendental and the local orders in RVS.

Chapter Five: Teacher Culture

1. There are 16 houses of which two (the senior boys' and girls' hostels) have more than one houseparent due to the larger number of pupils in them. Boys and girls live separately except in the two most junior houses where there are mixed dormitories.

2. Merton defines the 'role-set' as being 'that complement of role-relationships in which persons are involved by virtue of occupying a particular social status' (1957: 110).

3. Madan, in his study of institution-based doctors, suggests that a multiplicity of roles results in a 'role-blur' affecting role perception and creating strains in performance (1980: 298).

4. Woods defines 'strategies' in teaching as being, in essence, ways of achieving goals. They are 'individually motivated, culturally oriented and interpersonally adapted. They are also situationally adjusted' (Woods in Woods, 1980b). I have used the term more specifically in my discussion of teacher–pupil interaction in Chapter Eight.
5. The term 'situational adjustment' also has been used for coping with and adapting to a situation whereby an individual 'turns himself into the kind of person the situation demands' (Becker as referred to by Woods, 1979: 147).
6. These are given in Chapter Three, p. 32.
7. I am using the term 'renunciation' deliberately to stress the fact that something more than the sacrifice of material interests is involved in this choice: it points to an attitude to life according to which the choice that the teacher makes is morally superior to his earlier way of life. Needless to add, renunciation (*sannyāsa*) is a major ideal in Hindu and Buddhist cultural traditions but I am not using it in quite such a literal sense.
8. For an account of the impact of Krishnamurti on one such teacher and his decision to join as a teacher, see Jayakar (1987: 314–16).
9. I am using the notion of discourse in two related contexts. Essentially, it refers to the existence of a body of formally recorded reflections/knowledge pertaining to the aims and methods of education. As discourse it implies speakers/authors and interlocutors/readers. In the context of the discussion of the presuppositions of education (bearing upon the purposes of education in relation to individual and society) the discourse is axiomatic in character and I call it ideological discourse. In the related context of pedagogy, the aims, content and methods of the transmission and evaluation of knowledge are specified. I call this the educational discourse. Further, ideological discourse, whether implicit or explicit, serves as one of the criteria in terms of which educational discourse may be defined, evaluated and modified. In RVS, ideological discourse is located in the school's transcendental order whereas educational discourse is representative of the local order. These two orders and their representative forms of discourse signify the essential character of the school in terms of *value* and *activity*.
10. Denscombe suggests that noise emanating from the classroom constitutes the most immediate and significant source of information to others on the teachers' competence or lack of it. In particular, 'pupil initiated noise' is taken to be 'indicative of a lack of control in the classroom'. The recognition of control as being a precondition for teaching activity therefore becomes something to be learnt by new teachers as part of their 'rites of passage' (1980: 61–83).
11. Teacher–pupil interaction in the classroom and other settings is examined in Chapter Eight.

Chapter Six: Teacher Interaction

1. Woods defines the staffroom—'the main arena'—as the 'teachers' collective private area' (1979: 211). At RVS, however, this is not the case as the staffroom is used by several persons for various reasons.
2. I attended 18 such meetings during the course of my fieldwork.
3. The *sangha* is the Buddhist monastic community which has well-defined relations with the laity.

4. Hargreaves suggests that the 'occupational culture' of teachers is organized around the three themes of 'status, competence and social relationships' (1980). This may be seen as applying to the teacher culture at RVS with the additional theme of the ideology that has important ramifications for the same as has been noted in the text.
5. Teachers in the junior school are not however all young as those in the senior school are all not necessarily older teachers.
6. That the Management itself however fails to meet this expectation is evident, for example, in the special house system established for a few selected pupils in the school.
7. In Chapter Three, while discussing the role of the Principal, one factor considered responsible for the distance he maintains from teachers is the lack of adequate authority attached to his role.
8. Subsequently, the 'rebel' leader of the group left the school under a cloud and the group completely broke up.
9. On my return to the school in 1983, however, I observed that with an increase in the number of ideologue teachers, there is a definite tendency for them to stay together. Hence, in terms of informal interaction, the distinction between the ideologue and professional teachers is very pronounced.
10. On my visit to the school in July 1988 I found that ideologue teachers currently in RVS do not subscribe to this viewpoint and several of them are now married.
11. This has been observed by pupils of Standards Eight and Nine who, at a meeting with some teachers, commented on it. They were complaining about teachers who kept 'lecturing' to them about having a 'healthy relationship' with pupils of the opposite gender, for they asserted, such healthy relationships did not exist among the teachers themselves.

Chapter Seven: Pupil Culture

1. My analysis, in Chapters Seven and Eight, is largely based on the responses of 88 (out of a total of 92) pupils of Standards 10, 11 and 12 to a variety of questions. These pupils were selected for study as they were the senior-most pupils in the school and were seen as being able to express their views based on their long exposure to school processes. The views and activities of junior school pupils have also been included as far as possible. I have used the masculine pronoun for pupils unless otherwise stated. This has been done for the sake of convenience; moreover, the number of boys exceeds that of the girls.

   In presenting the quantitative data in this chapter, I have followed a somewhat different procedure from that in the corresponding chapter on the teachers. Since the number of questions to which answers were sought from the pupils was considerably larger, the data were marked by some complexity owing to overlap in responses in some cases. I have therefore considered it best to keep the description and analysis of the data in the text as free of numbers and percentages *as possible.*
2. Berger and Luckmann define socialization 'as the comprehensive and consistent induction of an individual into the objective world of a society or a sector of it'. Further, 'primary socialization is the first socialization an individual undergoes

in childhood, through which he becomes a member of society' (1967: 150). I am using the term 'primary socialization' in a similar manner.

3. Four Government of India merit scholars, admitted into Standard Four, are an exception but are not a major category and, therefore, do not affect the general trend in the kind of pupil gaining entry. There is also the category of 'school scholars' (usually one or two gain entry every year) whose admission is dependent primarily on the recommendation of senior Foundation Members.

4. I use the term 'group perspectives' as referring to 'modes of thought and action developed by a group which faces the same problematic situation. They are the customary ways members of the group think about such situations and act in them . . .' (Becker as quoted by Woods, 1976: 130). Woods suggests that such perspectives arise 'when people face "choice-points", where previous thought and experience does not guide their actions, . . .' (1976: 130).

5. It may be of comparative interest to note that in his study, Woods also distinguishes two main factors affecting pupils' subject choice, '. . . an affective one (liking or disliking) and a utilitarian one (career and ability) . . .' (1976: 132).

6. Hendry refers to the work of Murdock and Phelps who suggest that 'secondary schools in mirroring in miniature the social and ideological universe of the professional middle class reproduce the underlying "middle class" values of achievement, rational calculation, and deferment of immediate gratification' (1978: 26). This may be viewed as being applicable to RVS as well.

7. The distinction between 'hard' and 'soft' subjects has been made by the Headmistress in her assessment of the situation.

8. Pupil views on examinations would obviously differ in the junior school where there are no tests and comparison is kept to the minimal. The pupil would, however, necessarily enter the examination stream as soon as he is in the senior school.

9. The term 'muck-about' is used by Woods to describe a 'kind of seemingly aimless behaviour' (1979: 105) on the part of pupils and is similar to terms such as 'fooling around' and 'messing about'.

10. Relations between houseparents and pupils are discussed in greater detail in Chapter Eight.

11. Among other things, this results in pupil assessment of the teachers as 'hypocrites' particularly with reference to the ideology.

12. In his analysis of the 'public school phenomenon' in England, Gathorne-Hardy writes about the 'games obsession' in public schools. He suggests that this passion for games has been transmitted to public schools set up across the world and concludes, 'It is true that, . . . Britain's most significant contribution to the world at the present is not parliamentary democracy but the football, cricket and athletics invented by her public schools' (1977: 166).

13. In contrast, De Souza, for example, writes about the pattern of competitive games and sport he found in the public schools studied by him. These take the form of inter-house competitions, the organization of school teams competing with other teams, and the rewards, prizes and medals awarded to the pupils. He concludes that 'achievement in games is the traditional avenue to power and privilege in the school community' (1974: 81).

14. On one occasion, the cricket coach was asked by a teacher as to why he had bowled so often for the school team. He answered, 'That was the only way to

win', thus indicating his aggressive attitude towards the game which would inevitably influence pupil views.

15. Huzinga's observation is pertinent here: although the 'fun-element' characterizes the essence of play, in modern social life 'with the increasing systematization and regimentation of sport . . . something of the pure play-quality is lost' (1955: 197). The ideology makes a similar point in arguing for the removal of competition from the sports arena.

16. Moreover, the Physical Director, in disjunction with the ideology, expresses the need for competition in order to gauge the standard of sport in RVS and improve on it. He feels that 'running' is sufficient exercise to keep the pupils 'healthy' and that the school is wasting a large amount of money on coaches and equipment by not allowing extensive pupil participation in competitive sport. Such a view would necessarily be reflected in his attitude towards sport on the field and would also influence pupil views.

17. Bullying does not, however, exist in RVS to the extent that it does in other public schools where the authoritarian system of prefects and monitors encourages the activity.

18. There have been instances in the past where the school has had to ask the parents to withdraw a particular girl or boy because of the excessive involvement between two pupils.

19. The Principal, in fact, commented that the girls' participation in 'school affairs' (he meant at Discussion meetings, Culture lessons, and assembly) is low because 'they are too busy dressing up'. Although this indicates a certain derogatory attitude towards girl pupils, it is a fair assessment of the situation at the time.

20. This seems to be common across cultures as Woods suggests that evidence on pupil perspectives indicates that 'the majority of pupils have a basic orientation towards school which is largely and potentially supportive of the official programme' (1983: 62).

21. In a typology of pupil adaptations to school life, Woods identifies 'colonization', 'conformity', 'retreatism', 'intransigence' and 'rebellion' as the major modes of adaptation (1979: 63–83).

Chapter Eight: Teacher–pupil interaction

1. Goffman, for instance, refers to the 'furniture, decor, physical layout and other background items which supply the scenery and stage props for the spate of human action played out before, within, or upon it' (1959: 32–3).

2. Delamont writes about the 'physical, temporal, organizational and educational contexts in which classrooms are embedded' (1976: 26). The setting therefore comprises the 'temporal aspects of classroom interaction, the formal organization of the school, the social and educational context, and the physical surroundings in which they take place (Ibid: 27). My use of the term 'setting' and the different contexts, as suggested by Delamont, extends however to all teacher–pupil interaction in the school.

3. Delamont suggests that pupils view teachers 'more or less favourably on the basis of idiosyncratic features of their private lives'. They (the pupils) do not usually have access to 'guilty knowledge' (information not publicly available) but when they do acquire it, 'it becomes specially potent because the access is illegitimate'

(1976: 81–2). In RVS, the private knowledge the pupils had of a senior teacher's relationship with a lady teacher adversely affected their relations with him as they did not view such a relationship favourably since it lay outside the accepted social code.

4. Strategical action implies the use of a 'strategy' which Woods describes as essentially a way of achieving a goal. He suggests five prominent aspects of strategies related to their origin in interactionist theory: strategies are thus 'individually motivated, culturally oriented and interpersonally adapted. They are also situationally adjusted'. Finally, he relates strategies to structure and process (1980b: 18–38). I am using the term in a similar sense.

5. Elsewhere, Woods has used the concept of 'negotiation' as one example of the teachers' 'survival strategy' in their interaction with pupils (1979: 146).

6. Woods defines 'control' in this context as 'successfully dealing with an incident which fractures the teacher's peace, or establishing one's power in a situation which pre-empts such an occurrence' (1979: 146). This definition appears to refer primarily to situations of disorder. The use of control is also evident in orderly situations, in the teacher's attempts to seek pupil compliance to prevalent norms for pupil behaviour.

7. According to Woods, 'fraternization' is a 'prominent survival strategy': 'to work for good relations with the pupils, thus mellowing the inherent conflict, increasing the pupils' sense of obligation, and reducing their desire to cause trouble' (1979: 155).

8. While conducting the classroom study, I was interested in gaining an overall perspective on the nature of teacher–pupil interaction in the clasroom rather than collecting specific data on different aspects of this interaction. To that extent my analysis is based on a consideration of more descriptive data.

9. Goffman defines a 'situated activity system' in terms of an individual's 'face-to-face interaction with others for the performance of a single joint activity, a somewhat closed, self-compensating, self-terminating circuit of interdependent actions' (1961: 96). He further views the 'situated role' as emerging out of continued interaction in situated systems and defines such a role as 'a bundle of activities visibly performed before a set of others and visibly meshed into the activity these others perform' (Ibid.).

10. The curriculum for Standard 10 has been discussed in Chapter Three, pp. 49–51.

11. It has been suggested by Hargreaves *et al.* that a lesson generally consists of five phases: an entry phase, a settling down phase, the lesson-proper phase, a cleaning up phase and an exit phase (as referred to by Hammersley, 1977: 52). Although I am not dividing the lesson into phases for the purpose of analysis, the different aspects of the lesson are self-evident.

12. The term 'direct selection' is used as it is by Hammersley: 'tagging a question with a name or "one of you four", "you", combined with pointing, etc.' (1977: 57).

13. *Akka*, literally older sister in Tamil, is the term by which the pupils address lady teachers. It is also an example of the effort to induce informal and close relations between teachers and pupils.

14. Woods suggests that the essence of 'showing up' pupils as a punishment lies 'in the force with which an individual's deviation from the norm can be emphasized in the eyes of his peers' (1975: 123). I am not sure to what extent this was the intention of the teacher in Lesson Five. She, however, used this form of

punishment which proved to be functional inasmuch as she held the pupils' attention, established order in the classroom failing nonetheless to elicit sufficient pupil participation.

15. The Prep Section was however disbanded in 1982 as the pupils were considered too young for a boarding school. It was also not considered a viable unit as it comprised very few children for teaching whom special teachers had to be recruited. I have therefore not provided any illustrations of the lessons in the text.

16. This curriculum subsequently failed in its implementation as a result of several factors. In Chapter Six, I examined one such factor: the breakdown of communication between the teachers concerned resulting in the disruption of their work activity. I am here interested in only examining the extent to which it influences the nature of teacher–pupil interaction in the classroom.

17. These include the making of beds and keeping the house clean and tidy.

18. My analysis is based on house reports compiled for 21 pupils (12 boys, 9 girls) in Standard 10'B'. Teacher evaluation of pupils in the classroom is discussed on pp. 205–9 of this chapter.

19. Here, vertical age grouping means that there are two junior and five senior pupils living together. Of these, four are in the same class while the rest belong to different classes in the school.

20. Hammersley's observation is apt at this point. He suggests that one pupil orientation influencing their interest in teacher behaviour is 'the issue of consistency, or inconsistency between the teacher's moral pronouncements and his example'. That is, teachers present themselves 'as exemplary' in the moral terms they present to the pupils as morality'. When they fail to be consistent in their behaviour, the pupils view it as a 'warrant for deviance' (1977: 65).

21. Compare with Wood's analysis of pupils' comments on teachers which he interprets as depending on 'their (the teachers') degree of institutionalization, dislike arising from ultra-rule consciousness, uneven and irrational use of power, formal and depersonalized relationships, superior attitudes as well as certain aspects of pedagogy and personality' (1979: 100). The similarity with pupil views at RVS are apparent although the two study-schools are located in different cultural settings.

22. See also Geer (1971) who emphasizes the conflicting nature of teacher–pupil interaction in terms of the subordination of the taught to the teacher.

Chapter Nine: Concluding comments

1. As we have seen in Chapter Two in this work, Krishnamurti emphasizes both academic excellence and 'the other', namely, observing oneself. as being equally important in the pedagogic process.

Appendix A: The Theoretical Approach

1. Work in this area includes an attempt by Sharp and Green (1975) to merge the phenomenological and Marxian approaches in their study of a progressive primary school. The most significant Marxian analysis of schooling is that of

Bowles and Gintis (1976). I have not, however, used such an analysis in my study.
2 This term derives from Gorbutt (1972).
3. I have not referred to studies in the field of the sociology of education pertaining to India because my purpose here has been to outline the theoretical foundation for my own study (For an Indian case study of related interest see De Souza, 1974).
4. In a recent work, Bernstein has examined the possibilities of resistance to the code and the possibilities for its transformation. See Bernstein (1987).
5. See Thapan (1988) for a more detailed discussion of this problem of resistance *vis-a-vis* reproduction in the sociology of education.

Appendix B: A Note on Fieldwork

1. This procedure appears to be shared with others. For example, Béteille notes, 'When I went to Sripuram I did not have a definite preference for any particular aspect of its social life, and I certainly did not have a clearly formulated plan of investigation . . . I did have an interest in the problem of social inequality, but this interest took shape only in the course of my stay in the village' (1975: 102). Becker *et al.* have also pointed out that their study had no research design: '. . . we had no well-worked-out set of hypotheses to be tested, no data-gathering instruments purposely designed to secure information relevant to these hypotheses, no set of analytic procedures specified in advance' (as quoted by Burgess, 1982: 12).
2. This was one indication of the relations of power in the school—which were later revealed to me—in terms of who 'counted' in taking decisions.
3. I am using the term 'understanding', following Wax, to refer to 'a social phenomenon—a phenomenon of *shared* meanings' (1971: 11). That is, the ethnographer understands the field when she can interpret the words, gestures and nuances of the participants' lives as they do.
4. I use the term 'involved' as it has been used by Woods who defines his role in the field as that of an '*involved* rather than a participating observer'. He views his involvement in terms of 'the relationships entered into with staff and pupils, an identification with the educative process, and a willingness to go along with their perceptions of life' (Woods, 1979: 261).
5. Woods has drawn by attention to the term 'understanding through talk' which he describes as a research style, concomitant with participant observation, and which consists essentially of conducting 'interviews, discussions, conversations: in short, some form of "talk"' (1979: 263).
6. The 'ordinariness' of events has been identified by Woods (1981: 16) at three levels in relation to three levels of access. The first is the public image that is presented to the ethnographer in the initial few weeks at the school. With the passage of time, this front is relaxed and the ethnographer is allowed glimpses of life behind the mask. However, it is only with the building of rapport and trust that the participants begin to confide their feelings, experiences, attitudes which provide insights into the actual functioning of the school.
7. Some of my 'key informants' were among those at the school with whom I formed the closest and most lasting relationships. I could therefore never really view

them *only* as informants: they were also friends and confidants with whom I shared my anxieties and problems, usually related to some aspect of fieldwork.

8. In this context, Gluckman notes that 'the right to gossip about certain people is a privilege which is only extended to a person when he or she is accepted as a member of a group or set' (1963: 313).

9. Woods notes a similar experience in his study suggesting that 'talk assumes an onomatopoeic quality' thereby enabling the observer to directly experience the situation (1979: 267).

10. The term 'interventionist research strategy' is used by Lacey to describe 'episodes of innovation and change (that) can occur through research . . . ' (1976: 62) although in my case, it was not a planned episode but arose out of the circumstances.

11. Lacey states that what he did was to '"escalate insights" through moving backwards and forwards between observation and analysis and understanding' using different methods of data collection (1976: 61).

12. It has been suggested that both 'involvement and detachment' or belonging and distantiation as Ricoeur (1981) puts it, are the essence of the ethnographer's experience in the field: 'Involvement is necessary to understand the psychological realities of a culture, that is, its meanings for the indigenous members. Detachment is necessary to construct the abstract reality: a network of social relations including the rules and how they function . . . ' (Powdermaker, 1966: 9).

13. Cf. Geertz (1983: 55–70) who scoffs at the anthropologist's attempt to get 'into some inner correspondence of spirit' with participants who, he suggests, would not welcome such an intrusion. He is emphatic that the ethnographer cannot 'perceive what his informants perceive' and 'whatever accurate or half-accurate sense one gets of what one's informants are . . . comes from the ability to construe their modes of expression, . . . their symbol systems . . .'. He thus concludes that 'Understanding the form and pressure of . . . natives' inner lives is more like grasping a proverb, catching an allusion, seeing a joke—or, . . . reading a poem—than it is like achieving communion'.

References

Abbs, P. 1979. *Reclamations: Essays on Culture, Mass Culture and the Curriculum* (London: Heinnemann).

Anon. (G. B.). 1933. 'Some Impressions of Krishnaji's Visit to Ahmedabad', *The Theosophist.*

Ball, S. 1984. 'Beachside Reconsidered: Reflections on a Methodological Apprenticeship' in R. G. Burgess, ed., *The Research Process in Educational Settings: Ten Case Studies* (London: Falmer Press), 69–96.

Barnes, J. A. 1979. *Who Should Know What? Social Science, Privacy and Ethics* (Harmondsworth: Penguin).

Barton, L. and Meighan, R., eds. 1978. *Sociological Interpretations of Schooling and Classrooms: A Reappraisal* (Driffield: Nafferton Books).

Becker, H. S. 1970. *Sociological Work: Method and Substance* (Chicago: Aldine Publishing Co.).

Bedford, S. 1974. *Aldous Huxley: A Biography, Vol. II* (New York: A Knopf).

Bennett, S. J. 1974. *The School: An Organizational Analysis* (Glasgow and London: Blackie).

Berger, P. and Luckmann, T. 1967. *The Social Construction of Reality* (Harmondsworth: Penguin).

Bernstein, B. 1975 (1977). *Class, Codes and Control: Towards a Theory of Educational Transmissions* (London: Routledge and Kegan Paul).

———. 1987. 'A Sociology of the Pedagogic Context' in U. Ammon, *et al.,* eds., *Class, Codes and Communication in Sociolinguistics* (Berlin: Walter de Gruyter).

Berreman, G. D. 1972. 'Behind Many Masks: Ethnography and Impression Management' in *Hindus of the Himalayas: Ethnography and Change* (Berkeley: University of California Press), xvii–lvii.

Besant, A. 1938. *The Besant Spirit, Vol. I* (Madras: The Theosophical Publishing House).

———. 1942. *Essentials of Indian Education* (Madras: The Theosophical Publishing House).

Béteille, A. 1975. 'The Tribulations of Fieldwork' in A. Béteille and T. N. Madan, eds., *Encounter and Experience: Personal Accounts of Fieldwork* (Delhi: Vikas Publishing House), 99–113.

Blackburn, K. 1980. 'The Tutor: A Developing Role' in R. Best *et al.,* eds. *Perspectives on Pastoral Care* (London: Heinnemann Educational Books), 56–69.

258 *Life at School*

Blumer, H. 1976. 'The Methodological Position of Symbolic Interactionism' in M. Hammersley and R. Woods, eds. *The Process of Schooling: A Sociological Reader* (London: Routledge and Kegan Paul), 12–18.

Bourdieu, P and Passeron, J. C. 1977. *Reproduction in Education, Society and Culture*, Tr. R. Nice (London: Sage Publications).

Bowles, S and Gintis, H. 1976. *Schooling in Capitalist America* (London: Routledge and Kegan Paul).

Burgess, R. G. 1982. 'Early Field Experiences' in R. G. Burgess, ed., *Field Research: A Sourcebook and Field Manual* (London: George Allen and Unwin) 15–18.

Campbell. B. P. 1980. *Ancient Wisdom Revived: A History of the Theosophical Movement* (Berkeley: University of California Press).

Cassel, J. 1980. 'Ethical Problems for Conducting Fieldwork' in *American Anthropologist*, 82, 1, 28–41.

Cenkner, W. 1976. *The Hindu Personality in Education* (New Delhi: Manohar Book Service).

Chanan, G. and Delamont S., eds. 1975. *Frontiers of Classroom Research* (Windsor: NFER).

Coleman, J. S. 1961. *The Adolescent Society* (New York: The Free Press).

Davies, B. 1973. 'On the Contribution of Organizational Analysis to the Study of Educational Institutions' in R. Brown, ed., *Knowledge, Education, and Cultural Change. Papers in the Sociology of Education* (London: Tavistock), 249–95.

Delamont, S. 1976. *Interaction in the Classroom* (London: Methuen).

Denscombe, M. 1980. ' "Keeping'em Quiet": The significance of Noise for the Practical Activity of Teaching' in P. Woods, ed., *Teacher Strategies: Explorations in the Sociology of the School* (London: Croom Helm), 61–83.

De Souza, A. 1974. *Indian Public Schools: A Sociological Study* (New Delhi: Sterling Publishers).

Durkheim, E. 1961. *The Elementary Forms of Religious Life*, Tr.: J. W. Swain (New York: Collier Books).

Eliade, M. 1959. *The Sacred and the Profane* (London: Routledge and Kegan Paul).

Erikson, E. H. 1977. *Toys and Reasons: Stages in the Ritualization of Experience* (London: Marion Boyers).

Gathorne–Hardy, J. 1977. *The Public School Phenomenon 1597–1977* (Harmondsworth: Penguin Books).

Geer, B. 1971. 'Teaching' in B. R. Cosin *et al.*, eds., *School and Society: A Sociological Reader* (London: Routledge and Kegan Paul).

Geertz , C. 1983. 'From the Native's Point of View: On the Nature of Anthropological Understanding' in *Local Knowledge: Further Essays in Interpretive Sociology* (New York: Basic Books), 55–70.

Gluckman, M. 1963. 'Gossip and Scandal: Papers in Honour of M. J. Herskovits' in *Current Anthropology*, IV, 3, 307–16.

Goffman, E. 1959. *The Presentation of Self in Everyday Life* (Harmondsworth: Penguin).

———. 1961. *Encounters: Two Studies in the Sociology of Interaction* (London: Allen Lane Penguin Press).

Goode, W. J. 1960. 'A Theory of Role Strain' in *American Sociological Review*, 25, 4, 483–96.

Gorbutt, D. 1972. 'The New Sociology of Education' in *Education for Teaching* 89, 3–11.

Gouldner, A. W. 1976. *The Dialectic of Ideology and Technology: The Origins, Grammar and Future of Ideology* (New York: The Seabury Press, Inc.).

Hall, R. H. 1972. *Organizations. Structure and Process* (New Jersey: Prentice–Hall Inc.).

Hammersley, M. 1977. *Teacher Perspectives*. E 202 Schooling and Society. Units 9 and 10 (Milton Keynes: The Open University Press).

Hammersley, M. and Atkinson, P. 1983. *Ethnography: Principles in Practice* (London: Tavistock Publications).

Hammersley, M. and Woods, P., eds. 1976. *The Process of Schooling. A Sociological Reader* (London: Routledge and Kegan Paul).

Hargreaves, D. H. 1967. *Social Relations in a Secondary School* (London: Routledge and Kegan Paul).

———. 1980. 'The Occupational Culture of Teachers' in P. Woods, ed., *Teacher Strategies: Explorations in the Sociology of the School* (London: Croom Helm), 125–48.

Hendry, L. B. 1978. *School, Sport and Leisure* (London: Lepus Books).

Holroyd, S. 1980. *The Quest of the Quiet Mind: The Philosophy of J. Krishnamurti* (Northamptonshire: The Aquarian Press).

Hughes, M. G. 1976. 'The Professional-as-Administrator: The Case of the Secondary School Head' in R. S. Peters, ed. *The Role of the Head* (London: Routledge and Kegan Paul), 50–62.

Huxley, A. 1954. Foreword in J. Krishnamurti, *The First and Last Freedom* (London: Victor Gollancz), 9–18.

Huzinga, J. 1955. *Homo Ludens. A Study of the Play-Element in Culture* (Boston: Beacon Press).

Jayakar, P. 1981. *The Seer Who Walks Alone* (pamphlet).

———. 1982. 'Krishnamurti and Self-Knowing' in P. Jayakar and S. Patwardhan, eds., *Within the Mind: On J. Krishnamurti* (Madras: KFI), 19–28.

———. 1987. *Krishnamurti: A Biography* (New Delhi: Penguin).

Jayakar, P and Patwardhan S., eds. 1982. *Within the Mind: On J. Krishnamurti* (Madras: KFI).

Kanter, R. M. 1974. 'Commitment and Social Organisation: A Study of Commitment Mechanisms in Utopian Communities' in D. Field, ed., *Social Psychology for Sociologists* (London: Thomas Nelson and Sons), 126–46.

King, R. 1983. *The Sociology of School Organization* (London: Methuen).

Khare, B. B. 1988. *J. Krishnamurti: Things of the Mind* (Delhi: Motilal Banarsidass).

Krishnamurti, J. 1929. 'Speech at the Ommen Camp dissolving the Order of the Star' (mimeo).

———. 1954. *The First and Last Freedom* (London: Victor Gollancz).

———. 1970a. *The Penguin Krishnamurti Reader* (Harmondsworth: Penguin).

———. 1970b. *The Second Krishnamurti Reader* (Harmondsworth: Penguin).

———. 1972. *You are the World* (Madras: KFI).

———. 1973a. *Education and the Significance of Life* (New Delhi: BI Publications).

———. 1973b. 'A Statement from Krishnamurti' in *KFI Bulletin No. 4* (Madras: KFI), 2–3.

———. 1975. *Beginnings of Learning* (London: Victor Gollancz).

———. 1976. 'On the Formation of New Schools', *Krishnamurti Foundation Bulletin 30* (England: Krishnamurti Foundation Trust Ltd.).

———. 1978. *The Impossible Question* (Harmondsworth: Penguin).

———. 1981a. 'The Book of Life', *KFI Bulletin No. 1* (Madras: KFI), 3–14.

———. 1981b. *Letters to the Schools* (Madras: KFI).

———. 1982a. 'The Teaching' in P. Jayakar and S. Patwardhan, eds., *Within the Mind: On J. Krishnamurti* (Madras: KFI), 8–18.

———. 1982b. 'A Talk', *KFI Bulletin No. 3* (Madras: KFI), 25–32.

———. 1982c. 'Krishnamurti on Education' in P. Jayakar and S. Patwardhan, eds., *Within the Mind: On J. Krishnamurti* Madras: KFI), 145–52.

———. 1983. 'A Seminar in Madras', *KFI Bulletin No. 2* (Madras: KFI), 2–21.

Krishnamurti Foundation of India. 1983. *Memorandum of Association and Rules and Regulations*.

Lacey, C. 1970. *Hightown Grammar: The School as a Social System* (Manchester: Manchester University Press).

———. 1976a. 'Problems of Sociological Fieldwork: A Review of the Methodology of "Hightown Grammar"' in M. Hammersley and P. Woods, eds. *The Process of Schooling: A Sociological Reader* (London: Routledge and Kegan Paul), 55–65.

———. 1976b. 'Intragroup Competitive Pressures in the Selection of Social Strategies: Neglected Paradigms in the Study of Adolescent Socialization' in E. Fuchs, ed., *Youth in a Changing World: Cross Cultural Perspectives on Adolescence* (The Hague: Mouton Publishers), 287–314.

———. n.d. *Socialization as the Adoption of Appropriate Social Strategies* (MS).

Lambert, R. *et al.* 1970. *A Manual to the Sociology of the School* (London: Weidenfeld and Nicholson).

Leach, E. 1973. 'Ourselves and Others', *Times Literary Supplement.* 3, 722 (mimeo.).

Levi-Strauss, C. 1973. 'The Scope of Anthropology' in *Structural Anthropology*, Vol. II (Harmondsworth: Penguin), 3–32.

Lutyens, M. 1975. *Krishnamurti. The Years of Awakening* (New York: Avon Books).

Madan, T. N. 1980. Epilogue in T. N. Madan *et al. Doctors and Society. Three Asian Case Studies. India, Malaysia, Sri Lanka* (New Delhi: Vikas Publishing House), 289–304.

Malinowski, B. 1922. *Argonauts of the Western Pacific* (London: Routledge and Kegan Paul).

————. 1944. *A Scientific Theory of Culture and Other Essays* (New York: Oxford University Press).

McLaren, P. 1986. *Schooling as a Ritual Performance: Towards a Political Economy of Educational Symbols and Gestures* (London: Routledge and Kegan Paul).

Meltzer, B. N. *et al.* 1975. *Symbolic Interactionism. Genesis, Varieties, and Criticism* (London: Routledge and Kegan Paul).

Merton, R. K. 1957. 'The Role-Set: Problems in Sociological Theory', *British Journal of Sociology*, 8, 2, 106–20.

Morrison, 1989. 'Bringing Progressivism into a Critical Theory of Education' in *British Journal of the Sociology of Education*, 10, 1, 3–18.

Musgrave, P. W. 1968. *The School as an Organization* (London: Macmillan).

National Council of Educational Research and Training (NCERT). 1980. *Fourth All-India Educational Survey* (New Delhi: NCERT).

Peters, R. S. 1959. *Authority, Responsibility and Education* (London: George Allen and Unwin).

Powdermaker, H. 1966. *Stranger and Friend: The Way of an Anthropologist* (London: Secker and Warburg).

Ricoeur, P. 1981. *Hermeneutics and the Human Sciences*, Ed. and tr. by John B. Thompson (Paris: Maison des Sciences de L' Homme and Cambridge University Press).

Robinson, P. 1981. *Perspectives on the Sociology of Education: An Introduction* (London: Routledge and Kegan Paul).

Schutz, A. 1970. *On Phenomenology and Social Relations: Selected Writings* (Chicago: University of Chicago Press).

Sharp, R. and Green, A. 1975. *Education and Social Control. A Study in Progressive Primary Education* (London: Routledge and Kegan Paul).

Shils, E. 1968. 'The Concept and Function of Ideology' in *International Encyclopedia of Social Sciences*, 7, 66–76.

Skilbeck, M. 1976. 'Ideologies and Values', Unit 3 in M. Skilbeck and A. Harris, *Culture, Ideology and Knowledge* (Milton Keynes: The Open University Press), 3–49.

Skorupski, J. 1976. *Symbol and Theory: A Philosophical Study of Theories of Religion in Social Anthropology* (Cambridge: Cambridge University Press).

Stebbins, R. A. 1976. 'Physical Context Influences on Behaviour: The Case of Classroom Disorderliness' in M. Hammersley and P. Woods, eds., *The Process of Schooling: A Sociological Reader* (London: Routledge and Kegan Paul), 208–16.

Tambiah, S. J. 1981. *A Performative Approach to Ritual* (London: The British Academy).

Thapan, M. 1988. 'Some Aspects of Cultural Reproduction and Pedagogic Communication', *Economic and Political Weekly*, XXIII, 12, 592–6.

Turner, R. 1962. 'Role-Taking: Process vs. Conformity' in A. M. Rose, ed., *Human Behaviour and Social Processes* (London: Routledge and Kegan Paul), 20–40.

Turner, V. 1968. *The Ritual Process: Structure and Anti-Structure* (London: Routledge and Kegan Paul).

Tyler, W. 1988. *School Organisation. A Sociological Perspective* (London: Croom Helm).

Waller, W. 1938 (1965). *The Sociology of Teaching* (New York: John Wiley).

Wax, R. H. 1971. *Doing Fieldwork: Warnings and Advice* (Chicago: University of Chicago Press).

Weber, M. 1947. *The Theory of Social and Economic Organization*, Tr. A. M. Henderson and T. Parsons (New York: The Free Press).

———. 1978. *Economy and Society*, Vols. I and II (Berkeley: University of California Press).

Wilson, T. P. 1970. 'Conceptions of Interaction and Forms of Sociological Explanation' in *American Sociological Review*, 35, 4, 697–710.

Woods, P. 1975. '"Showing Them Up" in Secondary School' in G. Chanan and S. Delamont, eds., *Frontiers of Classroom Research* (Windsor: NFER), 122–45.

———. 1976. 'The Myth of Subject Choice' in *British Journal of Sociology*, 27, 2, 130–49.

———. 1978. 'Relating to Schoolwork: Some Pupil Perceptions' in *Educational Review*, 30, 2, 167–75.

———. 1979. *The Divided School* (London: Routledge and Kegan Paul).

———. ed. 1980a. *Pupil Strategies. Explorations in the Sociology of the School* (London: Croom Helm).

———. 1980a. 'The Development of Pupil Strategies' in P. Woods, ed., *Pupil Strategies. Explorations in the Sociology of the School* (London: Croom Helm), 11–28.

———. 1980b. *Teacher Strategies: Explorations in the Sociology of the School* (London: Croom Helm).

———. 1980c. 'Strategies in Teaching and Learning' in P. Woods, ed., *Pupil Strategies. Explorations in the Sociology of the School* (London: Croom Helm), 18–33.

————. 1981. 'Understanding through Talk' in C. Adelman, ed., *Uttering, Muttering: Collecting, Using and Reporting Talk for Social Educational Research* (London: Grant McIntyre), 13–26.

————. 1983. *Sociology and the School. An Interactionist Viewpoint* (London: Routledge and Kegan Paul).

————. 1984. 'Teacher Careers—Crises and Continuities', *End-of-grant report to the Economic and Social Research Council* (mimeo.).

Wuthnow, R. *et al.* 1984. *Cultural Analysis* (London: Routledge and Kegan Paul).

Young, M. F. D. ed. 1971. *Knowledge and Control: New Directions for the Sociology of Education* (London: Collier Macmillan).

Index

Abbs, P., on the inward world, 52, 53
academic
  assessment, 49
  system, organization of, 49–53
activity, 48
actor, *see* participant
Arundale, G., 31
asana, 136
asthāchal, 57, 58, 61, 65, 71
  purpose of, 61
  responses to, 61–2
authority, 47–8
axis mundi, the, 62

Berger, P. and Luckmann, T. on secondary socialization, 118; on society, 5, 221
Bernstein, B., on structure of social relationships, 36; on ritual, 56, 57; on the sociology of education, 225
Besant, Dr Annie, 30, 31
Bourdieu, P. and Passeron, J. C., 228
Buddha, the, 104
Bursar, the, 35, 38, 39, 42

Cenkner, W. on Rabindranath Tagore, 25
charisma, 8–9, 68
classroom
  control, 170, 171, 173, 175
  disorder in, 169-170, 171, 178–80, 181, 182
  observation, 237–9
  problems in, 181–3
co-curricular activities, 129–30
collective leadership, 43
commitment
  ideological, 80, 83, 87, 91–2, 98
  instrumental, 83, 91
  professional, 83, 91
  vocational, 83

communitarianism, 25–6, 43
Culture lessons, 184, 185–6
curriculum, 50–52
  incorporation of ideology, in, 50
Council for Indian School Certificate Examination, 28, 33, 34, 39, 51, 70, 77, 123, 182, 223

Davies, B., on organizations, 35
decision-making, 43–8
Delamont, S., on pupil strategy, 167
Democracy Board, the, 134, 135, 161, 187
De Souza, A., on Indian Public Schools, 33, 34, 122, 210
differentiation, 52, 55, 61, 121, 138
Dining Hall, the, 192
  Committee, 47
Discussion/discussion, 60, 100, 184, 186–9, 190–92
Durkehim, E., on ritual, 56

education, definition of, 9
educational
  order, 62, 71, 83, 97
  process/es in India, problematic in sociological study of 3–4, 5
Eliade, M., on sacred space, 62; on regeneration of the community, 71
Erikson, E. H., on *ritus*, 56
ethics in field work, 244–5
ethnographic study, purpose of, 3, 4
examinations, 63, 65–6, 70–71, 127–9; *see also* weekly tests
Executive Committee, the, 44, 46, 47, 240

faculty, 50
  head, 50
  meeting, 100, 101
  play, 111–12